INTEGRATIVE SOLUTIONS
Treating Common Problems in Couples Therapy

INTEGRATIVE SOLUTIONS
Treating Common Problems in Couples Therapy

Gerald R. Weeks, Ph.D.
and
Larry Hof, M.Div.

With chapters by

Bonnie Howard, Ph.D. • **Martha Turner, M.D.**
April Westfall, Ph.D. • **Paul R. Sachs, Ph.D.**

PENN Council For Relationships
(formerly the Marriage Council of Philadelphia)
and
The University of Pennsylvania

BRUNNER/MAZEL *Publishers* · NEW YORK

Library of Congress Cataloging-in-Publication Data

Weeks, Gerald R. and Larry Hof
    Integrative solutions : treating common problems in couples
therapy / Gerald R. Weeks and Larry Hof, with chapters by Bonnie
Howard . . . [et al.].
        p.   cm.
    Includes bibliographical references and index.
    ISBN 0-87630-781-0
    1. Marital psychotherapy.   I. Hof, Larry.
II. Title.
RC488.5.W443   1995
616.89′156—dc20   95-23803
                                                                            CIP

Published by
BRUNNER/MAZEL, INC.
19 Union Square West
New York, New York 10003

Manufactured in the United States of America

10   9   8   7   6   5   4   3   2   1

This book is dedicated to
DENNIS ALTER
Chairman of the Board of Trustees, Patron, and Friend,
The PENN Council For Relationships.

Your tireless energy and enthusiasm are contagious . . .
Your support for our efforts and our mission stimulates hope . . .
Your quickness of perception and continuous challenging of the status
   quo keep us alert to the possibilities and necessities of change . . .
Your generosity of spirit, time, and resources is deeply appreciated . . .

Much of what we are in the process of becoming has been imprinted by
your leadership. Thank you!

CONTENTS

PREFACE

Integrative Solutions: Treating Common Problems in Couples Therapy is the latest in a series focusing exclusively on marital and couples therapy. The series began with *Integrating Sex and Marital Therapy: A Clinical Guide* (G. R. Weeks & L. Hof, Eds., 1987), which built on the work of the then individually oriented sex therapies by adding the systems perspective, and it was the first among only a few books in the field to attempt the integration of sex and marital or systems therapy. *Treating Couples: The Intersystem Model of the Marriage Council of Philadelphia* (G. R. Weeks, Ed., 1989) followed with a more comprehensive presentation, which described the theoretical orientation of the PENN Council for Relationships (formerly the Marriage Council of Philadelphia) and offered contributions by staff members on the principles and process of couples therapy.

The third volume, *Couples in Treatment: Techniques and Approaches for Effective Practice* (G. R. Weeks & S. Treat, 1992), was atheoretical, practical, and pragmatic, and focused on the approaches, methods, and techniques of the couple/marital therapist and the clinician engaged in training those just entering this field. *The Marital-Relationship Therapy Casebook: Theory and Application of the Intersystem Model* (G. R. Weeks & L. Hof, Eds., 1994) provided in-depth, clinically rich cases to exemplify the unique skills and rigorous therapeutic stance required for effective couples therapy done from the perspective of the Intersystem Model. Chapter 1 in this volume also describes the Intersystem Model in detail. Basically, this model includes an individual, interactional, and intergenerational assessment of the problem and treatment from these three perspectives when appropriate.

This volume, the fifth in the series, focuses on some of the common problems with which the marital-relationship therapist is called upon to deal: instilling hope in the therapeutic process; commitment, intimacy, anger, and conflict; the treatment of depression in conjoint therapy; addiction and extramarital sexuality; marital adjustments to life changes associated with aging; and inhibited sexual desire.

Problems . . . problems . . . problems. We think most clinicians would agree that the problems addressed here are significant issues, requiring sound and knowledgeable intervention on the part of the therapist for effective resolution, and to facilitate the growth and development of the couples seeking our help. In each chapter, we try to balance the theoretical and the practical, giving the clinician a solid conceptual background and suggesting effective techniques for dealing with these problems that emerge so often in marital-relationship therapy.

The therapist who is unfamiliar with growth-oriented approaches or disinclined toward such work will stop with problem resolution. Unfortunately, we believe this thinking is consistent with the emphasis on diagnosis and pathology that has dominated individual psychotherapy. We believe that individual diagnosis and the treatment of individual pathology are important to the couple therapist, but that we should not lose sight of the fact that we can do more than restore normal functioning.

Couples who enter therapy for a problem should be given the option of moving to a higher level of functioning by doing some growth-oriented work. This value has been underemphasized in psychotherapy and is seriously challenged by managed care in the current marketplace. This book is also intended to help the clinician promote health or optimal functioning. If the therapist's only model for couple functioning is the elimination of problems, then how is the therapist going to help this potentially higher functioning couple?

ACKNOWLEDGMENTS

Special thanks to David Hof for his reproduction of Figure 6.1 (Neuro-transmitters, Addictions, and Mental Illness). Working on a Macintosh Quadra 605, after expressing that it would be "a piece of cake to do it in about an hour," he turned blatant skepticism and challenging disbelief from someone born in the precomputer era to humbled belief and awed appreciation. At least he gives us credit for having moved to the "on ramp" of the information superhighway.

THE AUTHORS

Gerald R. Weeks, Ph.D. Director of Training, PENN Council For Relationships; Clinical Associate Professor of Psychology in Psychiatry, University of Pennsylvania, School of Medicine.

Larry Hof, M.Div. Chief Operating Officer, PENN Council For Relationships; Clinical Assistant Professor of Pastoral Counseling in Psychiatry, University of Pennsylvania, School of Medicine.

With

Bonnie Howard, Ph.D. Therapist at Riegler, Shienvold and Associates in Harrisburg, PA, specializing in individual, couple, and family therapy.

Martha Turner, M.D. Private practice, in the field of psychiatry and addictions. Dr. Turner conducts an outpatient group therapy program titled Sexual Trauma and Recovery. Her office is in Bryn Mawr, PA.

April Westfall, Ph.D. Director of Clinical Services, PENN Council for Relationships; Clinical Assistant Professor of Family Study in Psychiatry, University of Pennsylvania, School of Medicine.

Paul R. Sachs, Ph.D. Associate Director, Center for Adult Families Under Stress (CAFUS), PENN Council For Relationships; Private practice.

1

THE ELUSIVE ELIXIR:
FOSTERING HOPE IN MARITAL-
RELATIONSHIP THERAPY

Larry Hof, M.Div.

Healthy, well-functioning couples have a positive view of their potential, a basic sense of trust regarding the world in general and their relationship in particular. When they are called upon to cope with difficult situations and resolve specific problems, a sense of optimism generally prevails and the presence of hope is clearly evident. On the other hand, dysfunctional couples have relatively greater degrees of negativism, distrust, pessimism, and hopelessness or despair (see Beavers, 1985).

The degree of hope or hopelessness/despair in the individuals and couples presenting for marital therapy is an important element in the therapeutic process, and the development of an individual's hopefulness is considered a key ingredient in enabling people who are burdened with despair and "learned helplessness" to develop "learned optimism" (Seligman, 1991).

Snyder (1994), through research based upon his own hope scale, described three significant characteristics of individuals who have high levels

---

Chapter 1 is reprinted in an expanded and modified form from *The Family Journal, 1(3)*, 1993, pp. 220–227. © ACA. Reprinted with permission. No further reproduction authorized without permission of the American Counseling Association.

of hopefulness. They have the ability to envision a much wider range of goals than most people, greater determination and more energy in the pursuit of their objectives, and the skills and competence needed to create a greater variety of ways and means to achieve their desired outcomes.

People with lesser degrees of these abilities perceive themselves to be proportionally less competent and less able to cope successfully with the vagaries of life. They are, in fact, less hopeful than those I have just described; and if that condition is not addressed and corrected, it can be detrimental to any therapeutic process.

The instillation and maintenance of hope is described as a crucial aspect in all of the psychotherapies (Frank & Frank, 1991; Yalom, 1970). Luborsky (1976) notes that several studies indicate that expectations of early benefits expressed in early sessions in the therapeutic process are the best indicator or predictor of later benefits. Frank and Frank (1991) reviewed the placebo response and the role of expectations in medical and psychological treatment, and go so far as to assert:

> (H)opelessness can retard recovery or even hasten death, while the mobilization of hope plays an important part in many forms of healing in both nonindustrialized societies and our own. Favorable expectations generate feelings of optimism, energy, and well-being and may actually promote healing, especially of those illnesses that have a large psychological or emotional component. (p. 132)

In the literature in the field of marital and family therapy, however, we find few references to hope. The entire *Journal of Marital and Family Therapy*, from the first issue in 1975 through the third issue in 1994, had only one article with hope in its title, and it was the only one that dealt with hope directly (Beavers & Kaslow, 1981). In addition, a survey of the indexes in 14 familiar and widely used books in the field yielded one, two-word reference, "pathological hope," in a chapter by Whitaker and Keith (1981) in the volume by Gurman and Kniskern (1981), and four references to hope in a book by Beavers (1985). Twelve of the 14 were totally silent on the subject (Becvar & Becvar, 1988; Glick, Clarkin, & Keesler, 1987; Goldenberg & Goldenberg, 1980; Gurman, 1981 & 1982; Gurman & Kniskern, 1991; Nichols & Schwartz, 1991; Sauber, L'Abate, & Weeks, 1985; Scharff & Scharff, 1987 & 1991; Stuart, 1980; Weeks, 1989).

Two notable exceptions are the recent work of Waters and Lawrence

(1993) and that of Sherman, Oresky, and Rountree (1991). Waters and Lawrence (1993) note that:

> In helping people to change, it is critical to understand what they were hoping for, their sense of possibilities, and what strengths and abilities they feel they can call upon (if any) to get them there. A competence approach works to engender a strong sense of positive possibility, of hope, while remaining respectful of people's sense of negative possibility and their realistic limitations (p. 82).

They suggest that hope and change are fostered, in part, through a therapeutic process that creates a *vision* in the clients (and in the therapist) of what is possible for themselves as multifaceted individuals or ''selves,'' a vision that respects and honors the past of the individual family members and the family unit, but is oriented towards the future. The process also requires a differentiation between clients' ''patterns'' and their ''person,'' between the often limiting habits developed over years of coping and surviving, and the ''real self'' with ''healthy impulses toward mastery and belonging'' (p. 87).

Sherman, Oresky, and Rountree (1991) deal with the issue of hope in referring to developing ''the art of encouragement.'' They discuss several structured techniques (e.g., the Appreciation Party and the Encouragement Meeting), and several ''tips and tactics for encouragement'' (e.g., affirmation rather than discounting, blocking tactics, affirming tactics).

Unlike the majority of the literature in the field of marital and family therapy, we find many direct and indirect references to hope in the lyrics, children's stories, and the folklore of American society. Frank Sinatra sang about it in a song that included reference to an ant, a rubber tree plant, and the part that hope played in helping the ant to move that rubber tree plant!

There is also the proverbial *Little Engine That Could* (Piper, 1990), at the foot of the mountain, one of a number of engines that would not, or could not, make the grade. Off the Little Engine went with the somewhat questioning, but also hopeful and optimistic words, ''I think I can, I think I can,'' until it was over the top of the mountain, and the words turned to an increasingly rapid, ''I thought I could, I thought I could, I thought I could.''

These two illustrations are contrasted against what might be called the "Eeyore syndrome." Eeyore is the rather pathetic donkey in *Winnie the Pooh* who is about as pessimistic a character as you would ever want to meet. If it is a beautiful day and Christopher Robin greets him with a joyful, "A good day to you, Eeyore," the lop-eared creature proceeds to hypothesize that the day will probably turn out to be at least a disappointment if not an outright disaster! Left to his own devices, Eeyore could influence those around him with his gloomy assumptions, creating a series of self-fulfilling prophecies and hopeless situations.

There is also what can be called the "Paul or Paula Pollyanna syndrome." For people infected with or enamored with this approach, life is always viewed as having a silver lining. This, in itself, is not necessarily harmful, but for people afflicted with this syndrome, even the most potentially dangerous, insidious, or pernicious aspects of life may not be avoided or attended to with an appropriate sense of balance, fear, or care. They could potentially "walk in where angels fear to tread," without appropriate evaluation of the consequences. (This is perhaps an example of the "pathological hope" of Whitaker and Keith [1981].)

Hope plays a key role in all of these examples. In the first two, the presence of hope leads to the successful accomplishment of a task and assists in the attainment of a goal. In the third example, the relative absence of hope contributes to a pessimistic outlook on life or a series of self-fulfilling negative prophecies and "learned helplessness" (Seligman, 1991). In the last case, the presence of unrealistic hope contributes to potential damage or disaster.

Many of the clients seen in treatment mirror the ant, the engine, Eeyore, or Paul/Paula Pollyanna. They are often alienated from each other, extremely angry, and almost always in significant pain. With those couples who enter treatment earlier rather than later, there is often a modicum or more of hope that the relationship can be different, that people can change. There is sometimes even a firm belief in the possibility of positive outcomes, and a commitment to the attainment of them.

With those couples who seek treatment in the later stages of marital decay, despair or fear may be felt, and there may be a belief in the impending death of the relationship, along with the virtual absence of hope regarding the future of the relationship. These couples frequently enter a therapeutic relationship as a last resort, long after preventive maintenance would have been helpful, and long after the optimal time has passed for effective intervention. Nonetheless, they frequently have the expectation, or hope (there is that word again), that the therapist will be able to perform some kind of a miracle and breathe life into a lifeless corpse of a marriage, or the hope that the clinician will at least be able to help the couple to end the marriage with as little acrimony as possible, perhaps for the sake of the children whom they will still be required to parent.

For those couples who are somewhere in between, there is usually some clear sense of fear regarding the future or the direction of the relationship, but also a clear sense of hope that the difficulties can be defined and resolved and that the relationship can continue.

In all of these instances, hope plays a crucial role in the therapeutic process, either to build the relationship or to end it constructively. If the therapist is to be helpful, s/he must be able to reveal, clarify, or instill hope within the couples who are presenting for treatment. To paraphrase the old proverb, "Where there is no vision, the people perish"; where there is no hope, the partners, their relationship, and the therapy either perish or it becomes extremely difficult to move to a level of healthy, well-functioning interaction. (Of course, where there is too much hope, unrealistic hope, or pathological hope, the therapist is frequently called upon to foster a balanced view of reality that will permit attention to areas of needed change and appropriate change efforts on the part of the clients.)

HOPE DEFINED

Webster's dictionary (*Webster's Ninth New Collegiate Dictionary*, 1985) defines hope in the following way: "to cherish a desire with expectation of fulfillment" (p. 581). Expanded a bit, it could be said that hope is to entertain or harbor in the mind, deeply and resolutely, a conscious impulse toward something that promises enjoyment or satisfaction in its attainment, with the expectation that it will happen. If individuals and couples in treatment believe in that definition, and have such a hope, that is close to half of the basic "battle for initiative" (Barnard & Corrales, 1979), a battle that the therapists must lose and the clients must win. The therapist cannot want them to be in treatment more than they themselves want to be, cannot want an outcome more than they do, and cannot be the driving force in their lives or in their therapy. But if the clinician can uncover hope, enable them to express hope, or instill hope in each of them as individuals and in the couple, then the prognosis for treatment becomes much more positive.

BLOCKS TO HOPE

What prevents a couple from experiencing hope, or prevents them from believing that they have hope or that the situation is hopeful? Some clients were raised in dysfunctional families in which little, if any, positive change was experienced. They often have no concept of change, and remain stuck in familiar, destructive patterns of interaction. If both marital partners had such a family-of-origin experience, there is often little belief in, or expectation of, positive change; there are significant skill deficits in the areas of problem solving and decision making; and there is little experience of positive reinforcement in marital/family interactions. This can contribute to continued failures in current interactions and change efforts, with increasing demoralization and, eventually, the apathy that can come from the conclusion, "It is hopeless."

Even where there was not a significant amount of dysfunction in the family of origin, clients might say, "We have waited so long!" and in that statement there is implied a major block, a history of negative interactions and relationship failures leading to loss of hope. For a significant number of couples seeking treatment, that would include a habitual aspect to the relationship, a homeostatic balance, a functional equilibrium, a negative reciprocal spiral or cycle (which may include object relations issues such as unconscious or preconscious primitive projections upon each other)—all of which provide some degree of predictability, control, and protection to the system. The latter, however, are not attained without significant cost to the individuals and the couple: continuous feelings of powerlessness, frustration, anger, and pain; perpetual cycles in which one or both partners vilify or blame the other; and cognitive distortions that become permanent or universal descriptions of each by the other and the relationship, with a disastrous impact on hope (Seligman, 1991).

Related to the idea of "we have waited so long," and the blocks to hope inherent in that statement, is the concept of the Dynamics of Negative Conflict. A conflict in which a couple presenting for treatment is embroiled can be viewed in the following way (reading from the left and the right simultaneously): Wish/Fear/Defensive Behavior/CONFLICT/Defensive Behavior/Fear/Wish.

In other words, the conflict exists between two persons, each of whom is engaging in defensive behavior because both are in fear that some wish will not be fulfilled. If the therapist and the therapeutic process cannot enable the clients to get to the wish on a consistent basis, the fears prevail, and in an attempt to protect themselves, the individuals who form the dyad feel justified in maintaining their defensive posture and conflict-oriented stance. The couple remains trapped in the cycle, with a predictable negative impact on hope. (Early in the treatment process, this theoretical construct can be used to demonstrate defensive posturing and reciprocal spirals of interaction to couples. For those whose preferred learning style is abstract conceptualization, its use may help increase awareness of their interactions and, thus, contribute to the hope that the relationship can change. See the following section, "Instilling Hope.")

Another factor that blocks the experience of hope and even contributes to its demise in couples is the negativism that appears so often when their romantic notions have collided with the realities of daily living, without any preparation or even the expectation that problems in relating are a normal part of building a relationship. This is what Vincent (1973, 1977) referred to as the inevitable consequence of the "myth of naturalism," the belief that all a couple has to do is to love each other and everything else will just somehow magically fall into place, without intentional effort and practice and surely without bad feelings or negative outcomes. This belief is only one of many possible cognitive distortions (Beck, 1976, 1988) that are prone to be used in couples' unique variations of the Eeyore syndrome ("You always treat me like that," "If you feel that way about this issue, it means that you don't love me," and so forth).

Many partners report that their hope for change was minimal, prior to entering therapy, and all they may have really hoped for was to survive or to reach some sort of an accommodation. One or both of them may feel a sense of powerlessness to effect change, after repeated failed attempts at problem resolution. One spouse may have a certain degree of hopelessness, while the other denies that any problems exist, effectively reinforcing and amplifying the other's hopelessness. They frequently have become entrenched in their patterns of relating, a process that has been reinforced by early learned family-of-origin styles of relating, primitive and unresolved intrapsychic projective identification issues, and a lack of skill in instilling and maintaining hope. After all, who among us, clients or clinicians, has taken a course in "hope"? (Many people who have participated actively in some religious heritage have a fundamental indoctrination into a philosophy or theology of hope, although they have rarely been taught how to apply this to human relationships.)

INSTILLING HOPE

One of the first tasks of the therapist is to uncover hope, to help create hope, or to instill hope. For, as Petronius, the Roman novelist and poet, wrote: "Just as dumb creatures are snared by food, human beings would not be caught unless they had a nibble of hope." At the beginning of therapy, that hope can be fostered, in part, if the clinician has hope in him- or herself, in the therapeutic process itself, and for people's efforts to change (Searles, 1977). Hope is also facilitated if the clinician helps the clients perceive that s/he likes them, that the therapist is similar to them in some ways, and that s/he hears them and understands their issues and accepts them as real issues. The therapist must also win the battle for structure (Barnard & Corrales, 1979)—that is, the therapist must be able to control the therapeutic process—and lose the battle for initiative (Barnard & Corrales, 1979)—that is, the therapist cannot provide the motivation and desire for treatment, that must come from the clients. S/he needs to demonstrate the communication and relationship skills that enable effective relationships to develop. The clinician must also "give the clients something" in the first session, and not just gather data (for example, provide some instruction, some connection, some personal self-disclosure) (Odell, 1992).

As therapy progresses, the therapist needs to offer what Beavers and Kaslow (1981) refer to as "the elements of genuine hope": (1) to be heard, acknowledged, and empathized with; (2) to experience successes according to their own definition; (3) to self-observe and evaluate themselves in relation to others; (4) to develop better interpersonal skills; (5) to reduce mistrust and increase trust; (6) to pick up and magnify positive feelings and accomplishments; (7) to distinguish between the past and the present and to focus upon the present, enabling them to function as adults rather than as small and powerless children; (8) to create and utilize a community of caring people; and (9) to have a transcendent belief system.

To accomplish all of these things, and to uncover, create, or instill hope, the therapist needs to deeply appreciate and understand the following: (1) the dynamics of change, (2) the learning styles of the individuals in treatment and the way they access information, (3) the stages of therapy, and (4) a variety of techniques for fostering hope.

The Dynamics of Change

The therapist needs to enable the clients to realize and trust that there is some predictable and universal aspect to the process or dynamics of change. Then the clients can sense that what they are going through in and out of treatment is normal and that they do not have to despair so much, thinking that they are the only ones going through the pain and difficulty. This can lead to a change in thinking, feeling, doing, and hoping: "If that is true, then maybe other aspects of the change process may be applicable to me (or us) as well, and perhaps there is hope for me (or us) to attain our relationship goals!"

As used here, the dynamics of change refers to the following points: people simply "go along and go along," that is, continue to live the way they are living until the pain gets too great, or they get bored (in reality, a form of pain), or they realize that there is perhaps a more efficient or productive way of doing what they are doing (that is, the realization that change is possible). When the pain, boredom, or realization that change is possible becomes sufficiently strong, individuals are placed in a position to do what is needed (that is, to risk a change in behavior of some kind). The risked new behavior requires support from one's self (including one's value or religious system) and from others as the change takes place. Continued support and reinforcement are needed as the changed behavior continues over time if the new behavior is to become an integrated part of people's lives as individuals and as couples. If the support does not continue, the individual and the couple may regress to the prior behavior, or to an even more primitive level of functioning. The inability to success-fully integrate a desired change in behavior is frequently accompanied by a sense of guilt and failure as a person and as a couple, with a diminution of hope. The successful integration of new, desired behavior, however, frequently leads and contributes to increased self-esteem and increased interpersonal effectiveness and satisfaction.

To reduce the possibility of the couple becoming demoralized, the clinician must also enable the clients to be aware that change occurs slowly, over time, and in incremental steps, and very rarely occurs in a rapid, continuous, nondeviating, positive manner. After the gradual development of a commitment to change, and after various skill-building efforts have yielded some success, a sense of "all right, we can change!" may emerge, followed soon after by a crash. This is a first testing phase, which results in the emergence of old behavior and a drop in satisfaction, which feels like it is just as bad as before, but, in reality, is not a return to the baseline condition. This is followed by returning to the use of skill and commitment, and a so-called second honeymoon, which is followed by a second testing phase, with a drop in satisfaction that is nowhere near what it was before. This can happen several times before the clients consolidate the new pattern of interaction (Stuart, 1980).

If therapists know, believe, and utilize the dynamics of change, emphasizing the slow, incremental nature of change, then they become bearers of hope when they predict what will happen before it does (the first testing phase), thus demonstrating the universality and normal nature of the process of change. The therapist can also instill hope by placing an emphasis on changing that which is more readily and easily changed *before* the couple tackles issues that are more difficult, and that involve more vulnerability, and therefore, more resistance, on their part.

Individuals' Learning Styles and Ways of Accessing Information

Kolb (1983) has identified four kinds of learning abilities or styles. The first is concrete experience, in which the person is fully and openly involved in new experiences (for example, giving a hand massage for the first time). The second is reflective observation, in which the individual observes and reflects on experiences from new and different perspectives (for example, the drawing of a marital life line by each partner, including high and low points, happy, sad, hurt, turbulent times, and so forth, and then the sharing and discussing of the drawings; thus, observing and reflecting on their experiences from new and different perspectives in order to increase their sense of inclusion and their ability to listen accurately and empathetically to each other). The third learning ability or style is abstract conceptualization, in which the person creates concepts that integrate observations or life experience (for example, someone might hear the "dynamics of negative conflict" described earlier and "catch" the principle of defensive reciprocal spirals, and then use that abstract conceptualization as the basis for attempting to behave differently the next time a conflict arises). The fourth is active experimentation, in which theories are used to make decisions or attempt solutions for problems (for example, a couple might share wants, needs, and fears in some specified area and then agree on and write a specific, achievable, time-oriented contract for changing one thing that they would like to be different; thus, actively experimenting with the theory of contract writing in order to make decisions and attempt solutions to problems).

If the therapist is aware that clients have different learning styles, then s/he should be sure to intervene in such a way that each person's preferred style will be accessed and utilized. This can increase hope dramatically by giving *each person* a sense of being spoken to and involved in a way that is meaningful and engaging. How many times has a clinician "hooked" one person of a couple into therapy because s/he could identify with the preferred learning style of the therapist, or that upon which a particular technique was based, only to have the other partner withdraw into silence, or feel left out? The left-out client has often been defined as resistant, when, in fact, s/he may not have been able to identify with or utilize effectively the learning style that was being accessed or focused upon. Thus, if the therapist uses interventions that potentially access multiple or different learning styles, especially at the outset of therapy, the likelihood of joining effectively with each partner is increased. This increases the likelihood that each partner will feel hopeful that s/he can learn from the therapeutic experience (for example, the technique represented by "My World of Feelings," [Hof & Miller, 1981; Weeks & Treat, 1992]).

Another approach to the different ways in which people learn is to be aware of how they access information, and for this we are indebted to the proponents of Neuro-Linguistic Programming (NLP) (Bandler & Grinder, 1975; Cameron-Bandler, 1978). NLP proponents suggest that some people are more visually oriented than others, some more auditorially oriented, some more kinesthetically oriented, and some more affectively oriented. It is believed that clients and therapists "reveal what they are thinking and feeling through sensory based statements ('I *see* what you mean'; 'I'm *touched* by your offer') and behavioral cues (for example, eye movements)" (Goldenberg & Goldenberg, 1980, p. 117). If the therapist happens to be visually oriented and keeps asking the clients how they see things, whereas they happen to be, respectively, kinesthetically and auditorially oriented, then they may somewhat freeze when they hear the question, and not be able to answer in a helpful manner. If, however, the therapist initially uses multiple openings such as "What is your sense about this?" and "How do you see/hear/feel about what we are discussing?" the clients may be more free to access the information from their preferred perspective and the sense of hope that comes from being in a relationship in which s/he is understood may increase quickly. If the therapist is a careful listener to their words, and observer of their body language, the clients' preferred ways of accessing information can be identified. The therapist can then use that information to speak directly to the person in a way that not only increases the client's sense of being understood but also increases the likelihood of the therapist being heard and responded to. The implications for instilling hope within the individuals and the couple are clear.

The Stages of Therapy

The therapeutic process unfolds in a number of predictable stages. One paradigm the author finds useful suggests that the stages include Magical Thinking, Parentification, Self-Reliance, and Self-Aspiration, with the therapist being more active in earlier stages and progressively less active in the later stages (Rado, 1956, 1962, 1969).

If the therapist understands these stages, then s/he can increase or decrease involvement and intervene according to the needs of the clients. For example, in the Magical Thinking stage of therapy, the couple is frequently low on morale, has depleted most adaptive reserves, and places their hope in the therapist rather than in themselves (Beavers, 1985). Their expectations of "cure" are "raised by the healer's personal attributes, by his or her culturally determined healing role, or, typically, by both" (Frank & Frank, 1991, pp. 111–112). The therapist is expected to draw a rabbit out of the hat, so to speak.

Suppose a couple has colluded in keeping silent about feelings of sadness related to a painful experience in their past. If the therapist senses the pain and the avoidance, an appropriate, well-timed, overt reference to feelings of pain can appear magical and foster getting into their feelings and, thus, increase their sense of hope that the therapist may be able to help them.

In this stage, the clients frequently protect themselves against being vulnerable. The therapist may be able to tap a little reserve of hope with the explicit verbalization that in the midst of significant hostility and the possibility of relationship dissolution they may have an unexpressed hope for some reconciliation. The use of NLP techniques, such as addressing deletions, distortions, and generalizations (Bandler & Grinder, 1975) can effectively, quickly, easily, and "magically" clarify communications at this stage and, thereby, foster hope.

In the Parentification stage, the therapist is viewed as less godlike and magical; however, significant transferences may still be present. If the transferences can be utilized to permit the therapist to play the part of a needed Nurturing Parent, providing support and encouragement to the clients and belief in their abilities, then such transferences may not only be permitted but also encouraged at this point. The clinician must be careful not to overly encourage such transferences, and to diminish dependence upon such "borrowed hope" (Beavers & Kaslow, 1981, p. 121) as quickly as possible, replacing it with a realistic hope based upon the couple's own skill development and accomplishments.

In the later stages of therapy, where Self-Reliance is present and the beginnings of Self-Aspiration have emerged, the prolonged silence of the therapist after a straightforward request for direction from the clients is frequently followed by a smiling comment from them, such as "So you want us to figure it out for ourselves," increasing the hope of the couple because they sense that they are trusted and able to solve their own problem.

Various Techniques for Facilitating Hope

In addition to the therapist's awareness and use of the dynamics of change, the learning styles of the individuals in treatment and the way they access information, and the stages of therapy, a therapeutic armamentarium that contains a variety of other techniques for the creation and instillation of hope is essential for therapeutic success. Some of these techniques follow.

GIVING SUPPORT, NURTURE, EMPATHY, AND AFFIRMATION

Providing genuine support, nurture, empathy, and affirmation, even the affirmation of what the clients cannot do now, and/or should not be able to do now (that is, that it is okay and normal to learn/change in steps or stages) increases hope because the clients feel heard, understood, appreciated, validated, and prepared for action. Alone, or in combination, these are essential building blocks of hope in the therapeutic process.

RELABELING AND REFRAMING

Relabeling and reframing (Weeks & Treat, 1992) can undermine the negative views and cognitive distortions (Beck, 1976, 1988) of the clients and increase hope, as they see the supposed negative in a positive light or interpret it as having a positive purpose instead of the negative and destructive view that they had before (e.g., conflict viewed as positive, distancing viewed as a means of maintaining the balance of the relationship for their own protection).

PRESENTING THE THREE ASSUMPTIONS

This technique was developed by Weeks (Weeks & Treat, 1992) and was designed to change the initial assumptions that many couples bring to treatment, namely, that the partner is less committed than they are, that the partner may want to hurt them, and that they themselves will not be able to understand the partner or be understood in return. The therapist invites each partner to adopt three new assumptions: the assumption of commitment, the assumption of goodwill and intent, and the assumption of understanding.

After specifically checking the validity of the first assumption with each of the partners, the commitment to each other and the therapeutic process can be validated and affirmed. The second assumption begins the process of enabling them to distinguish between intent and effect: "Sometimes you are hurt by something I have said or done, but my intention was not to hurt you; I wanted to be helpful." The third assumption paves the way for the couple to continue to struggle with their communications, by emphasizing that continued effort and use of communications skills will enable them to understand each other, although they may not be able to easily reach agreement on an issue. The clinician asks the couple to remind themselves of these assumptions each day, and also when their communications deteriorate, providing a hopeful assumptive base for ongoing work. (Also compare Doherty [1981a & 1981b] for a further discussion of the role of cognitive processes in intimate conflict, especially with regard to attribution theory and efficacy and learned helplessness.)

IDENTIFYING AND EXPRESSING STRENGTHS

Identifying and expressing individual and marital strengths, or positive potentials, trends, or realities is an important aspect of instilling hope (see Hof & Miller, 1981). These are often hidden by the "negative" interactions, ignored because of the current pain or anger, or overwhelmed by the cognitive distortions utilized by the couple.

Such identification and affirmation experiences can offer the hope of fertile, positive realities and possibilities rather than the bleak desert couples often present with and experience when they are blinded by the cognitive distortions related to the immediate problems.

MARITAL CONTRACTING AND BEHAVIORAL CHANGE

Marital contracting, behavioral change, "catching each other doing good" (for example, Stuart's [1980] "Caring Days" technique) (Hof & Miller, 1981; Sager, 1976; Sager & Hunt, 1979; Stuart, 1980; Weeks & Treat, 1992), and other similar experiences instill hope in several ways. Catching each other doing good teaches the effect of positive reinforcement and helps correct cognitive distortions. Through contracting, couples demonstrate that they can discuss wants and needs, and make commitments to each other. As they follow through on the commitments, behavioral change is demonstrated as possible. Positive feelings frequently emerge to begin to balance the negativism that often permeates couples' initial interactions in therapy, and the skill-based techniques underlying such interventions are identified as something that can be learned through training, practice, and rehearsal.

IDENTIFYING AND UTILIZING SPIRITUAL BELIEFS AND RESOURCES

Helping the clients to identify and utilize *their* spiritual or transcendent beliefs, values, and resources is an often underutilized hope-instilling technique in marital/relationship therapy. Because many of the religions, life philosophies, or ethical credos of the world offer comfort, support, encouragement, and hope in time of trouble, and a sense of meaning beyond oneself, the use of those beliefs, values, and resources can infuse some hope in a time of difficulty, pain, or even despair. Shame and guilt cause many individuals and couples to turn away from their religious and spiritual supports just when they need them the most. The clients frequently need simple permission and encouragement to access those resources, which can include, among others, prayer, private or communal worship experiences, and rituals of confession and forgiveness. At other times, a more direct, planned approach is needed. For example, the author referred a Roman Catholic couple to their priest for some work around the issue of forgiveness, and, in the experience of a Sacrament of Reconciliation, they were able to put the past behind them in a way that they were unable to do without the overt supports of their faith system.

Raider (1992) has suggested that the therapist, through specific questioning, can help the couple to assess ways in which religion influences their family structure (for example, "To what extent does the family's religion define family membership?" [p. 174]), their family processes (for example, "To what extent does the family's religion offer guidelines for family problem solving and decision making?" [p. 176]), their family boundaries (for example, "To what extent does the family's religion influence the degree of permeability of the family's boundaries with the neighborhood, community, and outside environment?" [p. 179]), and their family system equilibrium or integration (for example, "To what extent does the family's religion emphasize tradition, stability, and order?" [p. 180]). Careful assessment in these areas may uncover hopeful and helpful supports or guidance for the individuals and the couple as they work together at problem solving and decision making.

Griffith and Griffith (1992) discuss therapeutic change in religious families from the perspective of working with the "God-construct." With a sound base in object relations theory, they show how coping and interaction are impacted by introjects of ultimate images. Through interventive questions of a circular nature (for example, "About which relationship in the family do you think God would express the most/least satisfaction?" [p. 73]); a future nature (for example, "If you were to find your relationship with God changed at the end of therapy, in what aspect of the relationship would you most hope you might see the change? What aspects might you hope would remain unchanged?" [p. 73]); a reflexive nature (for example, "If God were to restructure this interaction, how do you think it would go?" [p. 73]); in addition to questions aimed at "unique outcomes," "unique accounts," "unique redescription," and "unique possibilities" ("What difference will your having learned how to trust God make in your learning how to trust your wife?" [p. 74]), they show how the therapist can prepare the hopeful "way for new conversations to be born between self and God-construct within the client" (p. 84). (For a more thorough discussion of spiritual/religious issues in relation to marital and family therapy, see Burton [1992], Prest and Keller [1993], Stander and colleagues [1994], and Worthington [1991]. For an interesting historical comparison, from an individual perspective, see Group for the Advancement of Psychiatry [1968].)

USING ABSURDITY, HUMOR, LAUGHTER, FOLKLORE, AND "FUTURIZING"

Hope can be fostered through the use of absurdity, humor, and laughter; lyrics, children's stories, and folklore; and, a planned look to the future, especially in problem solving. The use of lyrics, children's stories, and the folklore of the society or the clients' ethnic group(s) (as in the beginning of this chapter) can engage the clients and trigger the childlike imagination, playfulness, and creativity that are sorely needed in the therapeutic process, but so frequently lacking in couples who present for treatment. Absurdity, humor, and laughter can release creative energy and help the clients (and the therapist) to take themselves and the situation a little less seriously and negatively. This can lead to the hope that often emerges from reduced tension, and increased fun, creative play, and positive attempts to look towards the future with problem-solving techniques and processes. When clients and the therapist are relaxed, engaged, playful, and creative, true brainstorming and genuine learning can occur, relatively free of negativism and pessimism, blaming and criticism, hypervigilance and hopelessness. In such an environment, the possibilities for creating multiple and workable options, and utilizing those proposed solutions, are increased dramatically (compare also the "vision process" in Waters and Lawrence [1993]).

A virtually endless list of techniques that can foster or instill hope, if used correctly, could be created. *Correctly* is the key word, because the techniques have to be used with an appropriate sense of timing; with the sense that their use will result in the meeting of real, identified needs; with a sense of how their use can support the dynamics of change; and with a sense that their use will take into account the learning styles of the individuals in treatment and the way they access information, as well as where the clients are with regard to the stages of the therapeutic process.

CONCLUSION

Hope is a genuine elixir for many couples in therapy. With it, they feel nourished and somewhat healed, and are able to continue with the struggle to learn and change. Without it, they often drop out of treatment or out of the relationship. The therapist can do much to enable the client system to move beyond the pain, the pessimism, the powerlessness, the negativism, and the apparent hopelessness of many situations. The clinician can do much to make that elixir of hope less elusive, to help the clients experience the hope and the learned optimism (Seligman, 1991) that can provide significant fuel for the therapeutic endeavor.

REFERENCES

Bandler, R., & Grinder, J. (1975). *The structure of magic*. Palo Alto, CA: Science and Behavior Books.

Barnard, C. P., & Corrales, R. G. (1979). *The theory and technique of family therapy*. Springfield, IL: Charles C Thomas.

Beavers, W. R. (1985). *Successful marriage*. New York: Norton.

Beavers, W. R., & Kaslow, F. W. (1981). The anatomy of hope. *Journal of Marital and Family Therapy, 7(2)*, 119–126.

Beck, A. (1976). *Cognitive therapy and the emotional disorder*. New York: International Universities Press.

Beck, A. (1988). *Love is never enough*. New York: Harper & Row.

Becvar, D., & Becvar, R. (1988). *Family therapy: A systemic integration*. Boston: Allyn & Bacon.

Burton, L. A. (Ed.). (1992). *Religion and the family: When God helps*. New York: Haworth.

Cameron-Bandler, L. (1978). *They lived happily ever after*. Cupertino, CA: Meta.

Doherty, W. J. (1981a). Cognitive processes in intimate conflict: I. Extending attribution theory. *American Journal of Family Therapy, 9(1)*, 3–13.

Doherty, W. J. (1981b). Cognitive processes in intimate conflict: II. Efficacy and learned helplessness. *American Journal of Family Therapy, 9(2)*, 35–44.

Frank, J. D., & Frank, J. B. (1991). *Persuasion and healing: A comparative study of psychotherapy* (3rd ed.). Baltimore: Johns Hopkins University Press.

Glick, I., Clarkin, J. F., & Keesler, D. R. (1987). *Marital and family therapy* (3rd ed.). Orlando, FL: Grune & Stratton.

Goldenberg, I., & Goldenberg, H. (1980). *Family therapy* (2nd ed.). Monterey, CA: Brooks/Cole.

Griffith, J. L., & Griffith, M. E. (1992). Therapeutic change in religious families: Working with the God-construct. In L. A. Burton (Ed.), *Religion and the family: When God helps* (pp. 63–86). New York: Haworth.

Group for the Advancement of Psychiatry. (1968). *The psychic function of religion in mental illness and health*. New York: Author.

Gurman, A. S. (Ed.). (1981). *Questions & answers in the practice of family therapy*. New York: Brunner/Mazel.

Gurman, A. S. (Ed.). (1982). *Questions & answers in the practice of family therapy, Volume II*. New York: Brunner/Mazel.

Gurman, A. S., & Kniskern, D. P. (Eds.). (1981). *Handbook of family therapy*. New York: Brunner/Mazel.

Gurman, A. S., & Kniskern, D. P. (Eds.). (1991). *Handbook of family therapy, Volume II*. New York: Brunner/Mazel.

Hof, L., & Miller, W. R. (1981). *Marriage enrichment: Philosophy, process, and program*. Bowie, MD: Brady.

Kolb, D. A. (1983). *Experiential learning: Experience as the source of learning and development*. Englewood Cliffs, NJ: Prentice-Hall.

Luborsky, L. (1976). Helping alliances in psychotherapy. In J. L. Claghorn (Ed.), *Successful psychotherapy* (pp. 92–118). New York: Brunner/Mazel.

Nichols, M. P., & Schwartz, R. C. (1991). *Family therapy concepts and methods* (2nd ed.). Boston: Allyn & Bacon.

Odell, M. (1992, October). *Therapist factors, client factors, and their interaction in the first therapy session: Developing a model to predict a second session*. Paper presented in the Poster Session at the Annual Convention of the American Association for Marriage and Family Therapy.

Piper, W. (1990). *The little engine that could*. New York: Platt & Munk.

Prest, L. A., & Keller, J. F. (1993). Spirituality and family therapy: Spiritual beliefs, myths, and metaphors. *Journal of Marital and Family Therapy, 19*(2), 137–148.

Rado, S. (1956). *Psychoanalysis of behavior. Collected papers, 1922–1956*. New York: Grune & Stratton.

Rado, S. (1962). *Psychoanalysis of behavior. Collected papers, Volume 2, 1956–1961*. New York: Grune & Stratton.

Rado, S. (1969). *Adaptional psychodynamics: Motivation and control*. New York: Science House.

Raider, M. C. (1992). Assessing the role of religion in family functioning. In L. A. Burton (Ed.), *Religion and the family: When God helps* (pp. 165–183). New York: Haworth.

Sager, C. J. (1976). *Marriage contracts and couple therapy*. New York: Brunner/Mazel.

Sager, C. J., & Hunt, B. (1979). *Intimate partners*. New York: McGraw-Hill.

Sauber, S. R., L'Abate, L., & Weeks, G. R. (1985). *Family therapy: Basic concepts and terms*. Rockville, MD: Aspen.

Scharff, D. E., & Scharff, J. S. (1987). *Object relations family therapy*. Northvale, NJ: Jason Aronson.

Scharff, D. E., & Scharff, J. S. (1991). *Object relations couple therapy*. Northvale, NJ: Jason Aronson.

Searles, H. F. (1977). The development of mature hope in the patient-therapist relationship. In K. A. Frank (Ed.), *The human dimension in psychoanalytic practice* (pp. 9–27). New York: Grune & Stratton.

Seligman, M. (1991). *Learned optimism*. New York: Knopf.

Sherman, R., Oresky, P., & Rountree, Y. (1991). *Solving problems in couples and family therapy.* New York: Brunner/Mazel.

Snyder, C. R. (1994). *The psychology of hope.* New York: Free Press.

Stander, V., Piercy, F. P., Mackinnon, D., & Helmeke, K. (1994). Spirituality, religion and family therapy: Competing or complementary worlds? *American Journal of Family Therapy, 22(1),* 27–41.

Stuart, R. B. (1980). *Helping couples change.* New York: Guilford.

Vincent, C. E. (1973). *Sexual and marital health.* New York: McGraw-Hill.

Vincent, C. E. (1977). Barriers to the development of marital health as a health field. *Journal of Marriage and Family Counseling, 3(3),* 3–11.

Waters, D. B., & Lawrence, E. C. (1993). *Competence, courage, and change.* New York: Norton.

Webster's Ninth New Collegiate Dictionary. (1985). Springfield, MA: Merriam Webster.

Weeks, G. R. (Ed.). (1989). *Treating couples: The Intersystem Model of the Marriage Council of Philadelphia.* New York: Brunner/Mazel.

Weeks, G. R., & Treat, S. (1992). *Couples in treatment: Techniques for effective practice.* New York: Brunner/Mazel.

Whitaker, C. A., & Keith, D. V. (1981). Symbolical-experiential family therapy. In, A. S. Gurman & D. P. Kniskern (Eds.), *Handbook of family therapy* (pp. 187–225). New York: Brunner/Mazel

Worthington, E. L., Jr. (Guest Ed.). (1991). Religious values in psychotherapy (Special issue). *Journal of Psychology and Christianity, 10(2).*

Yalom, I. D. (1970). *The theory and practice of group psychotherapy.* New York: Basic Books.

2

COMMITMENT AND INTIMACY

Gerald R. Weeks, Ph.D.

Couples entering therapy often complain about the loss of those intense feelings of love or intimacy that existed at the beginning of the relationship. These intense feelings may have become the benchmark for how the relationship should feel. The partners indicate that their love just is not what it used to be. They talk about a gradual erosion of the early intense feelings of romance, love, intimacy, and so forth. Sometimes they begin treatment with the idea that, since love has been lost entirely, the relationship should be ended or simply endured. They have no hope or expectation that love can ever be restored. Some couples will talk directly about wanting to rediscover feelings of intimacy; for others, it is something the therapist infers from what is being said.

In cases where there has been or continues to be an affair, the partner having the affair experiences the intensity lacking in the ongoing relationship that existed in the affair relationship, and then compares the two relationships on that basis. Whether or not the ongoing relationship measures up to the benchmark can be a deciding factor in whether the marriage continues or ends.

Even when loss of love or intimacy is not presented as a problem to be resolved, it is useful to think in terms of what constitutes a healthy relationship. Most couples enter therapy in order to eliminate some problem. They may hope that in so doing they will rekindle some of the feelings discussed in this chapter. Whatever the case, the therapist may wish to facilitate greater intimacy once the problem-solving phase of

treatment has ended, or may integrate this work with the problem resolution phase. Some couples will readily accept or desire intimacy enhancement as the logical next step. Others will be satisfied with the fact that
the identified problems have been removed.

Every therapist has an implicit theory of personality, that is, the
assumptions s/he has about the structure and dynamics of individuals.
Part of the training to become a therapist involved learning about the
explicit personality theories of Freud, Adler, Sullivan, Erickson, Horney,
the behavioral approaches, the existential approaches, and so forth. These
theories inform the therapist as to what might be happening within the
individual client.

At this point, the field of couple therapy does not have explicit
theories of healthy functioning for couples, although it is possible to
extrapolate such theories from the different treatment modalities. The
couple therapist is essentially informed by his or her own implicit theory
of couple functioning. This chapter has the secondary purpose of focusing
on the concept of intimacy. Once the therapist has an explicit understanding of this concept, it may serve as a guide in helping the couple develop
their own ideas about intimacy and how to implement them.

Thus far the words "love" and "intimacy" have been used synony-
mously. Couples usually use these words as if they mean the same thing.
In fact, they are not the same. The concepts of love and intimacy have
been elusive in our field. These words virtually never appear in writings
about couple/marital therapy. They have been dismissed and relegated
to the softer disciplines of literature, philosophy, poetry, and drama.
Psychologists have not found these concepts easy to define. After all,
they would need to create operational definitions, which means the concepts would also have to be measurable, and researchable. Thus, it is
easy to understand why therapists trained in the scientist-practitioner
model would avoid overtly focusing on them.

In this culture, marital or ongoing relationships are based on love/
loving and have some defining characteristics that distinguish them from
all other relationships. These characteristics can create contradictions for
the therapist.

First, the relationship is voluntary, but affirmed to be permanent. A
child has a permanent relationship with a parent, but it is involuntary—
we cannot choose our parents. Friendships are voluntary, but not affirmed
to be permanent. Sometimes partners lose sight of the fact that their
relationship is voluntary; they talk about feeling trapped in a marriage.
As long as this feeling persists, the therapy is stuck. The therapist must

help the partners see options so that they attribute their staying in the relationship to a voluntary act.

Second, marriage is the only relationship in which sex is socially sanctioned and expected. It is expected that each partner will have sexual desire for the other and will express this desire behaviorally in ways that are mutually pleasing. This expectation that desire will occur works in concert with the myth that if partners are in love then desire must be naturally available on demand. When desire is expected and demanded, it can become more difficult to access.

Finally, marriage is based on the notion that the relationship is cemented through an emotional attachment. Partners expect to have, or at the very least believe they should possess, loving feelings for each other. Many relationships can be based on love—that between parent and child, between friends, between an individual and God.

Our contention is that love, in a couple relationship, is defined in a special way. Essentially, it involves voluntariness, permanency, sexuality, and a particular feeling that is called "love." Needless to say, trying to find satisfaction in such complex areas often leads to trouble.

Sternberg (1986a, 1986b) has developed a triangular theory of love based on the literature in the fields of social psychology and personality. This theory was the first these authors found that could be applied clinically. A part of this theory includes the concept of intimacy. We consider the concept of intimacy to be more complex than most people believe. It must be understood dialectically, that is, in terms of its contradictions. Intimate interaction occurs in a number of dimensions (for example, emotional, intellectual, physical). In an intimate relationship, a dialectic exists between thoughts or perceptions and feelings of closeness and distance, actions that lead to engagement and disengagement, and a relationship of togetherness and separateness. This dialectic allows each individual to exist both as a separate self and a self-in-relationship. Each self is intimate with that self and intimate with the self-of-the-other in these dialectical relationships.

THE TRIANGULAR THEORY OF LOVE

According to Sternberg (1986a, 1986b), marital love consists of three components. These components can be schematically shown as an equilateral triangle. This visual representation is designed to show that in the case of marital love the three components exist in approximately equal intensities. If the strength or intensity of any one component is altered, then another kind of relationship is defined. The three components are commitment, intimacy, and passion.

Commitment is known as the cold component; it is the decision to commit to another person. This component is cognitive. The second component, intimacy, is the warm component, and it is the emotional element of the triangle. Passion is the hot component, forming the motivational leg of the triangle. It is the component that motivates us to spend time with the other.

This triangle may serve as the template for much of the couple therapy. The therapist may choose to briefly describe the triangle and define each component. This can lead to a discussion with the couple of what is missing or is weak in their relationship. There are five questions that flow from this triangle, the answers to which provide diagnostic information from the outset.

1. The first question is whether each partner desires all three components. This is basically a yes/no or on/off question. Each partner either wants the three components or not. Passion and commitment are two areas where there are often discrepancies between partners. One partner may not want to commit to the relationship or may want to break the existing commitment, whereas the other wants to establish a commitment or wants to continue the commitment. In other cases, the problem may exist in the realm of passion, with one partner experiencing a lack of sexual desire, and the other demanding sex.

2. The second question is a refinement of the first. Assuming both partners want all of the components, do they desire the same level of intensity in each component? In many relationships there is a discrepancy between components. Intimacy and passion lend themselves to intensity. One partner might want more intimacy and the other less. The one who wants less might express it in terms of feeling smothered or engulfed by the other. The wife might desire more intimacy and the husband more sex.

3. The third question is whether both partners can identify and express the three components as being important in a loving relationship. Each partner should at least be able to identify the three components as important. However, identification is an intellectual function, and the clinician should be listening to determine whether any com-

ponent is just being given lip service. This requires clinical judgment and is a matter of listening for the emotion associated with each component. Although commitment is a cognitive component, the clinician must discern whether the partner really feels committed.

The more difficult task is to determine what might prevent the expression of these three components. The partners may be asked this question directly and their responses explored until the reasons become clear. This exploration takes place in the context of the Intersystem Model described in our previous volumes (Weeks, 1989; Weeks & Hof, 1994; Weeks & Treat, 1992), considering the many factors that may contribute to an inability to express these three components. Some may exist in one or both individuals, others in the relationship, and some may derive from the families of origin.

4. The next question deals with whether the partners have a realistic perception of what love involves. Many distortions exist regarding love. These distortions are commonly known as the myths of love. For example, a husband might define a loving relationship as one in which there is good sex. He may emphasize sex to the exclusion of almost all other aspects of the relationship. Conversely, a woman might underemphasize sex in order to focus on intimacy. She might define intimacy as closeness, but the description may more closely define engulfment. In some relationships, partners do not desire intimacy or passion. They want a highly committed relationship that looks like a marriage, but in fact is a permanent friendship or companionate relationship.

5. Finally, there is the three-part question of what in these three areas each partner is able to realistically offer, what each has actually offered, and how each perceives what has been offered. Often one partner will say s/he desires intimacy and believes s/he acts in intimate ways. However, the partner may strongly refute the statement and the therapist may come to agree with the refutation. A husband, for example, might claim he is intimate, and yet, not talk to his wife about his thoughts or feelings. He might equate intimacy with doing things with his wife such as going out to eat or watching a movie. He might further argue that he is always doing things for her.

Marital therapists seem to think that, with therapy, all partners will develop the capacity to give significantly in the three areas. However, we have treated partners over an extended period who never developed in some or all of these areas. Some partners lack the real motivation to do the work. Others are motivated, but so afraid that the fear prevents the development of the ability to commit, be intimate, or express passion and sex. The therapist should be aware of the strength of the fears, the client's motivation, and the investment s/he is willing to make in therapy. It is important to set realizable goals and discuss the probable limitations.

Asking these five questions and keeping this framework in mind helps the therapist decide what is missing when the couple talk about love and intimacy. The therapist may need to work in all three areas of the triangle or just in one or two.

At the outset, it was pointed out that Sternberg's triangular theory of love is one of very few theories of love that lends itself to clinical application. Rubin (1973) also conducted one of the first clinically applicable research projects on love, finding that love has four major components: (1) needing (the desire to be with and cared for by the other), (2) caring (wanting to help the other), (3) trusting (exchanging confidences), and (4) tolerance (overlooking the personal faults of the other). The results of this empirical study indicate that partners do not always desire these four components to the same degree.

Though it has been overlooked in the marital therapy literature, tolerance is an important component. Intellectually, partners know they are fallible. They realize they will sometimes hurt and disappoint the other. Yet, they do not always behave as if they believe it. Partners may become intolerant of the smallest acts. Couples sometimes sound like children telling on each other and complaining about trivial matters. Of course, to them these matters are not trivial, and the therapist must pay attention to the partners' perception of reality. However, it is possible to get lost in the trivialities and, as a consequence, buy into their intolerance. To avoid this, the therapist may remind them of the need to be tolerant and ask each partner to pick their issues (battles) more carefully. Tolerance is lost as problems mount and the relationship feels more and more negative. It is easier to be tolerant when some reciprocity returns to the relationship. The therapist can encourage the growth of tolerance by focusing the couple on expressing more caring, positive verbal and behavioral exchanges, and clarifying and fulfilling each other's expectations. When good feelings are being generated, it becomes easier to overlook negative events and feelings.

COMMITMENT

The decisions to commit and to what degree are complex and related to the other two components of love. The therapist may open this discussion by asking about what commitment means to each of them. Then it is possible to see how their definitions are similar or different. If they differ and the partners are in conflict over commitment, this aspect of the relationship requires work. The ideal situation is for the couple to begin treatment with a high degree of commitment to the relationship. Such an occurrence predicts a good outcome for the therapy. Couples who begin in a committed state may be less dysfunctional, or more tolerant of each other, and, therefore, more motivated to change. These couples should be congratulated for having maintained their commitment in spite of their problems. The therapist may wish to use some of the techniques that follow to affirm or strengthen this commitment.

Unfortunately, couples do not always enter therapy with a high level of commitment. One partner may be pushing for marriage, whereas the other is satisfied with living together. The issues for married couples may range from a lack of commitment on both sides (seeking divorce) to unequal commitment (one may want out or is having an affair) to ambivalence (not knowing what one wants) to a polarized commitment (one definitely wants out and the other definitely wants in).

The therapist's first task is to assess the status of the commitment in an open and direct fashion. Sometimes, partners are not honest about how they actually feel regarding their commitment. It is not uncommon for a couple to begin by stating they want to save the marriage only to later find that one partner has already decided it cannot be saved. The therapist may need to probe repeatedly for this material at the beginning of treatment in order to arrive at the truth.

When commitment is an issue for one or both partners, the risk of dropping out of therapy is great. If that happens, it is also possible that the relationship will struggle along for months or years without resolution. Before the issues of commitment can be worked on therapeutically, the couple must be committed to therapy. This fact may seem like a contradiction to the couple. However, the therapist can make clear that s/he is not invested in saving or ending the relationship until the couple have made their decision. The purpose of therapy will be to help them decide. Otherwise, they may continue going back and forth as to what they wish to do. The purpose of the therapy is defined as bringing the partners to the point of knowing what they want to do and then helping them to do it. The options might include staying together, trying a separation, or moving on to divorce.

A number of techniques may be used in clarifying and enhancing commitment. The first is to open the issue up and talk about what has brought them to their current thinking. As we stated earlier, problems in commitment may reflect problems in passion or intimacy. For example, if a partner feels sexually rejected, and, in turn, personally rejected, s/he may decide the relationship should be ended. The problem here is not one of commitment per se, but one resulting from a problem in another area.

The idea of ending a relationship is sometimes reactive. In some relationships, threats of divorce are made during heated fights and they fade away later. The person being threatened may not know it is just a threat—a reactive statement—and may begin to wonder where s/he stands. This kind of empty threat must be stopped so that attention can be focused directly on the issues that prompt the fighting.

For other partners, the idea of divorce involves a great deal of fantasy. They imagine that divorce will free them from their pain, promising a new life and another relationship that is without problems. This idea is often based on the assumption that this person did not contribute to the current relationship problems so all that is needed is to find a new partner. Once a systemic understanding has been reached, this idea often disappears. By systemic understanding we mean an understanding of what each partner has contributed to the problem that would be acted out again in another close relationship if the underlying issue is not resolved.

Another way to combat the fantasy aspect of divorce is to help the partner(s) think about this idea more realistically. Just talking about divorce, including all of the painful and difficult details, may begin to change the partner's perception. A phenomenon we have noted many times is that couples will get to the brink of divorce and then pull back. Perhaps it is the fear of loss or the reality of divorce that produces this reaction. Whatever the underlying cause, the therapist can use this phenomenon constructively. One technique is to use symptom scheduling (Weeks & L'Abate, 1982). The therapist may ask the person to imagine s/he has made the decision to divorce and think and act accordingly on a predetermined schedule. For example, one week the person acts as if divorce is imminent, and the next week acts as if resolution is likely. Another technique is to suggest that the couple go to an attorney in order to learn about legal rights and responsibilities should there be a divorce.

A visit to an attorney frequently brings the couple back to therapy with renewed motivation. One husband recently put this experience in a humorous context by saying that 20 years of therapy would be cheaper than a divorce. His wife laughed at this pronouncement and agreed that too much would be lost in a divorce.

The therapist may also notice a change in the attitude we alluded to earlier in this chapter when talking about partners who feel trapped. After seeing an attorney, these partners ascribe staying as a volitional act, having confronted the fact that divorce is possible and that they have chosen to stay and work on the relationship.

Although the concept of commitment may be missing in the marital and family therapy literature, it is not a phenomenon that has gone unnoticed in psychology. Social psychologist Harold Kelley (1983) reviewed the literature on why people commit and what sustains commitment.

The research shows that one factor in sustaining a relationship is improving the reward-cost balance. This idea may be used in several ways. First, the therapist might ask the couple to think about the past in order to help them see that the relationship had been rewarding and that it continues to be so in some areas, although the rewards are often overlooked. Asking the couple what they used to like about each other and the relationship may orient them in this direction. It is a question we ask all couples to help reactivate positive feelings. Second, the question may be future-oriented to discover what each wants to get from the other. In many cases, the answer is related to what they felt they received early on in the relationship. The partners may also affirm for each other that they want to do what will make the other happy as a way of instilling some hope about future rewards. Third, the therapist may begin developing some simple contracts to help each one feel more rewarded. Successful implementation of these contracts becomes evidence that the partners can give to each other.

A second factor in Kelley's (1983) work related to commitment is what has been called *irretrievable investments*. This factor is difficult to describe because the investments are intangible. In spite of the fact that it is difficult to define these investments, couples generally know what the therapist is referring to when this question is asked. The couple will often talk about losing what was special or unique about their relationship, the memories they share and can revive together, experiences, hopes, dreams, and familiarity. For example, one man who came to therapy to save a marriage frequently talked about their dreams of retiring and moving to a plot of land they had purchased several years prior. The man had created an image of his life in this new place that included fantasies of how his marriage would be and of his children and future grandchildren coming to visit.

The *understanding* that develops between partners is a third factor identified by Kelley (1983) that will be lost if the partners separate. As partners spend months and years together they come to understand each other and share a sense of we-ness, even if it is in terms of their projections. They may develop a unique language to describe feelings, behaviors, requests. Each partner is a "known" rather than an "unknown." One wife stated she knew her husband would always be faithful and even tempered. On one hand, she needed to be married to a man with these traits because her father had rejected her and was prone to violent outbursts. On the other hand, she found his lack of passion emotionally unbearable. The fact that she could "know" her husband was comforting and to lose that would be frightening.

The final factor in Kelley's (1983) work is that of the *attractiveness of the alternatives*. When a partner considers leaving a relationship it is to escape the pain of the present and move toward a relationship that holds the promise of being satisfying. The alternative is usually idealized, with fantasies of finding another person who will fulfill every need without the problems of the current relationship. Sometimes an already established affair is believed to be the answer. The problem is that an affair, the new relationship, has a carefully circumscribed life of its own. A marital relationship cannot compete with the idealized pattern of an affair. The therapist must help the client weigh the alternatives realistically, and this can be accomplished in three ways.

First, the therapist may suggest that unresolved problems in the current relationship, which are, in part, due to each partner, will mostly likely manifest themselves in subsequent relationships. For example, a woman may divorce one alcoholic just to marry another addict. Unless she resolves her own issues of codependency she will keep repeating the pattern. But, if she resolves her issues and confronts her husband, then maybe he will resolve his alcoholism.

Second, if there is an affair and the person is leaving to be with the "new love," then the affair must be examined. The intoxication that surrounds an affair is as powerful as any drug. The perspective on the relationship and the other person is clouded. When the honeymoon phase of the affair is over, clients often remark on how they "did it again"— picked someone just like the last partner.

Third, the ideal picture of the future needs to be challenged. Life is filled with difficulties that can be successfully navigated. In the idealized version of the future, relationship difficulties do not exist or they are minimized. All relationships take work. One husband in his 60s made the comment after beginning couple therapy that he never truly understood the work required in a relationship. This same man had, to this therapist's amazement, been in analysis for over 15 years and had had an 11-year affair. His analyst had encouraged the affair. The man lived over a decade of his life with the fantasy that he would one day leave his wife for the other woman. When the affair partner's husband died and she began insisting they marry, his perception of her changed and he began to see that she was much like his wife. His defenses of denial and projection had overpowered the reality of his situation.

INTIMACY

Several theories of intimacy are described here for the purpose of pointing out how they may be clinically useful. In treatment, these theories are secondary to eliciting the couple's views of intimacy and helping them clarify their ideas in light of these theories.

Sternberg (1986a, 1986b) defines intimacy as the sense of feeling close, connected, or bonded; having a sense of welfare for the other, wanting happiness for the other; regarding the other highly; being able to count on the other in time of need; experiencing mutual understanding, sharing oneself and one's possessions; talking intimately; giving emotional support; valuing the other; and finding the other person predictable (trustworthy). His definition is actually a list of descriptors for intimacy that is much like what many couples will say when they are asked about what constitutes intimacy in their relationship.

The early research in the field of intimacy was primarily aimed at being able to conceptually and operationally define this concept and develop an instrument to measure it. Schaefer and Olson (1981) differentiate between two types of intimacy. An "intimate experience" is a feeling of closeness or sharing with another person in one or more of seven areas of what they define as intimate behavior. They define an "intimate relationship" as one in which an individual shares in several areas with the expectation that the experiences and relationship will persist. They believe intimacy is a process that can never be fully completed, one that requires constant attention and work. Seven types of intimacy are identified: (1) emotional intimacy, which involves experiencing a feeling of closeness; (2) social intimacy, which involves, among other things, having common friends; (3) intellectual intimacy, which involves sharing ideas; (4) sexual intimacy, which involves sharing affection and sex; (5) recreational intimacy, which involves doing pleasurable things together; (6) spiritual intimacy, which involves having a similar sense regarding the meaning of life and/or religion; and (7) aesthetic intimacy, which involves sharing in the experience of a sense of beauty.

Schaefer and Olson (1981) state, "Intimacy is a process and an experience which is the outcome of the disclosure of intimate topics and sharing of intimate experiences" (p. 51). These researchers then go on to discuss how to measure intimacy using an assessment inventory known as Personal Assessment of Intimacy in Relationships (PAIR). The clinician may be interested in using this inventory as a quick way to assess intimacy as operationally defined by Schaefer and Olson. The conceptual definition is also useful in pointing us toward various types of intimacy that may exist in a relationship and that might be used to guide our clinical investigation.

Another researcher whose work is similar to that of Schaefer and Olson is Waring (1981, 1984). Waring (1981) defined intimacy as a multifaceted interpersonal dimension that describes the quality of a marital relationship and consists of eight variables: (1) affection, which is the feeling of closeness; (2) expressiveness, considered the degree to which thoughts, feelings, and beliefs are communicated; (3) compatibility, the degree to which the couple can work and play together; (4) cohesion, which is the commitment to the relationship; (5) sexuality, the degree to which sexual needs are met; (6) conflict resolution, which is how effectively conflicts are resolved; (7) autonomy, which is the degree of connection to family and friends; and (8) identity, which is the couple's self-confidence and esteem. The clinical application of this work is directed toward "cognitive self-disclosure." This approach refers to making ourselves known to others by revealing our thoughts, beliefs, attitudes, and so forth, as well as developing a better sense of self-awareness. The specifics of this approach are not delineated in the paper, but the eight concepts defining intimacy are useful in guiding our thinking about relevant areas for further examination. In a subsequent paper, Waring (1984) describes a 90-item true/false inventory that measures the quantity and quality of marital intimacy, known as the Waring Intimacy Questionnaire (WIC). This questionnaire could be employed to assess intimacy and to suggest areas in which the couple need to focus attention. The use of these kinds of intimacy inventories early on in treatment has the advantage of pointing out problem spots long before couples are able to identify or discuss such areas themselves, especially in the realm of sexual behavior.

The two previous researchers show that self-disclosure through a variety of channels is the major component of intimacy. In other words, there is a positive relationship between marital adjustment and self-disclosure (see Chelune, Rosenfeld, & Waring, 1985). These researchers also found that distressed partners being treated clinically showed little similarity in their self-disclosure patterns and that positive disclosures by one partner led to an increase in negative disclosures by the other. This finding suggests that the use of communication training for distressed couples would be useful to help minimize misunderstandings and keep the communication equitable and positive.

One of the most interesting empirical studies in the literature on intimacy deals with the question of how much intimacy is optimal. Harper and Elliot (1988) suggest that too much or too little intimacy could be detrimental. Their study shows that intimacy was curvilinearly related to the level of marital adjustment. Those couples who perceived a large discrepancy between the amount of intimacy they felt and the amount they desired reported the least amount of marital satisfaction. On the other hand, those with very low discrepancies were also low on marital satisfaction. Some middle point produced the greatest level of satisfaction. This study has significant theoretical and clinical implications. To what extent is intimacy a good thing and to what extent should the clinician encourage intimacy in the couple?

Interestingly, Wynne and Wynne (1986) wrote a theoretical article that warns us about enshrining intimacy. They define intimacy as "a subjective relational experience in which the core components are trusting self-disclosure to which the response is communicated empathy" (p. 384). Their concept of intimacy is embedded in their larger epigenetic or developmental model of relational systems. In this theory, there are four major relational processes, which unfold developmentally: attachment/caregiving, communicating, joint problem solving, and mutuality.

The last concept is the most important in understanding their concept of intimacy. Mutuality is defined as the selective integration of the preceding processes into a pattern of relatedness. The relationship between these processes is not simply linear, but circular or spiraling. Wynne and Wynne (1986) emphasize that mutuality incorporates both distancing and constructive reengagement. At one time, these theorists had postulated intimacy as the fifth stage in relational development, but they abandoned that idea as flawed for three reasons. First, they saw intimacy as a subjective corollary of the more basic relational processes, and not a process itself. Second, intimacy could occur prior to the development of mutuality, and finally, the concept was seen as too "elusive, episodic, and culture-dependent" to qualify as a primary process.

In Schaefer and Olson's (1981) theory, intimacy is viewed both as experiences, which are elusive, unpredictable, and spontaneous, and relationships, which take time and effort to maintain. Wynne and Wynne (1986) offer three misgivings about this view. First, they do not agree that the goal of a relationship is to maintain intimacy. To do so would be to establish a goal of symbiosis and impose a continual burden on the relationship that would deny selfhood. They believe a relationship thrives when the distance between the couple waxes and wanes. Second, using the term "intimacy" to apply to experience and relationship is confusing. They advocate using the term to refer only to subjective experience. Third, in focusing so much on intimacy researchers and therapists may overlook the relational processes that must be in place.

Wynne and Wynne's (1986) theory supports our contention that intimacy requires a balance between closeness and distance, separateness and togetherness, engagement and disengagement (Weeks & Treat, 1992). There are two clinical issues inherent in this idea. First, we need to recognize that different couples have different intimacy needs and we need to determine what will work for whom. Some couples need less distance; others need more. Schaefer and Olson (1981) and Clinebell and Clinebell (1970) suggest that there are many different types of intimacy, and propose that partners might differ not only in the degree of desire for a particular intimacy, but in the specific intimacy or intimacies preferred. One partner's intimacy needs might be satisfied if his or her primary intimacy is present; whereas the other partner might be dissatisfied even if seven intimacies are satisfied, but the one defined as "crucial" is lacking.

The second clinical issue that must be considered is that, after the partners become aware of their needs, they must be able to negotiate those needs. Partners usually negotiate for closeness. They request time with each other or suggest an activity that creates closeness. Distance is usually sought through action rather than words. A partner may go out to play golf, read a book, go to a different room, or start a fight. The clinician needs to clarify how the partners move back and forth between closeness and distance and discuss how intimacy needs are met by both positions. Distance represents the autonomous pole of the continuum. It is where the person experiences self as separate from other and brings that sense of selfhood back to the relationship.

A simple exercise can help the clinician understand the couple's thinking about this concept. The clinician asks the couple to draw circles showing the degree of closeness and distance in the relationship. The partners are asked to draw circles showing where they would place themselves and where they think their partners would place them. Next, the same exercise is repeated, but this time partners are asked to show the ideal positioning—where they would like to be. The therapist can then discuss the meaning of these circles and go on to the issue of negotiation.

Wynne and Wynne (1986) argue that efficacious marital therapy must examine the developmental processes of attachment/caregiving, communication skills, problem solving, and mutuality. These four relational processes can be reconceptualized in a framework developed by Weingarten (1991). Her review of the literature suggests that there are two types of discourses about intimacy. She refers to these as "individual capacity" and "quality of relatedness." The individual capacity discourse is based on the assumption that intimacy is a capacity that resides in the individual. She goes on to point out that the work of Bowen (1978) and Lerner-Goldhor (1989) represent this point of view. The quality of relatedness discourse is based on the assumption that intimacy is a product of relationships in which partners are able to know each other deeply.

Weingarten (1991) proposes a new definition within a social constructionist and feminist perspective. She states:

> Intimate interaction occurs when people share meaning or co-create meaning and are able to coordinate their actions to reflect their mutual meaning-making. Meaning can be shared through writing, speech, gesture, or symbol. In the process of co-creating or sharing meaning, individuals have the experience of knowing and being known by the other. Intimate interaction can happen with one or more people, in actual or imagined encounter. Refraining from meaning-making and providing, imposing, rejecting, and misunderstanding meaning are associated with non-intimate interaction. Repeated intimate interaction may produce an experience of intimacy, while repeated non-intimate interaction usually interferes with or inhibits relational patterns that lead to the sharing or co-creation of meaning. (p. 295)

This definition focuses on meaning and interactions. She suggests that language is imbued with meaning and the process of sharing and co-creating meaning can lead to a coordination of action. She also states that intimacy is made up of both intimate and nonintimate interactions. By analyzing these interactions she believes it possible to determine the meaning of these events in order to see whether they are used to connect with or dominate another.

As we stated earlier, intimacy is a complex phenomenon involving both the individual and the relationship. Weingarten's (1991) delineation of two types of discourse—individual capacity and quality of relatedness—is useful. We believe both discourses have merit. In the Intersystem Model of therapy (Weeks & Hof, 1994), we state that problems should be conceptualized and treated from a metatheoretical perspective of dialectics. Specifically, we look at the individual, interactional, and intergenerational aspects of the problem. Thus, we believe a synthesis of the two discourses identified by Weingarten is the most appropriate method. Problems with intimacy may be in the individual and in the relationship. It appears Weingarten (1991) may be inappropriately placing Wynne and Wynne's (1986) theory strictly in the quality of relatedness camp.

From our perspective, Wynne and Wynne's (1986) attachment/caregiving would also fit within the individual capacity discourse. A partner's ability to attach to another is determined early in life as a result of experiences in the family of origin. Later in this chapter we show how individuals come to relationships carrying a variety of fears about intimacy that impede intimate interactions. The relational processes of communicating, problem solving, and mutuality fit within the quality of relatedness discourse. Our point is that work on improving intimacy may take a number of directions. The therapist may need to deal with communication problems, problem-solving strategies, or the couple's ability to regulate distance in a self-aware and deliberate manner. This leaves us with the task of understanding what factors may interfere with the ability to attach.

Components of Intimate Interactions

Part of fostering intimate interactions requires helping the couple identify those behaviors that will lead to a greater feeling of intimacy. Each partner can be asked to develop a definition of intimacy and then to think about breaking intimacy down into its components. The therapist might simply say, "Make a list of those things that would be included in your definition of intimacy." The partners then make their lists and discuss the ideas in the session in order to know what the other would like and to arrive at some consensus. The partners need not agree totally. In fact, as the research shows, some discrepancy is actually intimacy enhancing. Once the components have been identified, the next step is to think about how to implement them behaviorally. Couple therapists need to move from the general to the specific, from the theoretical to the concrete. The ideas represent the partner's attitudes, which then must be translated into actions. Each idea is discussed in terms of who will do what. The affective part of each component also requires attention. The therapist may ask the partners how they will feel behaving or having the other behave in the way that is under consideration. The couple should also be encouraged to comment on the behavior when it occurs in order to affectively reinforce its occurrence. Something that appears to have been underemphasized in the literature is the fact that intimacy is an emotion. It is something partners feel for each other. Partners do not say, "Today we had an intimate interaction," or, "I thought about saying something intimate." They say they felt close, warm, loved, cared for, intimate. The partners are encouraged to comment on the emotion they experience when these interactions take place or to reflect on them later in terms of the emotional impact.

The list of ideas generated by the couple is the beginning. The therapist may want to suggest additions to the list based on both personal experience and the literature on intimacy. The most clinically useful discussion of the components of intimacy this author has used was developed by L'Abate (1975, 1977). He identifies seven components.

1. SEEING THE GOOD

By the time many couples get into therapy, it is difficult to tell whether they see any of the good in each other. Their descriptions of each other are largely negative. One of the first tasks is to help them become less negatively biased. Questions regarding what attracted them to each other and what they like about each other currently help to activate these perceptions. We use what we call the three A's exercise; the three A's being appreciation, affection, and affirmation. Appreciation refers to commenting on what the other person does that we like or on the qualities we like about them. For example, a partner might say, "I appreciate the fact that you brought me a cup of coffee this morning" or "I appreciate your thoughtfulness." Affection refers to showing signs of liking and loving with words or actions. Touching, holding, kissing, hugging, and verbal statements of affection are important. The most difficult concept is affirmation. Affirming statements may be used to affirm the value of the other person and affirm the value of the relationship. The partner might say, "I like you," "You are a very special person," "I'm glad we're married," or "I can't imagine my life without you."

It is axiomatic that people cannot like others more than they like themselves. Seeing good in another means that one must be able to see good in one's self or have a sense of self-esteem. Feldman (1982) shows that projective identification is a powerful and pervasive force in couples' relationships. Aspects of the self that are rejected or disowned may be projected onto the partner. The "bad" elements of the self are then fought with through the other person. It is impossible to see good in another when this process is in place. The projections must be owned on both sides in order to allow for goodness to emerge.

2. CARING

Caring means being concerned about another's welfare, happiness, needs, and feelings in a consistent and dependable way. It is an attitude of respect for others, which derives from our own ability to care about ourselves. Caring begins with an awareness of what we need in order to feel safe, secure, esteemed, growing. These needs must then be competently communicated to others and acted upon in order to achieve some level of satisfaction. Caring for another requires tuning in to what the other says s/he needs and being willing to meet some of those needs. At times, it is difficult for one partner to express what is needed. An empathetic response from the other partner is then expected. For example, suppose one's parent has just died. We would not expect the grieving person to actually ask for help. A caring partner will possess the empathy needed to respond appropriately.

3. PROTECTIVENESS

Partners need to protect each other and their relationship. Mutual protection means taking the other's side when necessary and seeing issues from the other perspective. Protecting the relationship means affirming the boundary that has been established as a result of being married or in the relationship. A relationship is always embedded within many other relationships. Various forces impinge upon the couple, and it is necessary to establish fluid boundaries for the three to four priorities that are found in most marriages: self, marriage, children, and work. Among clinical couples, there are two patterns often seen. Partners may not agree on what order the priorities should take. The husband may value work, self, children, and marriage, whereas the wife may value children, marriage, work, and self. Is it any wonder they are unhappy? In other cases, the couple may agree on priorities but not have ideas that work for them. They may give themselves entirely to children and work to the devastation of self and marriage. To protect the relationship requires reaching some agreement on the priorities and then carrying them out in ways that serve the relationship as a whole.

4. ENJOYMENT

Enjoyment refers to being together and doing things together that are pleasurable. Achieving pleasure may be accomplished by doing something for oneself or by sharing pleasure with another. Clinical couples often seem to have forgotten how to play with each other. They are generally depressed, lacking in humor, and focused solely on life's difficulties. Many couples emphasize doing and having. They busy themselves doing what they think is expected of them and acquiring the possessions they feel they must have to compete—pleasure gets left out of the picture entirely. Unfortunately, many people were reared in families that denigrated the idea of enjoyment in life and focused only on performance. Performance was measured against a standard of perfection—so the child was expected to be perfect. When this attitude is expressed to the child, nothing is ever pleasurable in itself, everything is seen as a means to an end. The therapist may need to examine underlying attitudes and learning about pleasure as well as help the couple identify ways they can interact more enjoyably.

5. RESPONSIBILITY

This concept deals with taking personal responsibility for what happens in the relationship. Among clinical couples, there is often a pattern of externalizing responsibility for problems. In other words, the partner is blamed when things are not working as expected. An optimal relationship is one in which partners are able to see their role in problems and do what is necessary to stop the behavior. Partners also assume responsibility for making the relationship work. They realize relationships require maintenance and that one partner cannot do all the work.

We also think of responsibility in terms of being able to express emotions in a manner other than reactive. An emotionally reactive response is raw or lacking in thoughtful modulation. Emotional reactivity simply means that emotion rules. For the most part, the emotion is driven by past events and leads a partner to respond to the mate the way s/he once responded to a parent. Thought and affect become blurred. The emotion is ventilated without knowing the source, needs, or proper target. Being emotionally responsible means the partner is emotionally self-aware and is able to ask for what is needed in order to resolve the feelings.

6. SHARING HURT

L'Abate (1977) believes that sharing one's hurt is a most intimate act. He points out that we can share our good feelings and success with most anyone. With whom do we share our hurt feelings? Pain is difficult for a lot of people to feel; many defend against the feeling by denying it or by transforming the feeling into something else, often, anger. It is no wonder we only share our pain when we trust someone deeply and can safely expect that person to be empathetic.

It is also impossible to live in a close relationship and not from time to time hurt the person we love. When this happens it is essential to be able to deal with the hurt directly and not focus on some feeling used to cover it up. Helping partners learn to recognize their hurt feelings and be able to express them promotes a sense of intimacy. Hurt may be buried under anger, depression, resentment, frustration, guilt. Learning to identify the feeling may be a difficult task; one that requires empathetic understanding on the part of the therapist and careful probing to reveal it.

7. FORGIVENESS

This concept is one that most couples overlook in their list of components of intimacy. Yet, it is implicitly working in every healthy couple relationship. As we have pointed out, we cannot live in a close relationship without sometimes hurting the other person. What happens if there is not a way to resolve the hurt through forgiveness? Forgiveness doesn't simply mean offering an apology. Forgiveness is achieved through an understanding of the other person's motivations in the act and being willing to forgive the act by cherishing the goodwill that pervades the relationship. The motivation of the person who does the hurting needs to be understood. If the catalyst is anger, for example, then another way of dealing with it must be found.

In addition, the person who is hurt must be acknowledged. Acknowledging a hurtful act or intent is difficult and empathizing with someone who has been hurt can also be difficult. In some cases, the hurtful behavior will be denied and will continue. The therapist will have to monitor this behavior in order to make a case for a deliberate, but unconscious pattern.

We believe the ability to forgive is based on the faith one person has in another: the faith that the partner will act with goodwill, exhibiting many of the components listed, such as seeing good, caring, and being protective and responsible. Forgiveness is similar to tolerance, which was discussed earlier. Just as it is easier to be tolerant when we can counterbalance the negative with good things in the relationship, it is easier to forgive when we are able to see the goodwill that exists. It is also important to forgive ourselves when we have acted hurtfully or had a hurtful effect on another.

Fear of Intimacy

When partners bring the fear of intimacy to their relationship, something will always happen to prevent intimate interactions. This fear is personally embedded and falls into the category of the *personal incapacity discourse* (Weingarten, 1991), which refers to the individual having an inherent incapacity for intimacy. In spite of the fact that the fear is within the partners, it only manifests in relationship. As long as a person is not in a relationship, the fear can be hidden or disguised from others and from the self. Fear often does not emerge until a relationship is well underway. Many of the cases we see involve couples who felt they had an intimate relationship at the beginning, but have lost something. The fact is that as they became closer, embedded fear was activated and a new pattern was created in the relationship.

Another interesting phenomenon has to do with the selection of one's mate. We do not believe that the choice of mate is a random process; instead, it is based on careful deliberation at both conscious and unconscious levels. A person with a strong fear of intimacy will select a partner with a strong fear of intimacy, although it may not always be readily apparent. One of the most deceptive phenomena we see as couple therapists is a relationship in which one partner is pushing for more closeness and the other is backing away. It appears that the one who is backing away has the underlying fear. However, if the one who is backing away stops and resolves the fear, the other person begins to find reasons why s/he cannot enjoy the closeness that had been demanded. In essence, the overt problem in one has served to hide or disguise the covert problem in the other (cf. Napier, 1978). The lesson from this experience is quite simple. As couple therapists, we must not forget our systemic understanding of the couple-system, in spite of overt appearances.

Fear of intimacy is learned in one's family of origin. It may be useful to normalize the fear with couples by stating that virtually everyone comes to a relationship with some underlying fear about too much intimacy. The therapy will aim toward uncovering the fear and helping the partners learn how to cope with its manifestations in the relationship. When the therapist is aware that fear of intimacy is operating, the first strategy is to work on the fear, not on creating a list of intimate interactions. If the fear is not strong or appears to be absent, then the other strategy may be used first as an enhancement technique.

The clinician begins by suggesting that each partner has entered the relationship with some fear of intimacy. The partners are asked to think about the fear they may have. Some partners only need to think about it in order to bring it to awareness. Others will require much more work. For those who are unaware, doing a genogram can be a great help. As we stated, the fear first develops in the family of origin. The genogram will reveal patterns of familial interaction that allow us to infer what forms the fear might take. For example, if an adult child had been emotionally smothered as a child, we would infer a fear of engulfment. The following list of types of fear represents some of the most common fears of intimacy that we have observed. This list may also be used as a guide in inferring what might prevent intimate interactions. On some occasions, we briefly review this list as a way to prime couples to begin considering their fears.

Fear of intimacy is directly related to the issue of conflict in the couple. The reader may recall that fear has a biologically programmed response. In humans, the response is to fight or to flee. Patterns of chronic fighting, intermittent fighting and making up, fighting and fleeing, or simple withdrawal from each other are common responses to a fear of intimacy. These patterns regulate the distance, but do so in a way that is unacceptable to most couples.

1. FEAR OF DEPENDENCY

In a relationship both partners depend upon each other. Partners are interdependent. Some partners have difficulty letting their dependency needs be known. Others have such a strong fear of dependency that they deny themselves these needs. Individuals with a strong fear of dependency are generally known as counterdependent. For these individuals, it is essential to be emotionally self-sufficient, insulated, and independent. In some of these cases, the counterdependent partner will select a very dependent partner who carries their dependency needs for them. They can then take care of the dependent partner without having to look at themselves, because the partner needs or demands so much. In less severe situations, the partner with a weaker fear of dependency will remain emotionally aloof from the relationship. These partners do not ask for much and often have trouble giving much, especially in the area of emotional support. In Sager's (Sager & Hunt, 1979) list of marital types, these partners would likely be what they call parallel partners. They present a facade of marriage without the emotional interconnections.

In our experience, men are more apt to present with this fear. Such men likely received messages from their fathers that they should be strong, and never cry or ask for help, and that they must take care of themselves because the world is a competitive place that coddles no one. As children, these boys were often pushed to be self-sufficient and competitive. They may have received little support and guidance from their parents, except to be told to do more and be more adultlike.

This pattern is illustrated well by one 40-year-old man who stated he could never ask his wife for anything. He believed that to ask her for something would mean he was weak and a nothing. As a child, he had been physically punished and ridiculed whenever he showed any emotional vulnerability. He was told he was a baby when he cried. He had internalized his father's injunctions so strongly that he felt he would die if he expressed his own needs. He actually had panic attacks when he found himself feeling emotionally weak. Although he realized how irrational his behavior was, he had been unable to stop it on his own.

Another example involved a man in his mid-40s who was in his second marriage. The presenting problem was inhibited sexual desire in his wife. After years of being sexually frustrated, the husband had finally made his unhappiness known. His history showed that he had been reared by his father from infancy on. His mother had died. His father was a successful businessman who lived the life of a playboy. He wanted his son to be successful and to lead the same kind of life he had chosen. His father never showed emotion, never wept when his wife died, and never spent much time with one woman. Father would sometimes play a game that involved bending his son's toes back and asking if it hurt. If the son said it hurt or showed that it hurt, the father would keep bending his toes. The father said this was a game to help toughen his son in preparation for life. The father also said a man never goes to a woman or asks her for anything, and that women are there to serve men and please them sexually. When the son reached 16 and was still a virgin, the father brought a prostitute home for him and told him to go upstairs for his initiation into manhood.

In both of his marriages, this man was unable to ask for anything emotionally or sexually. He expected his partner to carry the full burden of responsibility. Although it was the wife's problem that got them into treatment, this was clearly a relational problem and much of the therapy was directed toward the husband learning to be aware of his emotional/sexual needs and correcting his early learning about expressing these needs.

2. FEAR OF FEELINGS

In our review of the literature on intimacy, we have found that self-disclosure is important. Self-disclosure might include revealing thoughts, beliefs, attitudes, opinions, and, especially, feelings. The partner with a fear of feelings is not afraid of experiencing or expressing specific feelings, but, rather, all feelings. However, this fear might be actually based on a fear of specific feelings, which has since generalized to all feelings.

These partners appear devoid of feeling. They often have obsessive-compulsive personality disorders or traits. Something is so frightening about feeling that they must develop obsessions or compulsions to keep themselves distracted. They often hide behind rationality, denial, projection, rationalization, and intellectualization, and have a rigid sense of right and wrong. Satir (1967) was one of the first family therapists to recognize this pattern in the family. She called these partners "computers" because of their lack of emotionality. Computers would rather think than feel, do, or act. They detach themselves when emotional situations occur.

These types of people are prone to pair off with either partners who are like them or with their opposite, such as a histrionic partner. When they pair with like partners, they do so in order to avoid feelings entirely. Interestingly, when they pair with partners who are opposite, the pairing provides an excellent example of how projective identification works. What one lacks and cannot deal with must be found in another and then worked through in the other. At an unconscious level, the obsessive-compulsive partner derives vicarious gratification from the overemotionality of the histrionic partner.

Several familial patterns contribute to the development of this type of individual. One type of family is nonemotional. Such families may be quite successful in some instrumental ways, but lack emotionality and emotional connection. Parents may actively or passively discount feelings. Sometimes they actually tell the children what they should feel. For example, a child may feel disappointed about something only to have a parent say that the child should cheer up, that s/he hasn't the right to feel down when life is so good. Other parents passively discount feelings. These parents simply do not acknowledge or reinforce emotional expression.

Some individuals fear feelings for good reason. In their families, feelings were out of control. One or both parents might have been severely depressed, have had bipolar illness, or been emotionally unpredictable (angry and rejecting). A child is overwhelmed by such feelings when they are unexplained. The child begins to fear all emotion because any emotionality is equated with the uncontrolled and hurtful behavior s/he experienced when growing up.

When Joe began couple therapy he was 35. He had been in individual analytic therapy for several years. The problem that brought him to couple therapy was ejaculatory incompetence, that is, an inability to ejaculate during intercourse. Joe's affect was flat, but he was not depressed. He had been depressed for several years prior to entering couple therapy. Joe's mother was histrionic and his father was an alcoholic with a bipolar disorder who was neglectful, rejecting, and angry. Joe never saw a normal expression of feeling as he was growing up. He witnessed "crazy feelings" as far back as he could remember. Whenever he felt up, down, angry, or anything else, he would associate that feeling with the extreme emotionality he saw in his parents. He feared losing emotional control to the point that he would not let himself experience an orgasm. Joe could talk about painful events with no emotion. He equated loss, sadness, and grief with his father's bipolar reaction and feared going crazy.

3. FEAR OF ANGER

This fear may be manifested in two ways: to fear becoming angry with the partner and to fear being the recipient of the partner's anger. In either case, the result is the same. This partner attempts to keep emotionally distant in order to avoid stirring up this feeling. Unfortunately, close relationships inevitably invoke feelings of anger, hostility, rage, and aggression.

First, the individual who fears losing control over his or her own anger. One type of family system that generates this fear is one in which anger pervades. One parent might be abusive and chronically angry. The child's experience of anger is as an irrational emotion, expressed in hurtful and destructive ways. Both parents may fight and frighten the child. One parent may be passive and frightened by the anger of the other parent and transmit this fear to the child. The lesson for the child is that anger is nothing but a destructive force. When confronted by his or her own anger, the child becomes overwhelmed by the potential consequences and works hard to suppress or repress the feeling.

Another type of family that instills a fear of anger is conflict-avoidant. Such families do not allow angry feelings. The parents never show anger, and when someone does become angry the person is told that the feeling is unacceptable. The message is that people who love each other cannot be angry with each other.

The second pattern belongs to the partner who fears being the recipient of anger. This partner may keep emotional distance and, when s/he senses anger in the partner, will placate the partner in order to eliminate the feeling: conflict-avoidant. Conflict leads to anger and anger must be avoided. The same family patterns described can also contribute to this pattern. Frequently, the two patterns are different sides of the same coin. The partner who avoids anger in the self also avoids it in the partner.

Aside from established family patterns, there is another reason anger may be avoided. The couple may have had a number of conflictual and angry encounters, which have gone unresolved because of a lack of skills to deal with anger and conflict. Over time, the anger has built up to a point that it contaminates all issues that emerge. The anger may be smoldering beneath the surface. When something happens that would normally produce a small amount of anger, the issue is emotionally determined to be a release for all the pent up, unresolvable anger. Distancing may be used to avoid the anger until it cannot be contained any longer. The couple believes it useless to try to deal with the anger together, and there is no way to resolve it internally.

This case illustrates one of the patterns described. Ann and Jerry were in their mid-20s when they entered couple therapy. They had been married for two years and were on the verge of divorce. The problem was that they could never resolve any fight. Fights always ended with one of them saying it was a mistake to be married to each other. Both Ann and Jerry had been reared in conflict-avoidant families. Neither could ever remember their parents being angry. The anger genogram (Weeks & Treat, 1992) was done and it became apparent just how negative their attitudes were toward anger. They both equated anger with not loving. Thus, when one had a conflict with the other, the partner on the receiving end sensed the underlying angry feelings, and felt unloved. Fights were implicitly about whether they were lovable or not.

The fear of anger can be so strong that it blocks the expression or even the experiencing of pleasure. A number of cases of inhibited sexual desire have shown that underlying the fear of sexual pleasure and orgasm is really a fear of anger. One woman commented that she had so much suppressed anger that she chose the "biggest football player I could find" for her first sexual experience. She could not be orgasmic with her husband because he was "frail" and would not be able to withstand the release of her rage.

Finally, a specific type of family dynamic can create problems with intimacy based on the suppression of anger. This is a family that creates what has been called parentification (Boszormenyi-Nagy & Spark, 1973). A parentified child is expected to act like an adult. In fact, the child is expected to act as a kind of spouse, usually to a recently divorced parent. The parentified child sacrifices his or her childhood in order to take care of the parent, and because it also provides a sense of omnipotence to counter the fear of being insufficient to the task (Johnson, Weeks, & L'Abate, 1979). The emotional cost to the child is high. The child must tune in to the parents feelings while tuning out his or her own feelings. Normally, such a dilemma would produce anger and resentment, but not for the parentified child. This child manages to suppress these feelings. The parentified child becomes a parentified adult and tends to marry someone who needs caretaking. For a while this system works because it is familiar, but, over time, the adult may begin to resent the situation. However, s/he is thoroughly indoctrinated to not express feelings, especially feelings of displeasure with the parents. This phenomenon has not often been recognized in the marital therapy literature, yet it appears in many of the cases we treat. Getting back to the early parentification is one of the keys to successful resolution.

4. FEAR OF LOSING CONTROL AND BEING CONTROLLED

Control is an important part of every relationship. Healthy relationships are based on mutual control. Partners share the power and control in the relationship. When a partner fears losing control or being controlled by the other s/he may actively resist or passively give in to the other. The fear of loss of control appears to operate on two levels. On the first level, the partner fears being controlled by the other, afraid the other person will take over. This situation can be conceptualized from a transactional analysis viewpoint as one partner assuming a child role and the other a parental role. Individuals with this fear do not know how to assert themselves appropriately. They unconsciously sabotage themselves in order to have the other partner take control. These individuals may have been reared in families where there was a strong and controlling parental figure who undermined their confidence. As children, they may have been overprotected or expected to do tasks beyond their years, which then led to failure. Intimacy suffers in these relationships because of the parent-child nature of the relationship. Those who fear losing control will not let their guard down to let others know them. They assume this knowledge would be used against them to keep them in their place.

The second, deeper level, reveals a fear that is much more pervasive. In fact, these individuals feel they are engulfed in the relationship. They believe their sense of identity is at stake. Somehow the partner is given the responsibility for their lack of self. This deep-seated fear reflects a poor sense of self-identity, a lack of differentiation. Paradoxically, these people search out partners who will complete or define them, and then recoil from the relationship because they do not want to be defined by another. They simply do not know who they are or what they want. As a result, they move back and forth in the relationship between enmeshment and disengagement.

Martin, age 52, had married when he was in his early 20s and then separated, but had never divorced. When he entered therapy he was in a relationship, and he said he wanted to get married. He had only been able to spend short periods of time with his new partner. The couple would go out on a date and he would either cut it short, or he would just leave the woman alone at his house. Sometimes he would call his wife during the date. After a number of sessions, Martin stated that he would die if he got married. What this meant was that whatever sense of self he had would be totally lost. He was afraid the new partner would take it from him. Martin's mother was an overpowering and domineering woman who never let Martin mature. She treated him as if he were a child, insisting on daily contact. His loyalty to her meant he could not attach to anyone else, and his fear of losing his tenuously felt sense of identity kept him from getting close to anyone.

5. FEAR OF EXPOSURE

Most everyone is familiar with the fear of exposure. When we begin to date, we put our best foot forward. We want our new partner to see only the best in us. As the relationship develops, the facade slowly begins to break down. A zigzagging effect occurs. One partner discloses something and then the other reciprocates, and then the first discloses something more personal and so on. Individuals with a fear of exposure do not move beyond this first phase of a relationship. They must guard against the other person really getting to know them. They believe that if they were truly seen, the relationship would end because their worthlessness would be revealed. Exposing the inner self is too painful. All the defects, weaknesses, faults, and feelings of emptiness would emerge. These individuals simply do not feel worthy of being loved. They engage in a pretense with others. They *act* as though they deserve success, love, to be liked, and so on. The incongruence between how they feel inside and how they act leads them to see themselves as impostors: "If they only knew who I really am or what I really did, they would never. . . ."

In our experience, many of these individuals were reared by parents who made love contingent on performance. If they did a good job, the parent would praise them, but even the praise would be restrained because the performance always could have been better. The parents were demanding, critical, and never satisfied with the child's performance. Contingent love teaches the child to value doing well rather than valuing self. The child eventually realizes that the parent's love is not for the child, but for what s/he can do, which is never enough.

Steven entered couple therapy when he was 48 years of age. His wife complained that he had always been aloof and noncommunicative. Steven was a very successful executive who had earned a reputation in his field. He believed his success was due to sheer luck. He was afraid someone would discover what a fraud he really was. His wife had never heard him speak about himself in this way. He went on to say he could never let her know him because he did not like himself. If she were to know the person he thought he was, she would surely find him horrible and leave. He did not want her to feel she had made a terrible mistake in marrying him either. Steven felt he was an imposter in his work and in his marriage. He had no friends and kept himself emotionally isolated in the marriage. Steven's father was described as a passive man who never did much with his life. His mother constantly criticized his father. Steven was told he should do well in school, but at the same time his mother told him he was not too smart, so he should not worry if his grades were not A's and B's. He was also told he should consider a career that involved working with his hands. When he was accepted to graduate school, his mother said he was foolish to waste his money because he could never finish. He did finish and not only did his mother not attend his graduation but she never acknowledged his professional life. His parents had ever been able to tell him they loved him or were proud of his accomplishments.

6. FEAR OF REJECTION/ABANDONMENT

A person may experience rejection or abandonment in a variety of ways. Structurally, this can occur through death, desertion, or divorce. Divorce is a phenomenon common to many of the cases in treatment today. As divorce rates have climbed over the past 30 years, more and more of our adult clients have experienced the loss of a parent through divorce. Desertion is a phenomenon that may not be apparent to many therapists because of the types of cases seen. Desertion is more likely among lower-class families. Doing a genogram should reveal whether an adult child has experienced one of these situations and how the child felt about the parent who "left." Adult children may also feel rejected or abandoned psychologically. An intact family does not guarantee the absence of these feelings. Sometimes children are not wanted, perhaps even viewed as mistakes. In other cases, the parents ignore, neglect, or send rejecting messages to the child. A child may be told s/he is not wanted, that something is terribly wrong with him or her. Those who have experienced feeling rejected or abandoned may fear getting too close to another person. They anticipate a repetition of the same pattern, hence the same feelings, that they experienced in the past. They realize that if they get close to someone and that person rejects or abandons them, the hurt will be tremendous. As a child, the hurt was overwhelming. As an adult, this partner can only anticipate the same level of intensity.

The fear of rejection or abandonment is one of the most common fears in the realm of intimacy. This fear reveals itself early on in the development of many relationships. The problem may first appear as difficulty in making a commitment rather than as difficulty in being intimate.

Louise, a 36-year-old client, entered therapy with her partner of 12 years. They had never married although they considered themselves married. The presenting problem was lack of sexual desire on her part and controlling behavior on the part of her partner. Louise was one of four daughters. She said her father had been unlucky because he wanted boys. Louise was a middle child and felt she had gotten lost in the pack. She could not remember her mother even saying a kind word to her. What she could recall was that her sisters all received better treatment. Whenever a problem occurred, Louise would be blamed. She was given more responsibility and fewer privileges than her sisters. She felt her mother was too busy and too interested in her sisters to care about her. Louise had never been intimate in a relationship. In spite of her 12-year history with her current partner, it was clear that neither one knew what it meant to share themselves. Louise's main desire for a relationship was, as she put it, to "make her normal."

The fear of rejection/abandonment need not stem from childhood. This fear can develop in adult relationships that have ended traumatically. In one case, a woman was about to marry. Just prior to her marriage, her fiancé disappeared without explanation. The trauma of this event left her confused, depressed, and feeling abandoned. All subsequent relationships were colored by this experience. She felt she could trust no one. In another case, a woman in her 50s and married for a long time, lost her husband in a plane crash. She later discovered that her husband was having an affair and that his partner was on the plane with him. This trauma produced a number of reactions. She was not able to work through her grief, loss, and anger about his betrayal, and her new marriage was marked by chronic conflict, mistrust, sexual acting out on her part, and a need to obsessively spend all the money that had come to her as a result of her first husband's death (over 10 million dollars).

CONCLUSION

The subject of passion was left out of this chapter because it is the focus of Chapter 9 on inhibited sexual desire. However, the couple should be asked to define passion and to develop ideas to promote it. If sex is emphasized as the main component of passion, the chapter on inhibited sexual desire will provide the right perspective. If, instead, the couple stresses romance, nurturance, and the feeling of wanting to be with the other, the clinician should address these aspects. The three components of love are synergistically related, but are considered separately here for conceptual clarity.

The issues of commitment and intimacy may be presented as a problem in the couple's relationship when either is lacking, and intimacy issues may be discussed near the end of treatment in terms of a growth-enhancing issue. Knowing what commitment and intimacy mean helps the clinician understand what couples may be talking about when these issues emerge, and can also guide us in helping couples develop greater commitment and intimacy.

Our approach to intimacy, which is based on the Intersystem Model, suggests that barriers to intimacy may be found in the individual, in the interactional system (couple), or in the family of origin. An interplay is likely to exist between the individual and relational factors. A couple complaining of intimacy problems will often attribute the problem to one partner. From a systems perspective, this situation is highly unlikely. Partners choose each other on the basis of how much closeness/distance they can tolerate. When intimacy is a problem, it is a two-sided problem, although the difficulties of one partner may be masked by the other partner.

One of the great pleasures in being a couple therapist is seeing couples grow and feel good about their relationship. We are in a unique position to help couples develop a greater sense of commitment, intimacy, and passion. Couples often enter therapy with the single goal of eliminating their problems. As therapy unfolds, their goal is often expanded, with an additional emphasis on intimacy enhancement being woven into the problem-resolution phase, or done as a separate piece of work at the end of therapy. The therapist should be capable of providing help in both problem solving and enhancement.

REFERENCES

Boszormenyi-Nagy, I, & Spark, G. (1973). *Invisible loyalties.* New York: Harper & Row.

Bowen, M. (1978). *Family therapy in clinical practice.* New York: Jason Aronson.

Chelune, G., Rosenfeld, L., & Waring, E. (1985). Spouse disclosure patterns is distressed and nondistressed couples. *American Journal of Family Therapy, 13,* 24–32.

Clinebell, H. J., & Clinebell, C. H. (1970). *The intimate marriage.* New York: Harper & Row.

Feldman, L. (1982). Dysfunctional marital conflict: An integrative interpersonal-intrapsychic model. *Journal of Marital and Family Therapy, 8,* 417–428.

Harper, J., & Elliot, M. (1988). Can there be too much of a good thing? The relationship between desired level of intimacy and marital adjustment. *American Journal of Family Therapy, 16,* 351–360.

Johnson, G., Weeks, G. R., & L'Abate, L. (1979). Forced holding: A technique for treating parentified children. *Family Therapy, 6,* 123–132.

Kelley, H. (1983). Love and commitment. In H. Kelley et al., *Close relationships* (pp. 287–314). New York: Freeman.

L'Abate, L. (1975). A positive approach to marital and family intervention. In L. Wolberg & M. Aronson (Eds.), *Group therapy 1975—an overview* (pp. 63–75). New York: Stratton.

L'Abate, L. (1977). *Enrichment: Structural interventions with couples, families and groups.* Washington, DC: University Press of America.

Lerner-Goldhor, H. (1989). *The dance of intimacy: A woman's guide to courageous acts of change in key relationships.* New York: Harper & Row.

Napier, A. (1978). The rejection-intrusion pattern: A central family dynamic. *Journal of Marital and Family Therapy, 7,* 5–12.

Rubin, Z. (1973). *Liking and loving.* New York: Holt, Rinehart & Winston.

Sager, C., & Hunt, B. (1979). *Intimate partners.* New York: McGraw-Hill.

Satir, V. (1967). *Conjoint family therapy.* Palo Alto, CA: Science & Behavior Books.

Schaefer, M., & Olson, D. (1981). Assessment of intimacy: The PAIR inventory. *Journal of Marital and Family Therapy, 7,* 47–60.

Sternberg, R. (1986a). A triangular theory of love. *Psychological Review, 93,* 119–135.

Sternberg, R. (1986b). Love, sex, & intimacy. *Psychological Review, 93,* 119–135.

Waring, E. M. (1981). Facilitating marital intimacy through self-disclosure. *American Journal of Family Therapy, 9,* 33–42.

Waring, E. M. (1984). The measurement of marital intimacy. *Journal of Marital and Family Therapy, 10,* 185–192.

Weeks, G. R. (1989). An intersystem approach to treatment. In G. R. Weeks (Ed.), *Treating couples: The Intersystem Model of the Marriage Council of Philadelphia* (pp. 317–340). New York: Brunner/Mazel.

Weeks, G. R., & Hof, L. (Eds.). (1994). *The marital-relationship therapy casebook: Theory and application of the Intersystem Model.* New York: Brunner/Mazel.

Weeks, G. R., & L'Abate, L. (1982). *Paradoxical psychotherapy: Theory and practice with individuals, couples, and families.* New York: Brunner/Mazel.

Weeks, G. R., & Treat, S. (1992). *Couples in treatment: Techniques for effective practice.* New York: Brunner/Mazel.

Weingarten, K. (1991). The discourses of intimacy: Adding a social constructionist and feminist view. *Family Process, 10*, 185–192.

Wynne, L., & Wynne, A. (1986). The quest for intimacy. *Journal of Marital and Family Therapy, 12*, 383–394.

3

ANGER AND CONFLICT: THEORY AND PRACTICE

Gerald R. Weeks, Ph.D., and Larry Hof, M.Div.

Two of the most common problems treated by the couple's therapist are anger and conflict. The content may vary within the couple and among couples, but the underlying problems with anger and conflict are relatively constant and common. Articles and books documenting anger and conflict as factors in marital dysfunction abound (L'Abate & McHenry, 1983; Tavris, 1989).

Anger and conflict, however, are inevitable in close relationships, and their presence is not, in any way, an indicator of a dysfunctional, or less than satisfying, relationship. Conflict (and the anger that frequently accompanies it) has too often been viewed exclusively as something negative, a battle or war to be either avoided or fought and won, rather than as the potentially positive use of the divergent or apparently opposi- tional differences between partners. As a result, many couples have never learned how to deal with conflict and anger in a helpful, even intimacy- enhancing way. They use instead a variety of less than helpful strategies, including avoiding it, ignoring it, denying it, withdrawing from it, acqui- escing in the face of it, scapegoating or attacking and destroying in the midst of it, or deflecting the current situation by creating a new conflict or focusing on an old one. One way or the other, the "it," the conflict, will be "handled."

Our experience with clinical and nonclinical couples suggests that happily married couples may actually report slightly more conflict than unhappily married couples. These couples have often developed more of the individual and relationship skills needed to resolve problems than their unhappy counterparts. They have been able to move through the feelings of anger to experience a sense of mastery in being able to resolve their difficulties. A sense of "coupleness" is derived from being able to compromise and negotiate an agreement that is for the good of the relationship.

The literature on conflict resolution has generally been behaviorally oriented. Even when other aspects of conflict are being discussed, the behavioral components are emphasized. In order to provide a more balanced approach, we examine the affective processes and the cognitive processes and attitudes within conflict, as well as the behavioral skills required to effectively resolve it. Anger is discussed as a separate topic.

THE MEANING AND FUNCTION OF ANGER AND CONFLICT

Anger and conflict are intimately related. Where conflict exists there is usually anger. Anger may be a problem for both the therapist and the couple. A common reaction for therapists, especially beginning therapists, is to overcontrol the expression of anger. Sometimes therapists even experience countertransference in reaction to anger, which draws them into a destructive relationship with the angry partner.

It is common for couples to have a number of cognitive distortions and fears about anger. Some partners believe it is their right to be as angry as they like, others fear the feeling so much that they avoid it at all costs. Anger is often associated with losing control, hurting someone, or being hurt. For those couples who can manage anger effectively, the clinician may move on to the conflict-utilization work. Otherwise, the feelings associated with the problem must be looked at initially. When a couple is in conflict, they often have two problems: the problem itself, and then the feelings about the problem (anger, hurt, fear). Dealing with the feelings must come first. If the feelings of anger cannot be diminished, placed in perspective, shared, and worked through in the couple, no amount of skills training will be effective.

The first task is to understand the anger. The following list of questions is given to the couple to take home and answer. In the next session, the responses are thoroughly discussed. The therapist may educate and work on changing beliefs about anger in a positive direction. A partner who believes anger is bad will not discuss or express anger. The belief must be changed in order to make it possible for the couple to deal with the feeling.

The Meaning and Function of Anger

1. What is anger?
2. What does it mean when you are angry?
3. What does it mean when you are angry with your partner?
4. What does it mean when your partner is angry?
5. What does it mean when your partner is angry with you?
6. How do you respond to your partner's anger?
7. How do you respond to your own anger?
8. How do you let your partner know you are angry?
9. How long does your anger usually last?
10. What are the other feelings that are associated with or underlie your anger?

The questions are deceptively simple. An entire session may be devoted to just one question, such as, "What is anger?" These questions may keep the clinician and clients busy for several sessions.

The last question is one that may take considerable time to explore. We use the iceberg model to explain this concept. Only the tip of an iceberg is visible. Anger is just the tip of many underlying and associated feelings. We draw an iceberg, placing anger at the top, and then we ask each partner to think about the feelings that lie beneath the waterline when they experience anger. Some of the more common feelings are hurt, fear, rejection, depression, guilt, insecurity, and shame. The partners are told to notice the underlying feelings each time they experience anger. These feelings need to be discussed just as much as, if not more than, the anger itself. For many partners, anger is actually a defense against experiencing the underlying feelings. Thus, if a man feels depressed, he might not want to be aware of, or express, that feeling, so he looks for reasons to be angry. What he really needs to do is get in touch with the unacceptable feeling—not act it out in anger. In our society, which too often views emotions such as hurt, pain, and sadness as weak, for men especially, anger may serve as an acceptable form of expression of other feelings.

Two feelings deserve special attention. Hurt is a feeling that often goes hand in hand with anger. Hurt is the genotypic feeling. Men may find it difficult to feel hurt and to show it. They will often cover this feeling with an over-expression of anger, or "translate" the softer feeling into anger. They may then strike out, expecting their partner to somehow recognize that what they want is to have the hurt feeling recognized. It is useful for the clinician to ask whether hurt is present and whether the person would know it if it were. If s/he says that hurt has never, or rarely, been felt, the question is, why?

Conversely, many women are taught to deny or avoid their anger. They often convert, or translate, the anger into tears or sadness/depression, rather than express the unacceptable feeling. The clinician needs to focus on the legitimacy of the anger. If s/he says that anger has never, or rarely, been felt, the question is, why? With either gender, the focus needs to be on facilitating a balanced expression of all of the feelings present.

The second feeling that warrents further attention is fear. Fear is a primary emotion. We instinctively know how to feel fear. Yet, none of us likes the feeling. Anger is commonly used to defend against fear. The reader may recall that humans respond to fear by either fleeing or fighting. This connection between fear and fleeing or fighting is also related to the earlier material in this book on the fear of intimacy. When a fear of intimacy is invoked, the partner will either avoid the other or start a fight.

The meaning attributed to anger derives from our experiences in our family of origin and with our mate. The early experiences are highly salient in the development of our attitudes about anger. We developed an anger genogram to help us understand the source and content of these attitudes. Individuals are encouraged to reflect upon the following questions vis-à-vis their family of origin, and to discuss their answers with their partner. The reflection and sharing process enables each person to realize how early learning has contributed to the development of their beliefs and behaviors regarding anger. This can effectively pave the way for learning something new—an alternative way of dealing with anger and conflict that is consciously chosen rather than merely assimilated and utilized in a habitual, unexamined way.

Anger Genogram

1. How did your parents deal with anger/conflict?
2. Did you see your parents work through anger/conflict?

3. When members of your family (name each one) got angry, how did others respond?
4. What did you learn about anger from each of your parents?
5. When your parents became angry with you, how did you feel and what did you do?
6. When you got angry, who listened or failed to listen to you?
7. How did members of your family respond when you got angry?
8. Who was allowed/not allowed to be angry in your family?
9. What is your best/worst memory about anger in your family?
10. Was anyone ever hurt as a result of someone's anger? Who?

Recognizing Anger

When anger is expressed appropriately, it is not difficult to recognize. The anger is expressed verbally, with congruent affect, without judgment or blame, without punishing or fearful withdrawal and distancing, and without oppressive control, intimidation, or overt physical or emotional abuse. It is then followed by constructive attempts at conflict utilization and problem solving, and attempts to breach the emotional distance that may have emerged, in order to increase the closeness and intimacy between the partners.

Unfortunately, this appropriate and potentially constructive expression of anger is often not the norm. Sometimes, the expression of the anger is designed to overwhelm the partner, to protect the self against a perceived attack, to gain control of the situation or of the partner, or even to punish or injure the partner emotionally or physically. When narcissistic vulnerability is present, the experience of self-fragmentation, diminished self-esteem, and perceived rejection often leads to the experience and expression of narcissistic rage and projective identification, with unconscious and conscious cognitive distortions regarding the self, the partner, and the nature of the interaction itself (Feldman, 1982). This narcissistic rage is differentiated from more common anger by its uncontrolled, furious nature, by the presence of those significant and tenaciously held cognitive distortions, and by the often desperate attempts to preserve self-esteem by vicious verbal, emotional, or physical attacks on the partner. This extreme anger requires special handling, which is discussed in the conflict-utilization section.

Anger is also often expressed in ways that are difficult to recognize. Bach and Goldberg (1974) identify eight ways anger may be expressed indirectly. They refer to these methods of expression as "hidden aggression." One means of such expression is through collusion. Collusion means that both parties work together to deny the fact that anger exists, yet they continue to act in hostile ways toward each other. The anger may be subtly expressed, such as when one person enables another to drink, use drugs, or engage in self-destructive behavior.

The second method is passive-aggressive behavior, a phenomenon that is quite familiar to therapists. Common examples include forgetting, procrastinating, misunderstanding, and attributing meanings to another person's behavior that were not intended.

With the third approach, moral one-upmanship, one partner takes the position of being morally right or superior, and often tries to instill a sense of guilt, doubt, or unworthiness in the partner.

Intellectualization is sometimes overlooked as a way to express anger. Taking the fourth tack, the person only responds intellectually to issues, hiding behind rationality and using it to show how the other person is wrong or "crazy" because s/he is "so emotional."

The fifth option is to be nonrewarding. This method involves never giving any positive feedback, even when it is appropriate and needed. In this context, the lack of positive feedback communicates anger toward the other. A similar method is to create doubt, with the doubter choosing critical moments in the relationship to create anxiety and insecurity in the partner. For example, in the middle of a fight this person might say the marriage was a mistake from the beginning.

The last three methods employ the use of weakness as the vehicle for expression of anger. The "helpless aggressor" uses his or her psychological fears, such as hurt, weaknesses, and the like, as an excuse to avoid responsibility and thereby control the relationship. The "sickness tyrant" uses physical illness (psychosomatic illness) in the same fashion. Finally, the "Red Cross nurse aggressor" has an unconscious need to keep others dependent and helpless by perpetuating their weaknesses. They pretend to help the helpless, but actually feed off of the other's need to be taken care of.

Functions of Anger and Conflict

Part of the therapist's task is to understand, and enable the couple to understand, the function anger and conflict play in the relationship. The function may be healthy or unhealthy. Anger and conflict are natural and healthy when used to maintain boundaries for the self, partner, or family system. The individual has certain rights and needs that should be respected by members of the family, and the same is true for the individuals in a couple relationship. When others cross the boundary or interfere with the functioning of these systems, interests come into conflict and anger results. In order to preserve the integrity of these systems, the individual, couple, or family must assertively struggle or "fight" for preservation of their boundaries.

Anger and conflict may, however, serve a number of unhealthy functions. They may be used to regulate distance in the relationship, one of the most common uses of anger and conflict. When one partner feels too much closeness or too much distance, s/he may create a conflict to either push the other away or bring the other closer. Of the two, creating distance is probably the more common. Partners who come to the relationship with an underlying fear of intimacy will only be able to tolerate so much closeness before needing distance. Unfortunately, rather than ask for some distance, which would require that they be consciously aware of the need, they create anger in themselves, followed by a conflictual situation, in order to produce the necessary distance.

A kindred function of anger and conflict is to test the commitment of the partner. Individuals who use this function usually have a strong fear of rejection or abandonment and, before they will risk being close, will push their partners away to test whether they will return. As they believe that they cannot tolerate being rejected, the test can never be conclusive and the trials will continue, keeping the relationship in a perpetual state of uncertainty. Testing also protects these people from rejection and abandonment—when closeness cannot be achieved, it cannot be lost.

Anger and conflict may also be used to assert power and control. Some partners believe they must maintain their power and control or else be controlled by the other. Anger may be used to intimidate the partner into submission and conflict may be generated because this person is not willing to negotiate.

The unhealthy functions that conflict may serve in a relationship can perhaps best be viewed in the following way (read from the left and the right simultaneously):

Wish/Fear/Defensive Behavior/CONFLICT/Defensive Behavior/Fear/Wish.

In other words, the *conflict* exists between two persons, each of whom is engaging in defensive behavior because s/he fears that some wish will not be fulfilled. If the therapist and the therapeutic process cannot enable the clients to get to, and attain, the wish on a consistent basis, the fears prevail, and in an attempt to protect themselves, the individuals who form the dyad feel justified in maintaining their defensive posture and conflict-oriented stance. The couple remains trapped in the cycle, with a predictable negative impact upon the relationship.

CONFLICT UTILIZATION

In the literature on conflict, two terms are commonly used to refer to work in this area. These terms are "conflict resolution" and "conflict utilization." Turner (1982) suggests that the term conflict resolution connotes that the ideal goal for a couple to achieve is to resolve conflict. On the other hand, conflict utilization refers to an active, dynamic process that connotes the idea that the couple can make use of the conflict for more than simply resolving a problem. He believes conflict can be positive, productive, and growth enhancing, and he lists 8 positive functions of conflict, including: (1) using energy rather than repressing it, (2) using conflict creatively to raise new questions and ideas, (3) surfacing heretofore hidden thoughts and feelings, (4) creating new methods in the couple for handling conflict, (5) reassessing power in the relationship, (6) creating a climate of cooperation, (7) learning to see problems rationally, and (8) renegotiating old contracts and changing expectations in the relationship. Clinebell and Clinebell (1970) and Hof and Miller (1981) even spoke of "Conflict Intimacy," which can be defined as facing and struggling with differences together, in such a way that association, connectedness, contact, warmth, and affection are increased.

One of the first tasks in dealing with conflict is to help the couple develop some positive ideas about that which they have been avoiding or dealing with poorly. The therapist should ask the couple about their beliefs regarding conflict. Once these beliefs have been made explicit and challenged, the therapist may suggest looking at conflict as a positive and constructive force in the relationship, one that could be intimacy enhancing if handled well, but relationship debilitating if handled poorly. The couple can be asked to list positive aspects of conflict. As we suggested earlier, if the couple does not have a positive attitude toward conflict and anger, no amount of education, coaching, or therapy will help. The couple will resist efforts to begin the work because their belief system tells them it is something to be avoided.

At the beginning of therapy, some bibliotherapy may help to instill this positive attitude. A book such as *The Intimate Enemy* (Bach & Wyden, 1968) makes this point both implicitly and explicitly. A positive attitude can also be demonstrated through self-disclosure or sharing specific case examples demonstrating the many benefits of conflict.

Cognitive Approaches to Conflict

ATTRIBUTION AND EFFICACY

In spite of the fact that cognitive therapy is a major force in psychotherapy and attribution theory is a major force in social/clinical psychology, very little has been written on cognition and conflict. Doherty (1981a, 1981b) published two articles describing cognitive processes in conflict, both of which were primarily theoretical in nature, although there are many practical applications. His work helps us to better understand the nature of conflict from the inside out. He clarifies the underlying mental processes that occur when conflict exists and identifies the factors that inhibit and facilitate conflict being utilized.

The two key concepts in his theory are attribution and efficacy. Attribution theories deal with causal explanations—how we attribute meaning to an event and the information on which it is based (Kelly, 1973). For the partner in a relationship the basic question is, ''Who or what is causing this problem?'' In a sense we are all attributional theorists. This question is ubiquitous in couple therapy. The causal attributions have several dimensions. In other words, there are several possible sources of the problem. This is the ''who'' or ''what'' of the problem. Partners may assign blame and responsibility to self, partner, relationship, context, and possibly to theological sources or to just plain luck, fate, or chance.

The therapist must discover how the partners conceptualize the conflict, that is, the ''who'' or ''what.'' In most couples, blame is assigned to the other partner. As long as this kind of attributional strategy is present in the couple, change will not occur. In a previous book, Weeks (Weeks & Hof, 1994) discusses the importance of helping the couple shift from a linear to a circular attributional strategy. A linear strategy involves the partners blaming each other or externalizing responsibility. A circular strategy involves partners defining the problem in terms of their relationship or system. In order to help couples make this attributional shift, the therapist uses reframing (Weeks & Treat, 1992). Reframing has been defined as changing the meaning of an event, and is used in two ways. The first is to redefine an event (behavior) that had been viewed negatively as one that is viewed positively. The second meaning is most applicable here. For couples, to reframe is to redefine behaviors so that they are no longer seen in terms of cause and effect but rather as circular, interlocking, or reciprocal. The technique of reframing is described in previous volumes (Weeks & L'Abate, 1982; Weeks & Treat, 1992).

Doherty (1981a) also identifies several other attributional dimensions and strategies that contribute to marital conflict and that need to be examined; namely, intent, stability, voluntariness, and specificity.

Intent refers to the meaning attributed to the person who performed the behavior. The partner is trying is determine the real meaning of the behavior. In most cases, intent actually refers to the judgment the partner makes regarding whether a behavior was perceived as having a positive or negative impact. For example, if a wife tells her husband to change his clothing because the outfit does not match, he might ascribe negative or positive intent to her statement. He could say to himself that she cares about him and how he looks. On the other hand, he might feel personally criticized and ascribe negative intent to her statement. As we pointed out in the chapter on communication, intent and effect often become confused in couples. Just because something "feels" negative, or is perceived to be negative, does not mean it was intended to be negative.

In couple therapy, it is important to help the partners eliminate distortions and projections around intent. Having each partner discuss what was actually intended is a beginning. If the other partner persists in seeing the behavior differently then two issues need exploration. First, why might the partner be distorting the intent? Perhaps, the response to a behavior is overdetermined. If, for example, s/he had learned to respond in only one way to a particular behavior in the family, the original conceptualization, and its corresponding responses, may persist, regardless of partner or context. The other possibility is that the initiating partner does not know the real intent of his or her behavior. S/he may be in denial of the actual intent or distort the meaning of the behavior. The therapist will have to use some judgment in sorting out what the real intent might be. If the same behavior persists, then it should become apparent that actual intent is being distorted. For example, if a partner does something hurtful, says it was not intended, but then does other hurtful acts, it is clear that the intent is to hurt the partner. Apologies, excuses, and denials cannot disguise the truth.

The second attributional dimension is *stability*. Stability refers to the extent to which the behaviors represent stable personality characteristics in the other person. A behavior may be viewed as an isolated event or it may be viewed as representing some stable characteristic in the other person. For example, when a partner becomes angry, the anger may be seen as a single isolated event related to some environmental situation, such as getting angry when the car has a flat tire, or it may be viewed as a behavior that is a stable trait in the person—"He is always angry; therefore, he is an angry person."

This attributional phenomenon helps to explain why therapists find it useful to frame problems in terms of behaviors rather than personality traits or characteristics. A personality trait is, by definition, believed to be rather stable. If it is stable, it probably will not change very easily. When the partner believes that a trait is being dealt with, as opposed to a behavior, s/he may be less likely to attempt to change the situation. In fact, the person may be likely to give up immediately because a favorable outcome is not foreseen. The couple may feel they cannot change when problem behaviors are defined as immutable traits. By redefining the problem in terms of behaviors, which are transitory and determined by context, a greater sense of hope and change potential is inspired.

Voluntariness or deliberateness of a person's behavior is the third dimension of attribution (see also Weeks, 1994). Partners make assumptions about how voluntary behaviors may be, and are likely to believe the behavior was voluntary or involuntary, controllable or uncontrollable, spontaneous or contrived. When the behavior is defined as voluntary, or in any of the parallel ways listed, the behavior carries much more import. Obviously, if one partner has done something that is perceived as hurtful, and the behavior was deliberate, the other partner will feel personally attacked. It may be easier to forgive a hurtful behavior if it is defined as involuntary.

The clinician needs to assess how the partners define problematic behaviors along this dimension. If there is a misattribution, then it needs to be corrected.

Mark and Jane had been married for three years. Mark had never said he loved Jane, withdrew from physical contact, and was rarely sexually interested. Jane's patience with Mark had reached its limit, and she initiated therapy. She firmly believed Mark was deliberately withholding these behaviors from her. As a result, she felt unloved and rejected. The family history revealed that Mark had been emotionally abused as a child. He feared getting close to anyone, and the closer he got the more anxious he became. They were both unaware of the impact of Mark's history on his current functioning. Once aware, Jane could see that Mark wanted to be closer but, for reasons that were unconscious to him, he could not accomplish what he consciously wanted to do. Mark was interested in using therapy to correct his deficiencies, which gave Jane further hope of getting what she wanted. Of course, this example only rendered half the story. Jane had her own unconscious difficulties with intimacy, which is why she had married Mark. She had grown up around a rejecting father and was repeating that pattern with Mark. His pathology was simply more overt and served to cover up her difficulties.

The final attributional dimension is *specificity*. The attributions made may generalize to the person or the relationship; they may range from global to specific. More problems occur when the attributions generalize, assuming these are negative attributions. For example, a newly married couple may have a few fights. They may begin to believe that all they ever do is fight. They become defined as a "fighting couple," and they believe they should divorce because that is all they will ever be. The generalization could have been to the individual in this example. One partner could be defined as always wanting to fight. Global negative attributions are demoralizing for the couple and represent a distortion.

The therapist can work toward specificity by challenging these distortions directly. A cognitive therapy approach may be used in which the couple are taught about distortions, how to identify them, and how to stop them (Burns, 1977). The therapist's use of language and the questions asked also lead the couple in the direction of seeing the problem specifically rather than globally. Specific questions about the who, what, where, when, and how of the argument encourage less global thinking in the partners.

It is now possible to review and synthesize the model proposed by Doherty (1981a). The main sources of conflict tend to be attributed to *self*, other, relationship, or environment. The first task is to determine which of these sources is seen as the problem and help the couple define the problem in terms of the relationship so that each can see his or her part. For each of the four main sources of conflict, there are four possible ways the conflict may be described—intent, stability, voluntariness, and specificity. After the source has been determined, the next step is to assess the attributions made along these four dimensions and work to change these attributions as needed. Let us assume a husband attributes the cause of a problem to himself (self). The problem might be that he becomes violently angry at times. He might think that his intent was not to hurt anyone, but to just let off some steam. He might see this behavior as a personality trait, saying he has always had a bad temper, just like his father. He might further think he cannot control his temper because he never has and does not want to do so, and he believes his anger is part of his global personality style of being uptight and always on edge.

The foregoing concepts in Doherty's (1981a, 1981b) model are all useful diagnostically and therapeutically. The next concept is the key to getting started—readiness. All couple therapists have had the experience of beginning conflict work with a couple only to have the couple abruptly stop treatment or fail to follow through on any of the principles of fair fighting. In order to do this work, the condition of couple readiness must be ascertained. A couple ready to work will begin the process. They may exhibit resistance, but there is a clear sense of engagement and commitment to move forward.

Doherty (1981b) uses the concept of *efficacy* to refer to beliefs about future events, a central aspect of readiness. He proposes that "efficacy refers to the individual's expectation for the couple or family as a group to engage in effective problem-solving activity" (Doherty, 1981b, p. 4). Bandura (1977) proposed that it was the individual's expectation for being able to bring about a particular outcome. Efficacy is similar to having *hope*, feeling masterful and competent, and being able to make a positive prediction happen. (See Chapter 1 for an in-depth discussion of these issues.) For the couple, the question is, "Can the problem be solved by us?" Doherty (1981a) suggests that if the efficacy expectations were low, the members of the family would not be persistent in trying to solve their problems and they would show a learned helplessness response. One of the goals of therapy, therefore, is to help create a generalized high efficacy belief and response, a sense of hope.

The level of efficacy determines the amount of effort partners expend in trying to solve a problem. Individuals with high efficacy expectations will predict positive outcomes and be very persistent in their problem-solving efforts. Low efficacy results from repeated failures in problem solving. Doherty (1981b) states that individuals with low efficacy expectations develop a cognitive deficit of ceasing to learn new information; a motivational deficit of giving up; a behavioral deficit of avoiding the issues or the partner, or ritualizing the conflict; and, an affective deficit of "feeling" that the conflict is uncontrollable.

The theory also assumes that causal attributions and efficacy expectations interact and have implications for how the conflict is handled. For example, when the attribution is that the other is the source of the problem, intent is positive, and efficacy is high, there is a positive attempt to change the partner. If efficacy is low, no attempt at change is made. If intent is negative and efficacy high, there is a great deal of blaming of the partner. If efficacy is low, there may be some retaliatory response (probably indirect). The clinician can assess the various dimensions and make some predictions about how conflict will be managed or, conversely, work backwards from how the conflict is managed.

The concept of efficacy has significant clinical implications. In order to carry out the work needed, the couple with low efficacy expectations must develop higher expectations. In addition to those discussed in Chapter 1, a number of other strategies may be used to develop these expectations. Suppose we are working with an individual who cognitively and motivationally gives up and ceases to learn new information. One approach with such a person would be to make the cognitions about conflict explicit. The therapist can discuss the concept of efficacy, how low efficacy expectations develop, and how they serve to undermine the ability to get started.

Specific cognitions might be examined next, including negative statements about the nature of conflict ("Conflict is destructive, harmful, bad") and self-defeating statements about the ability to change self, partner, or relationship ("My partner will never change"). The partner(s) can be asked to either adopt more productive ideas regarding efficacy, or, at the least, act as if such ideas could be true.

Several behavioral strategies may also be used to promote efficacy. First, the tasks to utilize the conflict must be broken down into small, incremental steps. These steps are approached one at a time in order to facilitate success, which will, it is hoped, lead to higher efficacy expectations. Second, these steps are first implemented in the therapist's office under close supervision and coaching. The partners may begin by role playing conflict in order to learn the skills and then proceed to the conflicts that carry the least emotional impact. Third, the couple needs to practice the skills repeatedly and regularly. Once conflicts have been identified, and utilization skills have been practiced successfully in the office, the couple can practice at home with highly structured tasks and agreed upon rules for "fighting." Finally, the therapist can change the affective experience by giving positive feedback in the office and asking the partners to give themselves and each other positive emotional feedback. They might make statements such as, "I'm feeling more personally empowered" and "I feel hope that you are trying to understand me and work cooperatively.'' After every successful behavioral interaction in the office, the therapist can ask the partners to give each other some emotional feedback. The combination of these strategies can reverse the low efficacy expectations and generalize over time to other aspects of the relationship.

Rational-Emotive Therapy

Albert Ellis (1976) describes how the theory and techniques of his Rational-Emotive Therapy (RET) can be applied in working with anger. His theory is based on the assumption that anger stems from irrational beliefs held about one's partner or relationship. It is an individually oriented approach, because the change must take place within the individual and not the relationship. The dissipation of the anger is accomplished through the A-B-C-D theory of rational therapy. *A* is the activating event, *B* is the belief system, *C* is the emotional and behavioral consequence, and *D* refers to the act of disputing the irrational belief. This particular theory and cognitive therapy in general are described in Weeks and Treat (1992).

Ellis (1976) proposes that much marital anger grows out of the "shoulds," "oughts," and "musts" in relationships. For example, if one partner thinks, "I absolutely must feel loved by my partner all the time and s/he must verbalize it," then disappointment, anger, and conflict will result. By eliminating the irrational ideas, the basis for the anger and conflict is removed.

He suggests two strategies for dealing with anger, the first of which simply involves a cooling off period in order to set the stage for thinking the anger through. The second strategy incorporates the following eight steps: (1) acknowledging the anger to oneself; (2) assuming full responsibility for the anger; (3) accepting oneself with anger; (4) putting an end to making oneself anxious and depressed, and being self-deprecating; (5) looking for the belief leading to the anger; (6) differentiating among wishes, demands, and commands; (7) removing the absolute musts; and (8) changing the behaviors and emotions that support the feelings of anger.

This model can work well when it is applicable. In some cases, the anger and conflict *is* certainly being driven by irrational thoughts and an individually oriented approach is appropriate. Each partner may need to change some thinking in order to remove the anger.

Ralph initially believed he had a right to express his anger in whatever fashion he felt. His expression was often blaming and cruel. He argued that because he had never been allowed to have feelings in his family of origin, he must have them in his marriage. Betty showed a complementary pattern. She initially believed she must be the source of all of Ralph's anger. She would say to herself, "If he is angry, then I must have done something." She would feel depressed, withdraw, and eventually become angry and show it passive aggressively. The unhealthy thinking in each of these partners had produced a highly dysfunctional system of behavior. Changing their thinking was one of the early interventions before moving on to teach behavioral skills for conflict utilization.

The disadvantage of the RET approach is that it is asystemic or nonrelational. In the intersystem model described by Weeks (1994), the partners codetermine the relationship and the relationship influences the partners. The Ellis approach does not examine how the relationship influences the thinking or actions of the partners. For example, assume the relationship is based on the unconscious premise that too much closeness is not desirable. Both partners, therefore, need a relatively distant relationship. Anger may be one of the mechanisms used to control distance. However, looking exclusively at the anger from the perspective of each individual misses the fact that the relationship has been defined in a particular way.

Affective Approaches to Conflict

L'Abate (1977) states that in most cases anger is the result of feeling hurt and the fear of being hurt. The hurt feelings may be based in unresolved grief, past frustrations and anger, loneliness, poor self-esteem, past frustrations or failures, and feelings of personal inadequacy. The failure to recognize these feelings means the clinician only treats the symptom and not the underlying emotional difficulties. This idea is similar to the iceberg model of anger discussed earlier, in which the feelings that underlie anger are considered.

L'Abate (1977) and L'Abate and L'Abate (1977) suggest five steps in dealing with the feeling. The first step is to recognize that when anger is experienced, there is also an underlying feeling of hurt. The second step is for the partner feeling the hurt to express it directly and appropriately to his or her partner ("I felt hurt when . . . "). Third, the individual with the feeling must assume responsibility for the hurt and not project it onto the partner. Normally, it is the anger that is projected, in terms of blaming the partner as the source of the anger. Fourth, the person must be able to forgive him- or herself for denying the hurt and not being invulnerable to this feeling. Finally, one must recognize that feeling hurt is a human reaction. It is important to redefine oneself as having weaknesses and vulnerabilities. Only by accepting this can the person stay in touch with the hurt. In the first section of this chapter, we emphasized the importance of dealing with the feeling of anger. This aspect of conflict utilization, dealing with the feelings of hurt and anger, too often has been underemphasized or ignored in the literature.

Behaviorally Oriented Approaches to Conflict

Three well-developed approaches to conflict are found in the literature, approaches that are not strictly behavioral because the theorists discuss conflict from several perspectives. All three, for example, address some of the intrapsychic and relationship variables involved in conflict. However, they have such a strong behavioral component that we have classified them as "behaviorally oriented." Each theorist outlines a number of specific steps that are useful in conflict utilization and "fighting fairly."

FAIR FIGHTING TECHNIQUE

Bach and Goldberg (1974) and Bach and Wyden (1968) are probably the best known because their books were written for the layperson. Bach and Goldberg (1974) identify 15 steps in their Fair Fighting Technique (FFT). These steps emphasize communication, focusing on a single problem, asking for a specific change, and expressing goodwill on the part of both partners at the close of the argument. In addition, they developed a system for rating whether the aggression was expressed positively or negatively and categories to rate the fairness of the fight (e.g., hurt, information, fear, catharsis).

NEGOTIATION

Dayringer (1976) developed a series of steps very similar to that of Bach and Goldberg (1974). He views the goal of fighting as learning how to negotiate. He sees anger as a response to being blocked from attaining one's goals. Some of his steps include learning how to engage to fight, selecting a "beef," giving feedback, asking for change, discussing change and different alternatives, and closing with goodwill. In order to develop a truly comprehensive approach, his steps in effective negotiation need to be compared, contrasted, and merged with the steps developed by Fisher and Ury (1981) and Ury (1991).

They stress the following points for effective negotiating: differentiating the problem from the persons involved, with each person treating the other in an empathic and respectful manner; actively listening to oneself as well as the other, while attempting to resolve the issues on merit, in an objective, unbiased fashion; avoiding polarized and combative stances, focusing instead on specific concerns; creating a variety of potentially mutually satisfying outcomes; and, using standards of judgment that are fair, reasonable, and impartial.

Ury (1991) developed their negotiation model further by focusing on modifications that need to be made when the other person is strongly confrontational. He emphasizes the following: the need to maintain the ability to mentally separate oneself from the interaction and "observe" what is happening, rather than responding in an oppositional or aggressive manner; the need to respond in an empathic manner to the ideas, issues, and feelings raised by the other person; the need to positively reframe the issue at hand; the need to search for ways to enable both persons' expressed and unexpressed interests to be met in a win/win manner, avoiding I win/you lose or I lose/you win outcomes; and openly and clearly identifying the consequences for both parties if a mutually satisfying, negotiated agreement cannot be reached.

The need for conscious utilization of negotiation skills in a relationship is nowhere more evident then when marital roles are being addressed. Sherwood and Scherer's (1975) concept of "planned renegotiation," as expressed by Hof and Miller (1981) highlights the need for such skills.

Such roles can be established overtly or covertly, by open and explicit decision making or by tacit agreement. In either case, there are certain clearly definable stages that are evident. The first stage can be labeled "Sharing Information and Negotiating Expectations." During this stage, each person communicates in some way his or her wants, wishes, expectations, or demands regarding the role in question. Through a verbal or nonverbal process, a negotiated settlement is reached, agreement is made, and the couple moves to the second stage, which can be labeled "Commitment to the Role," or the "Period of Consensus and Trust."

During this stage, each person appropriately indicates, by word or actions and internal acceptance, that agreement on that particular role has been achieved. A period of "stability and productivity" follows, during which each person behaves in accordance with the agreed upon role, internally accepts the role as appropriate, and is content with the situation.

Inevitably though, a period of "Disruption of Shared Expectations" emerges. We say inevitably, because people change over time as do their expectations of each other. In addition, some expectations and information (for example, feelings) may have been withheld initially, either by conscious choice or simply because the person was not aware of the thoughts or feelings at that time.

As many people have been taught that conflict is bad or to be avoided at all costs, the emergence of the period of "disruption of shared expectations" is frequently not highly valued. The result may be the denial of warning signs that something is wrong, or of the so-called "Pinch Choice Point." This point can be defined as a period of discomfort in which the realization that everything is not all right anymore, that one or both partners are dissatisfied with some aspect of a marital role, begins to take shape.

If "Disruption of Shared Expectations" can be viewed as inevitable, and as an indicator of needed change rather than as an indictment of a relationship or person, individuals and couples need not fear rocking the boat. Instead, they can be sensitive to the beginning phases of the stage of disruption, the pinch choice points. They can then express their feelings and perceptions, the need for role renegotiation, *before* deep feelings of hurt, anger, and resentment accumulate, before blame is placed, and before the situation becomes so disruptive or destructive that goodwill is threatened or destroyed.

When a destructive spiral has gained momentum, constructive change is extremely difficult and sometimes even impossible to achieve. In such a situation, feelings of uncertainty and anxiety frequently abound, along with anger, pain, and fear. Resignation to living with things the way they are even when unsatisfactory, attempts to kiss and make-up and return to the way things use to be, forced renegotiation ("we'll reach a new agreement or else . . ."), and possibly even resentful termination of the relationship are all possible outcomes when pinch choice points are avoided or overlooked and a destructive spiral is permitted to gain momentum. However, careful attention to pinch choice points opens up the possibility for planned renegotiation of marital roles (and if necessary, planned termination of the relationship). If planned renegotiation is chosen, the process begins all over again, with the sharing of information and the negotiating of expectations.

CONFLICT RESOLUTION

This model was developed by Strong (1975) and combines education with specific skills training. The belief here is that couples need to be educated about the nature of conflict, learn basic communication skills, and follow prescribed steps in negotiating.

Six assumptions about conflict are initially shared with the couple. First, conflict arises because there are alternatives or choices. People see the world in different ways, which leads them to make different choices. Therefore, partners are going to be in conflict over which choice is preferred.

Second, conflict involves personal values and past experiences. One partner might value one activity, whereas the other does not value the activity. Third, the conflict may become manifest as a symptom, rather than the underlying need. It is important to look beyond the content of the conflict to the underlying psychosocial need. Fourth, conflicts are often not addressed openly and if they are, they may be handled badly. Fifth, conflict can bring about personal growth and relationship enhancement. It can be a positive force in the couples relationship. Finally, when conflict is not resolved, it blocks satisfying interactions by creating a defensive posture. Unresolved conflict is a negative force in a relationship.

The communication skills needed to resolve conflict consist of listening, speaking, understanding basic needs, creating alternative choices, and detaching from the process in order to be more objective about it. The negotiation process involves recognizing the conflict, setting up a time to talk, identifying the surface and basic needs, giving each other feedback, looking for alternatives, selecting an alternative, and evaluating the agreement at a later time.

CONCLUSION

Anger and conflict are two of the most common problems that couples bring with them into marital or relationship therapy. The therapist needs to be well grounded in the theory and practice of anger and conflict utilization, from cognitive, affective, and behaviorally oriented perspectives. With that foundation in place, the therapist can then create or synthesize a conflict utilization model for use with couples. An example is presented in the following chapter.

REFERENCES

Bach, G., & Goldberg, H. (1974). *Creative aggression.* Garden City, NY: Doubleday.

Bach, G., & Wyden, P. (1968). *The intimate enemy: How to fight fair in love and marriage.* New York: Morrow.

Bandura, A. (1977). *Social learning theory.* Englewood Cliffs, NJ: Prentice-Hall.

Burns, D. (1977). *Feeling good: The new mood therapy.* New York: Signet.

Clinebell, H. J., & Clinebell, C. H. (1970). *The intimate marriage.* New York: Harper & Row.

Dayringer, R. (1976). Fair-fight for change: A therapeutic use of aggressiveness in couple counseling. *Journal of Marriage and Family Counseling, 2,* 115–130.

Doherty, W. J. (1981a). Cognitive processes in intimate conflict: I. Extending attribution theory. *American Journal of Family Therapy, 9*(1), 3–13.

Doherty, W. J. (1981b). Cognitive processes in intimate conflict: II. Efficacy and learned helplessness. *American Journal of Family Therapy, 9*(2), 35–44.

Ellis, A. (1976). Techniques of handling anger in marriage. *Journal of Marriage and Family Counseling, 2,* 305–315.

Feldman, L. B. (1982). Dysfunctional marital conflict: An integrative interpersonal-intrapsychic model. *Journal of Marital and Family Therapy, 8*(4), 417–428.

Fisher, R., & Ury, W. (1981). *Getting to yes: Negotiating agreement without giving in.* New York: Penguin.

Hof, L., & Miller, W. R. (1981). *Marriage enrichment: Philosophy, process, program.* Bowie, MD: Brady.

Kelly, H. (1973). Commitment. In H. Kelly et al. (Eds.), *Close relationships* (pp. 287–311). New York: Freeman.

L'Abate, L. (1977). *Enrichment: Structured interventions with couples, families, and groups.* Washington, DC: University Press.

L'Abate, L., & L'Abate, B. (1977). *Help for troubled marriages.* Atlanta: John Knox.

L'Abate, & McHenry, S. (1983). *Handbook of marital interventions.* New York: Grune & Stratton

Strong, J. (1975). A marital conflict resolution model: Redefining conflict to achieve intimacy. *Journal of Marriage and Family Counseling, 1,* 269–276.

Sherwood, J. J., & Scherer, J. J. (1975). A model for couples: How two can grow together. *Small Group Behavior*, 6(1).

Tavris, C. (1989). *Anger: The misunderstood emotion*. New York: Touchstone.

Turner, N. W. (1982). Conflict utilization in marital-dyadic therapy. *Psychiatric Clinics of North America*, 5(3), 503–518.

Ury, W. (1991). *Getting past no: Negotiating your way from confrontation to cooperation*. New York: Bantam.

Weeks, G. R. (1994). The Intersystem Model: An integrative approach to treatment. In G. R. Weeks & L. Hof (Eds.), *The marital-relationship therapy casebook: Theory and practice of the Intersystem Model* (pp. 3–34). New York: Brunner/Mazel.

Weeks, G. R., & Hof, L. (Eds.). (1994). *The marital-relationship therapy casebook: Theory and practice of the Intersystem Model*. New York: Brunner/Mazel.

Weeks, G. R., & L'Abate, L. (1982). *Paradoxical psychotherapy: Theory and practice with individuals, couples, and families*. New York: Brunner/Mazel.

Weeks, G. R, & Treat, S. (1992). *Couples in treatment: Techniques for effective practice*. New York: Brunner/Mazel.

4

CONFLICT UTILIZATION:
A SYNTHESIS OF THE WHOLE

Gerald R. Weeks, Ph.D., and
Larry Hof, M. Div.

The purpose of this chapter and the preceding one is to enable the practicing therapist to develop a comprehensive Conflict Utilization Model. The clinician needs to integrate ideas from all of the approaches mentioned in the previous chapter, balancing cognitive, affective, and behavioral components. We hope to provide a basic framework in which this integration may occur. In the following pages, ideas are presented that actually synthesize much of what has already appeared in the literature on conflict, communication, problem solving, and contracting. It is not that all of the ideas are original, but that the particular combination of ideas is new and comprehensive.

In order to help the reader synthesize the concepts presented, we have developed a flowchart (Figure 4.1) that shows the various assessment areas, decisions to be made, and the techniques that follow.

A word of caution: This approach works when the anger and conflict have not reached the level of abuse. If violence has erupted, this approach may be contraindicated. In situations where violence exists, it is necessary to first assess the nature of the violence and if the violence is instrumental, then the partners should be seen separately or referred for individual therapy. Safety is always the primary concern in these cases. Instrumental

Figure 4.1   Conflict Utilization Flowchart

---

1. Normalize Conflict
2. Bibliotherapy
3. Assess Meaning and Function of Anger
4. Assess Meaning and Function of Conflict
5. Assess Conflict Utilization Skills:
   Cognitive, Affective, Behavioral
6. Assess Level of Conflict:
   Low, Medium, High

7a. Anger & Conflict: Under Control and Resulting from Current Issues	7b. Anger & Conflict: Historically Based	7c. Intense Anger & Conflict
8a. Employ Conflict Utilization Approach	8b. Explore Family of Origin	8c. Treat Partners Together and Separately; No-Violence Contract
	9b. Employ Conflict Utilization Approach	9c. Employ Aspects of Conflict Utilization Approach as Possible
		10c. If Unsuccessful, Couple May Need Separation or Divorce

---

violence is designed to control or coerce the partner. It may be frequent and unrelated to the emotional life of the couple. The reader should consult one of our previous works for a description of how to work with spouse abuse (Mack, 1989).

Another factor that must be considered is the therapist's own ability to work with anger and conflict. Beginning therapists are sometimes afraid of losing control of the session, so they keep feelings of anger to a minimum and do not encourage enough emotional intensity to emerge. The therapist must balance how much affect occurs at any given time and pace the couple in how quickly they move into conflicted areas. It would be inappropriate to move into highly conflicted areas in the evaluation phase. During this phase the therapist is collecting information about the different conflicts, but not actually encouraging the couple to talk to each other until certain conditions have been met, that is, setting up some ground rules for fighting.

The therapist may also have a number of countertransferential reactions to dealing with anger and conflict. We believe it is also useful for the therapist to do an anger genogram and to answer the questions regarding the meaning and function of anger and conflict. Perhaps there is an inclination on the part of the therapist to minimize, ignore, or deny some of the anger and conflicts in the couple. S/he may have grown up in a family that minimized conflict or where conflict was out of control, and so the therapist may fear these feelings just as much as the clients.

A pattern we have commonly observed with therapists in training is that of the female therapist who is afraid of the anger in men and frequently sides with women in arguments. This obviously causes an imbalance in the therapy and is counterproductive. Another pattern is that of the male therapist who becomes angry about the passivity of the female partner in a couple. Some may identify with their own passive parent, feel the anger not expressed toward the mate, and express it in the therapy session.

Any number of countertransferential reactions are possible. Therapists in training need to be monitored carefully and asked about these types of reactions directly. Some therapists may need supervision or therapy to help them work through unresolved feelings of anger, fear of conflict, or other feelings that hinder doing this kind of work effectively.

LEVELS OF CONFLICT

Before beginning direct work with the couple in the area of conflict utilization, it is important to assess the level of conflict that is present within the couple (compare the "stages of marital conflict" in Guerin et al., 1987). Low-level conflict is often issue-focused, with minimal projection, and the individuals are able to maintain a responsible, balanced, and differentiated view of the situation, themselves, and their partner. There is usually a strong sense of "coupleness" present, and a willingness (though skills are often lacking) to engage each other affectively, cognitively, and behaviorally. There are legitimate differences or preferences and the negotiation process generally works quite well. This level of conflict often responds well to education and skill-building efforts alone.

Medium-level conflict often involves deeply ingrained family-of-origin patterns of relating, and significant, individual life "script" issues (James & Jongeward, 1971). There is a modicum of projection and some loss of "self focus" (Guerin et al., 1987), with an increase in emotional reactivity and blaming. One or both partners appear less differentiated, responsible, objective, and balanced (affectively, and/or cognitively, and/or behaviorally) than those people in the low-level conflict category. Unresolved, historically based issues may have prevented the individuals and the couple from learning or employing the appropriate conflict utilization skills. This level of conflict often responds well to insight (for example, Hendrix's [1988] approach to the resolution of projection-related issues) and to resolution of life "script" issues and family-of-origin issues through "reparenting" (James & Jongeward, 1971) and to a significant focus on differentiation and individuation, along with an appropriate emphasis on addressing deficits in social learning through modeling, skill practice, and reinforcement.

High-level conflict has a chronic quality to it. There is a high degree of emotional reactivity, blaming, and vilification. The couple is consistently and negatively polarized, and there is little sense of positive "we-ness." In one or both partners, differentiation is low, as is responsibility, objectivity, and balance within and among the affective, cognitive, and behavioral dimensions of the individuals. There are severe object relations issues, with significant narcissistic vulnerability and the use of rampant projective identification as an ego defense. The more severe and primitive or early the trauma, the greater the narcissistic vulnerability, and the greater the likelihood of the unhelpful use of projective identification.

This level of conflict generally requires long-term therapy, including the following: a conjoint emphasis to build the "coupleness," providing a buffer against the intrusion of the early trauma and an experience of healing intimacy, and frequent individual sessions to provide individual support and nurturance to diminish the severity of the emotional wound and promote healing. The relationship therapist may not be able to do the individual therapy for several reasons, including narcissistic vulnerability, fear of abandonment, or jealousy of one or both of the partners.

Even if there is a positive transference and scrupulous balance and fairness on the part of the therapist, the narcissistically vulnerable individuals may feel abandoned or rejected by the therapist doing the couple work. Great care must be exercised if the therapist is endeavoring to do both aspects of the therapeutic work, and an appropriate referral for concurrent individual therapy is often the best course of action. If the therapists can work together towards goals agreed upon by all parties involved, successful resolution of high-level conflict is more likely. (See "intractable conflict," below, for a more detailed discussion of high-level conflict).

At all levels, skill deficits, unhelpful patterns learned in the family of origin, and intrapsychic issues may be at work, contributing to the perpetuation of the conflict. The therapist needs to assess the individuals and the couple from an intersystem perspective, ascertaining the nature of the individual/intrapsychic issues, the interactional/relational issues, the intergenerational issues, and the psychosocial/broader-world context issues (for example, issues of race, ethnicity, and spirituality; current economic conditions) involved in the couple and the conflict in order to decide at which level(s) to intervene.

Once an assessment has been made of the meaning and function of the anger and conflict, of the extent of the couple's conflict utilization skills, and of the level of the conflict, the therapist can utilize the following steps to enable the couple to develop or enhance their ability to use conflict creatively.

Normalize and Educate

The first step is to normalize anger and conflict in relationships. Many couples have a negative view of anger and conflict and do not believe it is normal, much less healthy and potentially constructive. The therapist can explain that conflict is inevitable in every relationship, using any number of explanations and rationales. Sometimes the couple will offer information that may be used in providing a rationale for why it is normal. Perhaps they have said that not fighting has lead to resentment and distance. The therapist can turn this around and suggest that fair fighting will relieve the resentment and bring them closer. Some couples have the idea that a good marriage should be conflict free and if they fight it means they have failed and have a bad marriage. These ideas should be challenged and positive ideas offered to replace them.

The therapist starts with the assumption that conflict is inevitable and can become a useful force in the relationship. The question for the couple then is, "How do the two of you handle your anger and conflict?" If the couple begin by discussing how they avoid conflict and see it as negative, the therapist will need to focus on changing beliefs or attitudes first.

The goal is to educate the couple about the nature of anger and conflict, to normalize it, and then to provide some information about how to work with conflict more productively. Certainly the therapist cannot accomplish all of these steps in the session. Part of educating the couple involves bibliotherapy. A number of popular books are available that may be useful. Three stand out: Lerner's (1985) *The Dance of Anger* points out some of the sources of anger, makes clear that it is normal, and offers some suggestions on how to express it. *Your Perfect Right*, by Alberti and Emmons (1983), covers a number of areas, but the primary focus is on becoming more assertive. Several chapters deal with close relationships, and a chapter on anger is included. Issues covered include communication, assertiveness, anger, negotiation, and a variety of other therapeutic techniques that the couple can use. Bach and Goldberg's (1974) *Creative Aggression* is useful in describing many facets of anger and conflict, including a number of fair fighting techniques. Other books may be recommended to fit specific needs or deficits in the couple.

Feelings and Attitudes First

Most conflict programs skip this step and go directly into the behaviorally oriented skills training, which assumes that the couple is ready to begin the work. In our experience, this assumption is often erroneous. When the couple views anger and conflict negatively, they will be reluctant to begin any program that requires dealing with anger and confronting conflict.

The goal at this stage is to assess the attitudes toward anger and conflict and replace negative attitudes with positive attitudes. The material discussed in the first part of this chapter is used to facilitate this attitudinal change. It is also important to understand the array of feelings associated with the conflict. The iceberg model of anger described earlier is used to accomplish this task. The partners are asked to describe their feelings about anger and conflict, as well as their feelings about the conflict itself. The therapist acknowledges these feelings and encourages the partners to acknowledge each other's feelings.

A major task in this stage is to assess efficacy. This topic is discussed in the previous chapter. Unless the partners have sufficiently high efficacy expectation, the work will not proceed. If efficacy expectations are high and some of the other associated factors are in place, such as intent, stability, and specificity, the therapy is ready to proceed to the issue itself. Otherwise, the therapist will need to spend time working on these process variables in order to facilitate work on the content.

The final problem to assess is whether the partners have a win–lose or a win–win attitude. Some couples define the success of arguments in terms of whether one person wins and the other loses. These arguments are doomed to fail because a win–lose argument is really a loss for both. The framework does not promote cooperation or a spirit of compromise. The couple need to see the futility of such a framework and change it in such a way that they both agree in principle that negotiation leading to compromise will work best for both.

When they can put aside their strategies for winning they can focus on compromising. In essence, couples sometimes lose sight of the fact that all agreements are not just about issues, but about the relationship. If winning is at the expense of the relationship, the price of victory is too high. Once couples begin to realize an argument always has to do with the relationship, they will begin to be more concerned with how they are doing during an argument. This awareness can help to eliminate personal attacks and feelings of personalization. In fact, during the course of the argument, statements may be made to affirm the other person even while disagreeing with his or her position.

Assess the Source of the Conflict

Prior to stating a complaint to one's partner, it is useful to understand the source of the feelings and the conflict. The individual partner can look within in order to first determine why s/he is feeling the feeling. Basically, this process is cognitive therapy with the self. The individual should think about the basis for the feelings and try to determine whether expectations are rational, realistic, or workable.

For example, a husband became angry that his wife did not respect his desire that she not talk about any aspect of their relationship in front of their friends. This was a newly married couple and they were still discovering each other's likes and dislikes. He assumed she absolutely should have known his desires and became enraged when she commented about their liking something different. When this belief was examined, he realized he expected her to know something by reading his mind. He was then able to release the anger he felt, and make a request that she be sensitive to his need for privacy because he was extremely sensitive about what others knew about him.

This awareness changed the focus from the relationship to the individual. In most arguments, the focus may be on the individual or on the relationship depending upon the rationale for the anger. In all cases, the therapist needs to keep a balanced perspective. The partner may bring personal irrationality to the conflict, which further escalates the argument. In the example above, the wife had a strong response to her husband's anger. She assumed partners should always be fair and reasonable. When he did not behave according to her expectations in this area, she began to think and say that the marriage was a mistake.

Fighting as a Skill

Being able to use a fight constructively does not come naturally. Fighting is a skill that takes time and practice to develop. Couples sometimes believe they should automatically know how to have an argument. They need to be told that it is something that is learned and that they will not immediately begin to have constructive fights. Mistakes will be made and rules of fair fighting will be violated. Patience and tolerance are needed at the outset. An overview of the program may be given to the couple. They will need to agree to some basic ground rules to fair fighting, beginning with small fights first, and sticking to the basic steps for fair fighting until the process is mastered. Once the process is working, a step may be skipped if the partners believe it is not needed.

As the practice begins, the couple is asked to identify several ongoing fights or areas of conflict in their relationship. They are further asked to divide these into three categories—cold, warm, and hot. The therapist begins the practice exercises in the office with the cold arguments. Sometimes couples will say everything is hot. When this happens, it is important to have completed all the steps up to this point in order to determine whether there is an underlying issue that drives the belief that every issue is hot.

Segmenting Fights

Fighting takes time. Many couples attempt to resolve their differences in a matter of seconds or minutes. The dialogue is often truncated. A general rule is to discuss an argument as soon as one is aware of it and has had some time to think it through. Once the person is ready to say something, s/he should let the other know s/he wants to talk and that the talk is an argument and will require some time. If it is not an appropriate time to talk, or if the time is limited, it is advisable to agree on a time to talk later. The time should be fixed, otherwise the person with the problem may feel that there will not be an opportunity to express the complaint.

When the couple fight at home, it may be useful to designate a fighting place. This place should not be the bedroom or any other place the couple spend intimate time together. Most couples have some place in the house that is relatively free of distractions. The partners need to focus on each other during this time.

They may agree on the amount of time they have to talk before they begin. We have found that an hour is about the limit, because after that time partners begin to tire and issues start to recycle. Some arguments can be resolved in an hour; many of the hot issues will take many hours to resolve. The couple needs to know that certain issues may require many hours to solve and, therefore, learn to segment their fighting.

Segmentation simply means breaking the fight up into manageable increments. For the couple beginning therapy, the fight may be confined to the therapist's office and, for others, some combination of work at home and in the office. At the end of each segment at home, the partners agree on when to talk next and then say something positive about the process and about each other. The statement might simply acknowledge that some progress was made in the discussion and indicate appreciation for the understanding received from the other.

Sometimes a fair fight becomes nasty. Rules may be broken, emotions may begin to rule, and personal attacks may be mounted. The partners may not be able to get back on track. We have an escape clause in place for such an occurrence, which stipulates that either partner may unilaterally call a time-out, without a veto from the other person. When a time-out is called, it may be with or without feedback, for the shortest time possible. If a long time-out is called, the person calling it is also responsible for proposing the next time to talk. Long time-outs should be avoided if possible; shorter time-outs may be used to regain perspective and cool off. A partner may call a time-out because of the actions of the partner or for oneself. If a partner is feeling too upset or angry, some time alone may be needed.

Rules to Keep the Fight Clean

The partners need to agree that a fight must have rules in order to keep it clean and constructive. The following list of Do's and Don'ts (Weeks & Treat, 1992) may be used as a guideline for keeping the fight fair.

The couple may be asked to consider which rules they tend to adhere to and which they tend to violate during an argument. Generally, these rules are given at the end of a session as homework.

Essential Do's and Don'ts

1. Be specific when you introduce a gripe.
2. Don't just complain, no matter how specifically; ask for a reasonable change that will relieve one gripe at a time.
3. Confine yourself to one issue at a time. Otherwise, without professional guidance, you may skip back and forth, evading the harder ones.
4. Always consider compromise. Remember, your partner's view of reality is just as real as yours, even though you may differ. There are no totally objective realities.
5. Do not allow counter-demands to enter the picture until the original demands are clearly understood, and there has been a clear-cut response to them.
6. Never assume that you know what your partner is thinking until you have checked out the assumption in plain language; never assume or predict how your partner will react, or what your partner will accept or reject.
7. Never put labels on your partner. Do not make sweeping, labeling judgments about your partner's feelings, especially about whether or not they are real or important.
8. Sarcasm is dirty fighting.

The partners are told to read the rules during the week and come back with a list of which rules they adhere to and which they violate, in rank order. They may also add ideas to the list if they do things not mentioned. The therapist then goes through the list of each partner, affirming what they do that is helpful and asking them what they can do to avoid the behavior that interferes with fair fighting. If the strategy makes sense, the therapist goes on to the next item. If the client cannot state how to avoid the behavior, or if the approach does not seem workable, the therapist helps the person develop a strategy. After each partner has gone through his or her list, the therapist can turn to the other and ask if there are any additional partner behaviors that either further or interfere with the process. These points are then discussed and if the partner needs to change, a strategy is developed.

At the end of this discussion about rules, the therapist once again asks that each partner make a commitment to the rules. The therapist may point out that the commitment is actually to oneself and not to the partner. In other words, one person violating a rule(s) is no excuse for the other to then violate the rules. To do so only escalates the argument. Each person is responsible, and there is no excuse for violating the agreement.

However, the therapist must suggest that no one is perfect and that bad habits are hard to break. It is normal to violate some of the rules from time to time. When this happens the partner should try to catch it, apologize for the violation, and proceed. Otherwise, the partners may fall into the trap of becoming fixated on the violation and then arguing about whether the person really wants to fight fairly. By normalizing slips in the recovery, the therapist is helping the couple stay focused on the process and to keep moving forward.

Sometimes one person does not recognize that s/he has violated a rule, at least not before the partner has noticed it. Therefore, it should be agreed that one partner may calmly and nonjudgmentally confront the other when a violation occurs. When a violation is pointed out, the partner should stop, think about the feedback, and respond accordingly. If the partner cannot see the violation and persists in enacting the behavior, the other may need to call a time-out until the next therapy session.

The situation described can be difficult to tease out from the descriptions offered by the couple. A simple way to avoid this problem is to tape-record all the arguments that occur at home. Consequently, when the couple agree to talk about a problem, they meet at the agreed time, in the prescribed place, turn on the tape recorder, and begin. If they get stuck and cannot get unstuck, they can review the tape and process the interaction, or, if they have different perceptions about the process, they can bring the tape to the next therapy session so the therapist can play that segment and everyone can discuss the process.

Additionally, using a tape recorder puts some couples on their best behavior, which may be helpful in the beginning. Another way to use the tape is to have the partners listen to their arguments in order to do a self-appraisal. The instructions are as follows: "Listen only to how you sounded, what you said, and whether you followed your own rules and the process for constructive fighting. Don't worry about your partner. S/he will do the same thing you are doing."

Steps to Fair Fighting

The next task for the therapist is to teach the couple the mechanics of fair fighting. The steps are described in the following.

Steps to Fair Fighting*

Step 1: Listen to yourself. Identify and express that you own your feelings to yourself and to your partner ("I feel angry and hurt right now"). To "own" feelings means to accept them as your feelings in a responsible manner, and not to blame your partner for the way you feel. The overt and underlying angry and hurt feelings must be identified and expressed appropriately before effective and mutual problem solving can be accomplished. This requires a willingness to become vulnerable to your partner, to actively listen to each other in an empathic manner, and to express yourself clearly and concretely.

Step 2: Identify the real issue, which frequently is not the issue originally presented. For example, beneath the statement, "I am angry that you don't spend enough time with the children," may be another issue, "I feel overwhelmed by my responsibilities with the children and abandoned by you, and I want and need some direct support and help from you." Immediate problem solving regarding "more time with the children" by one partner would not necessarily lead to the exposing of the other partner's feeling of being overwhelmed and abandoned. Work together to identify the real issue(s) facing your or your partner.

Step 3: Stay here and now. In other words, don't drag up the past to score points. What is important is what is happening now, what the feelings and issues are now. The past cannot be modified, the present can. (This is not to say that long withheld feelings should not be expressed. At an appropriate place and time, such a disclosure can be extremely helpful to you and your partner.)

Step 4: Use polarization constructively. People sometimes desire or need to get away from each other in the midst of a conflict, either because anger has escalated beyond manageable limits, or just to

---

*Modified from Hof & Miller (1981).

think more clearly. Such polarization or time apart should be used constructively, to cool off or figure out how to move closer together on the issue at hand and resolve the conflict. Such time should not be used destructively, to figure out how to get even with your partner or perpetuate the conflict. Whoever requests the break or the time-out is responsible for telling the partner when s/he will reinitiate contact and for following through on the commitment.

Step 5: Find out what each of you has in common regarding the issue at hand. The common ground, or items both of you agree on already, is frequently overshadowed by the differences between you. Identification of the common ground helps you to see the differences in perspective, and frequently provides a positive starting place from which you can build a constructive solution.

Step 6: Do mutual problem solving. The two of you identify as many possible solutions to the problem as you can, without prejudging any of them, and then list the positive and negative consequences of each. Make a joint decision to pursue one proposed solution. After you have reached a decision, create an agreed upon action plan that includes specific steps, a time sequence, and an agreement to revisit the problem after some specific period of time to both reassess how the agreement is working and make changes as needed. Consider also what you might do to undermine the agreement and express that to your partner. (Speak only for yourself; let your partner speak for him- or herself.)

Step 7: Come together in celebration. Give some signal to each other, through the use of words or touch, to signify resolution of the conflict, or that you have at least agreed to disagree, that you have gone as far as you can at this time, or that conflict will not remain a permanent barrier between you. Congratulate each other for the hard work and willingness to compromise. Reaffirm your relationship in as many ways as possible. For example, you could use a hug, kiss, or other constructive use of physical touch, including sex. Words might be used, such as, "I love you and I'm glad we worked this out," "Thanks for hanging in there with me," or "Let's put it aside for now and come back to it later." This step should also include processing the experience, identifying what each of you individually and as the couple did that was helpful or unhelpful, and what has been learned.

The seven steps can be divided into two phases, with each step and phase being explained to the couple. The first four steps constitute one phase, the purpose being to help the couple talk about their feelings and gain a clear definition of the problem.

When a couple have a problem, they actually have two problems: the problem itself and the feelings about the problem. Many couples, and especially the male partners, will want to skip this stage. When partners attempt to skip this stage, it is virtually impossible to fully resolve the issue and unlikely that the following steps can be accomplished. When one partner does not attend to the feelings of the other about a problem, that person feels discounted, unheard, and will often say the other partner does not care. Acknowledging the feelings and sharing in the same meaning about the problem helps to affirm the relationship.

One reaction the therapist should expect is that of the partners confusing acknowledgment with agreement. In many cases, the male partners have said that if they acknowledge how their wives feel, they have already lost the argument. As a result, they ignore the feelings and refuse to see the partner's point of view. The therapist needs to watch for this pattern.

The last three steps deal with the problem-solving process and the negotiations that are a part of it. These steps should not be attempted until the first four steps have been successfully traversed. In some cases, the last steps are not needed at all. For example, in some situations the partner just wants to talk about some problem that may be outside the relationship. Basically, s/he wants the partner to know what is happening and how they feel about it, and get some validation for the feelings and some emotional support. The last thing the partner may desire is to be told what to do or how to fix the problem, yet this is exactly what some partners want to do.

Unfortunately, some men tend to operate solely in a problem-solving mode. He assumes the only way to be helpful is to "fix" the problem and make the unpleasant feeling disappear. The woman may want the validation described and a clash then occurs. This gender difference is useful for couples to understand. An additional step might be for the partner with the problem to state the need at the outset ("I want you to listen to my feelings and give me some emotional support so that I can solve this problem on my own"). We sometimes offer the rule of "don't offer advice unless asked."

The second set of steps enables the couple to generate alternatives and then choose from among them. This process is time-consuming, and the couple need to appreciate just how much time it may take. These steps are first practiced in the therapist's office, beginning with small nonemotionally laden issues. The therapist coaches the partners through the process, and it is common for the initial practice to take more than one therapeutic session. As the couple becomes more proficient with the model, the time required decreases. Couples also gain a sense of when they may skip steps because they have naturally done what is needed. Over time these steps feel less and less mechanical and more natural.

INTRACTABLE CONFLICT

Many couples will respond to the approach to treatment described up to this point. However, there are couples who continue to be angry and fight in spite of all of these efforts. In most conflict-resolution models, the assumption is that couples lack the interpersonal skill they need to resolve their differences. Thus, the method of treatment is behavioral and skills oriented. Our general approach to treatment is the Intersystem Model (Weeks, 1989). This model takes into account individual, interactional, and intergenerational factors in the development of problems and treatment. In those cases where a straightforward behaviorally and interactionally oriented approach does not work, it is important to examine the individual and intergenerational factors.

We examined some of the individual factors in the preceding chapter, where we looked at the meaning of anger and conflict in the individual, and using the anger genogram, the learning acquired in the family. Individual meanings and attitudes toward these feelings are an integral part of the model. In addition, a further exploration of individual/intrapsychic factors may be necessary.

The anger and conflict may be driven by unconscious individual conflicts and psychopathology. For example, an individual with a characterological problem, such as a passive-aggressive personality disorder, will not respond to this model. The person may have a conflict over being dependent. This hostile-dependent partner denies the emotional need for the other, but cannot escape the feeling of dependency. Rather than admit to being dependent, s/he responds to the other in a hostile, passive-aggressive manner, in order to not feel dependent. The lesson to be learned in such a situation is that when the model described does not work, we must go back to the Intersystem Model and examine individual psychopathology and unconscious conflicts. The couple work may need to be suspended while the therapist works on the characterological problems in one partner.

Feldman (1982) developed an intrapsychic-interpersonal model of marital pathology, which accounted for conflict. The underlying cause of conflict in his model is what he calls "narcissistic vulnerability." This phenomenon refers to low self-esteem, self-fragmentation, and a poor sense of self-identity. When individuals experience narcissistic vulnerability they become hypersensitive and manifest narcissistic expectations. Sensitive to rejection, disapproval, criticism, not being loved and cared for, they have difficulty controlling emotions and behavior. In order to compensate for the feelings of vulnerability, they develop unconscious expectations that are impossible for anyone to fulfill. They expect intimate others to be unfailingly admiring, attentive, loving, and so forth. Obviously, no one can meet these expectations, and the failure results in the partner being perceived as rejecting and nonempathic.

The narcissistically vulnerable partner's perception of the other then leads to narcissistic rage and anxiety. Should the interactive process stop at this point, the other partner is simply scapegoated, seen as the bad partner. In many cases, however, the process involves more dynamics. The narcissistically vulnerable individual splits off parts of the self s/he finds unacceptable. These disowned parts of the self are then projected onto the partner—a phenomenon known as projective identification. The other partner is then defined as all "good" or all "bad." Usually, the projection is of that which is defined as bad.

Once the projection has occurred, the individual then attempts to destroy the projected behavior in the other person, by whatever means possible. Needless to say, in such a situation, the perception of the other must be grossly distorted. Of course, the other partner is not a passive recipient. Usually rejecting the role in which s/he is placed, the conflict ensues or continues between the partners.

This process is shown schematically in Figure 4.2. Next to each dynamic is the corresponding treatment technique that might be used to stop or reverse this process. As is evident, this model requires in-depth work with both the individuals and the couple.

A final way to deal with conflict in a couple is to employ a paradoxical intervention. Weeks and L'Abate (1982) describe cases that involve the use of one or several paradoxical strategies. The two most common techniques are to positively reframe the conflict and then prescribe it.

Figure 4.2 Dynamic Process and Treatment Techniques in Feldman's Approach

DYNAMIC	*APPROACH OR TECHNIQUE*
Narcissistic Vulnerability	Emotional Awareness Training; Dream Work
Blocked Empathy	Communication and Empathy Training
Narcissistic Expectation	Cognitive Awareness Training
Narcissistic Rage	Self-Instruction/Control Training
Cognitive Distortions	Cognitive Awareness Training; Focusing on Positives in the Relationship
Overt Marital Conflict	Behavioral Contracting and Problem Solving

From L. Feldman, "Dysfunctional Marital Conflict: An Interpersonal-Intrapsychic Model." Reprinted from Vol. 8, No. 4, of the *Journal of Marital and Family Therapy*. Copyright © 1982, American Association for Marriage and Family Therapy. Reprinted with permission.

The *positive reframe* helps the couple see that there is something they derive from the conflict, that it serves some function in the relationship. The *prescription paradox* brings the heretofore out-of-control conflict under their control.

For example, the therapist might say the following: "It is clear the two of you care a great deal for each other. You keep a fight going almost constantly in order to protect each other from having to confront your depression. For now, you should continue to help each other by carefully noticing when the other person looks 'down' and picking a fight immediately. If you miss how your partner is feeling, then you should cooperate fully by fighting back when your partner picks a fight with you." If the couple follows this directive, they learn to see how fights are connected to depression and begin to take some control over the process. If they do not follow the directive, then they do not fight, which was one of the goals of the therapy.

A well-constructed paradoxical intervention is a win–win proposition. This particular approach requires a good deal of skill to implement. It should be attempted only after some study and, ideally, with the help of a supervisor experienced in this approach.

CONCLUSION

The experience of conflict intimacy is a genuine possibility for some couples. Other couples can only learn to make their angry expressions and conflicts less destructive or hurtful. In either case, the therapist's initial tasks are to normalize anger and conflict, assess the meaning and function of each individual's anger and conflict, assess the conflict utilization skills of the couple, and assess the level of their conflict. Once this has been done, the therapeutic effort shifts to a focus on intervening in an appropriate manner to facilitate the resolution of the conflict(s) and to enabling the couple to continue to utilize anger and conflict in as helpful and creative a way as possible.

REFERENCES

Alberti, R., & Emmons, M. (1983). *Your perfect right: A guide to assertive living*. San Luis Obispo, CA: Impact.

Bach, G., & Goldberg, H. (1974). *Creative aggression*. Garden City, NY: Doubleday.

Feldman, L. B. (1982). Dysfunctional marital conflict: An integrative interpersonal-intrapsychic model. *Journal of Marital and Family Therapy, 8*(4), 417-428.

Guerin, P. J., Fay, L. F., Burden, S. L., & Kautto, J. G. (1987). *The evaluation and treatment of marital conflict*. New York: Basic Books.

Hendrix, H. (1988). *Getting the love you want*. New York: Holt.

Hof, L., & Miller, W. R. (1981). *Marriage enrichment: Philosophy, process, & program*. Bowie, MD: Brady.

James, M., & Jongeward, D. (1971). *Born to win*. Reading, MA: Addison-Wesley.

Lerner, H. (1985). *The dance of anger*. New York: Harper & Row.

Mack, R. (1989). Spouse abuse—a dyadic approach. In G. R. Weeks (Ed.), *Treating couples: The Intersystem Model of the Marriage Council of Philadelphia* (pp. 191–214). New York: Brunner/Mazel.

Weeks, G. R. (1989). An Intersystem approach to treatment. In G. R. Weeks (Ed.), *Treating couples: The Intersystem Model of the Marriage Council of Philadelphia* (pp. 317–341). New York: Brunner/Mazel.

Weeks, G. R., & L'Abate, L. (1982). *Paradoxical psychotherapy: Theory and practice with individuals, couples, and families*. New York: Brunner/Mazel.

Weeks, G. R., & Treat, S. (1992). *Couples in treatment: Techniques for effective practice*. New York: Brunner/Mazel.

5

A HAPPY MARRIAGE:
PAIRING COUPLES THERAPY
AND TREATMENT OF
DEPRESSION

Bonnie Howard, Ph.D., with
Gerald R. Weeks, Ph.D.

Depression has been called the mental health common cold of our time
(Jessee & L'Abate, 1985), and the extensive clinical and research literature on depression mirrors its importance. The overwhelming majority of
the literature, however, conceptualizes depression as a biological disease,
which the individual "has," as an internal state of the individual, or as the
product of distorted individual cognitive processes. Systemic treatment
models for depression, including marital therapy when one or both partners are depressed, is rare. In fact, clinical research looking at outcome
for marital therapy for depression is extremely limited.

   Of interest here is a group comparison study of behavioral marital
therapy, individual cognitive therapy, and wait-list control groups by
O'Leary and Beach (1990). In the study, both treatment groups showed
clinically significant reduction in the women's depression, but the wives
participating in marital therapy showed greater increases in marital satis-

faction, a difference maintained at one-year follow-up. Research at the University of Washington looked at outcome in a group comparison study of individual cognitive-behavioral therapy with the depressed spouse, behavioral couple therapy, and a treatment combining the two (Jacobson, Dobson, Fruzzetti, Schmaling, & Salusky, 1991). The behavioral couple therapy was at least as effective as the individual therapy in leading to significant pre- to posttreatment reduction in depression among maritally distressed couples, and was the only therapy leading to significant increases in marital satisfaction in these couples. For the subset of couples with a depressed spouse but without marital distress, the combined treatment was the only one leading to significantly improved marital interactions and marital satisfaction. In a follow-up study, Jacobson, Fruzzetti, Dobson, Whisman, and Hops (1993) found that relapse rates did not discriminate among the three treatments.

The interpersonal effects of depression on family and other close relationships are widely recognized, but a broader systemic or interactional perspective on etiology, maintenance, and treatment of depression is rare. The application of the Intersystem Model developed at the PENN Council for Relationships (formerly the Marriage Council of Philadelphia) in treating couples when one partner is clinically depressed can be particularly helpful in addressing the systemic issues underlying the individual diagnosis. However, it should be clearly understood that with depression, as elsewhere, the interactive (interpersonal) or intergenerational perspective on the condition need not and should not becloud the individual biochemical and genetic perspectives. In fact, the prevailing clinical impression is that the judicious use of antidepressant medications may greatly facilitate marital therapy in depression, even though outcome research on this type of therapy is hard to find.

MARITAL FUNCTIONING AND DEPRESSION

Clear cause-and-effect relationships cannot be established, but the associations between depressive symptoms and clinical depression and marital dysfunction are strong. Marital discord is the most common life stressor reported by women as a precursor to depression (Paykel, Myers, Dienelt, Klerman, Lindenthal, & Pepper, 1969). One half of all patients receiving psychiatric treatment sought help because of marital problems, and in 30 percent of couples with marital problems, one spouse is clinically depressed. Further, in 50 percent of maritally discordant couples seeking treatment, at least one spouse is depressed (studies cited in Jessee & L'Abate, 1985, p. 1133).

The associations do not result only from the negative worldview of the depressed person, as spouses corroborate their depressed partners' negative reports about the marriage (studies cited in Coyne, Burchill, & Stiles, 1991, p. 338). It also cannot be assumed that the depressed spouse presenting for treatment is the only dysfunctional member of the couple. Partners of depressed individuals often have personal and family histories of psychopathology, including depression. For example, Merikangas and Spiker (1982) found that more than half of partners of patients with an affective disturbance met the criteria for a lifetime diagnosis of psychiatric illness. Depressed women are also more likely than nondepressed controls to have a husband with an alcohol or drug problem or personality disorder (Coyne & DeLongis, 1986). There is also evidence that spouses of depressed people have increased emotional and physical complaints during an acute depressive episode of their partner (Quinton, Rutter, & Liddle, 1984), and this distress can clearly exacerbate the distress of the depressed patient. One review found that about 40 percent of spouses of currently depressed patients were classified as suitable for referral themselves, in contrast to 17 percent of partners of depressed patients who were not currently in a depressive episode (Coyne, Kessler, Tal, Turnbull, Wortman, & Greden, 1987).

Studying the importance of loss and stressful life events to depression in women, Brown and Harris's (1978) classic research shows that a confiding relationship with a spouse is a strong mediator between stressful life events and depression. Women lacking such a relationship were three times more likely to be depressed following such an event. Other researchers have reanalyzed the data and suggest that the effects of lack of intimacy on depression are independent of whether the depressed person had a serious life event in the preceding six months (Cleary & Kessler, 1982). More recently, the Yale Epidemiologic Catchment Area Study (Weissman, 1987) looked at the relationship between being married, but unable to confide in one's partner, and found a greater than 25-fold increase in risk for depression when one is not able to talk to one's spouse.

The impact of marital dysfunction on depressive symptoms does not disappear with treatment of the depression. Many studies have shown marital problems to be associated with poor response to individually based treatment for depression, irrespective of the treatment modality. There is also a significant relationship between the resolution of marital disagreements and the modification of depressive behaviors of the patient. First, marital problems are a negative prognostic variable in studies of the response to antidepressants (Rounsaville, Weissman, Prusoff, & Herceg-Baron, 1979). In addition, relapses after acute depressive episodes and following treatment with antidepressants are often precipitated by marital disruption (Hooley, Orley, & Teasdale, 1986; Rounsaville et al., 1979). Four-year follow-up studies of depressed people with marital problems who were treated only with antidepressants suggest that they continue to be vulnerable both to depression and to marital problems (Rounsaville, Prusoff, & Weissman, 1980).

In addition, marital distress has also been found to be related to poor response to individually based nonmedication treatments for depression. For example, despite the relationship themes emphasized in individual interpersonal therapy for depression, those with unresolved marital conflict were the most likely to be showing depressive symptoms at the end of an eight month maintenance treatment (Rounsaville et al., 1979). Depressed persons with marital problems have also been shown to benefit little from cognitive therapy—despite other outcome research finding cognitive therapy to be an effective treatment for depression (Jacobson, Holtzworth-Monroe, & Schmaling, 1989). In another study, criticism by the spouse during an interview while the depressed partner was hospitalized, rather than individual factors, was found to be the most powerful predictor of subsequent relapses (Vaughn & Leff, 1976). Similarly, Hooley and Teasdale (1989) found that the best predictor of relapse was the depressed patient's rating on the single-item question, "How critical is your spouse of you?"

The previous evidence for a strong association between depression and marital dysfunction certainly supports an interactional, systemic perspective on depression—a perspective that counters the view of many lay people and professionals that depression is an internal state. Showing the links between depressed clients and the interpersonal context of their marriage is descriptive rather than explanatory, however. During the last 15 years, there has also been increased attention to developing more theoretical interactional models of the way that behavior of depressed people and their partners contributes to the etiology and maintenance of depression. It is important, therefore, briefly to examine several examples.

MODELS FOR PROBLEMATIC COUPLE INTERACTIONS IN DEPRESSION

Mate Selection

First, a systemic perspective suggests the role of mate selection in the relation between depression and marital problems. This explanation is supported by the associations between psychopathology and interpersonal difficulties in the spouses of depressed persons reported earlier. Also, Quinton, Rutter, and Liddle (1984) found that poor adjustment of women raised in an institution was related to their spouses' current alcohol, drug, or criminal status. Further, their spouses' self-reports of adolescent deviance were predictive of the wives' current adjustment. Similarly, Brown, Bifulco, Harris, and Bridge (1986) found that two-thirds of women with coexisting depression and marital difficulties were married to husbands judged to be "grossly undependable." Thus women made vulnerable to depression by histories of loss, abandonment, or abuse may marry men who are less likely to provide the interpersonal support shown to be a powerful mediating factor between these histories and subsequent problems with depression.

Clinical experience with the couples seen at the PENN Council for Relationships provides examples of other ways that mate selection can lead to depressive patterns best addressed through couple therapy. The partner presenting as depressed when a distressed couple begins treatment may not be the depressed partner at mid-treatment, as denial of depression can play a role in mate selection. One middle-aged couple was referred for treatment of the wife's chronic clinical depression. By the fifth session, it was apparent that the husband had a family history of unresolved loss—including the death of his mother during his adolescence—and family coping responses of minimizing loss and avoiding negative feelings. His unacknowledged depression emerged early in treatment and the couple and therapist hypothesized together that he had selected a depressed partner to "carry" the negative affect he was unable to acknowledge. In turn, the openly depressed wife had selected a partner who would show the optimism and emotional energy she could not.

In another case, a couple in their 20s were referred for adjunct marital therapy after the wife was diagnosed with a major depressive disorder and started on an antidepressant. The couple failed to respond to initial strategies of reframing the wife's depression and shifting to an interactional focus. The couple talked about commitment to the marital therapy, but seemed to be waiting for the wife's depression to respond to medication before addressing their problems. The impasse was broken after the partners completed a genogram during the sixth session. As an out-of-session assignment, each was then asked to describe each family member using five brief descriptors. During the initial session, both partners had denied a family history of depression. Reviewing the genograms in the seventh session provided new information. A theme in the labels applied by the nondepressed husband to his mother and an aunt, who had been a significant caretaker during part of his childhood, clearly suggested untreated depression. After briefly exploring his key relationships with depressed women, both spouses realized that in many ways the husband was comfortable with the depressed partner he had selected. His focus on taking care of his wife felt familiar, but was a critical factor in the relationship patterns that helped maintain her depression.

Interactional Models

Second, several interactional models of specific behavioral and affective exchanges between a depressed person and a nondepressed partner have been offered. While recognizing the role of stressful life events and problematic relationships, these models focus on how the behavior of the depressed person and the spouse coevolve over time to maintain a marital system that inadvertently maintains both distress and conflict.

MENTAL RESEARCH INSTITUTE MOOD DISORDERS CENTER MODEL

Coyne, Burchill, and Stiles (1991) emphasize the role of the inhibition of the anger felt by the spouse of the depressed person in generating an unsatisfactory interpersonal cycle. A basic feature of intimates' reactions to the distress of depressed people is often an increased sense of responsibility for the relationship. The depressed behavior of the mate may be aversive and may induce negativity in the nondepressed spouse. With the shift of the interactional burden to the spouse, however, the depressed person's distress will also induce guilt and initially inhibit hostile reactions. The nondepressed spouse may try to control the impulse to defend against the aversive nature of the demands placed on him or her by seeming to respond positively and to provide what is requested—while "leaking" impatience, hostility, and rejection. This disguised rejection and anger then validate the depressed person's insecurity and low self-esteem and lead to further expression of distress, which perpetuates the pattern.

In addition, the Mental Research Institute (MRI) Mood Disorders Center model can include the pattern of overt hostility found in many marriages where at least one partner is depressed. Established coping strategies involving inhibition of anger and avoidance of direct conflict may break down when life situations include problems that must be faced. Marital interactions then are burdened by the accumulated unresolved issues and negative feelings between the couple, with the likely result that attempts to talk about the current problem will be marked by high emotional reactivity and hostility. The marital exchanges will be unproductive and aversive—further strengthening the unhelpful beliefs that it is not safe to confront problems or express anger and interpersonal differences cannot be resolved (Coyne et al., 1991). A circular pattern is thus established, since marital conflict will again be avoided until the accumulation of unresolved problems leads to another explosion of intense negative affect followed by another withdrawal.

OREGON RESEARCH INSTITUTE MODEL

A related model is the Oregon Research Institute's application of Patterson and Reid's coercion theory in creating a model of depressive behavior as a form of aversive control. When a person displays depressive behavior, hostile behavior by the partner is temporarily inhibited and compliance with requests is increased. At the same time, truly caring responses are suppressed and the probability of hostility in the context of a long-term marital relationship is increased. Using sequential analysis, researchers at the institute showed that in couples with a depressed wife and marital distress, the wife's depressive behavior decreased the spouse's subsequent verbal aggression and the husband's aggression reduced the wife's subsequent depressive behavior. In the short run, each was able to exert aversive control over the other's undesired behavior and thus obtain immediate but short-lived relief (Biglan, Hops, & Sherman, 1988).

A COGNITIVE MODEL

Feldman (1976) provided a model of the depressive process in couples, which emphasizes cognitive schemata. The nondepressed spouse "innocently" makes a comment that strikes at the depressed partner's shaky sense of self-worth. A depressed or guilty response triggers a cognitive schema of overprotectiveness and omnipotence in the nondepressed partner and leads to increased attention, reassurance, and overprotective concern. Using a conflict model, Feldman then hypothesizes that the autonomy-seeking and competency-oriented part of the depressed person's personality is frustrated by the partner's overconcern. Feeling helpless and resentful, the depressed person then may respond with withdrawal, passive-aggressive behavior, open hostility, or a move toward defensive self-assertion. Each stimulates a cognitive schema of frustration and self-depreciation in the nondepressed spouse, who is motivated to shift again to the role of rescuer, and the cycle goes on.

A MICROLEVEL MODEL

In a study examining the interaction process in severe depression at a microlevel, Rubenstein and Timmins (1978) found a cyclical pattern of behavioral responses between the depressed patient and the partner that repeated every few minutes. Initially, the depressed spouse's verbal behavior included a very slow speech tempo and low pitch, a hesitant quality, a whining tone, little inflection, and few verbalizations. Nonverbally, there was little body movement or eye contact and the sitting posture was fixed. The nonsymptomatic partner mirrored the verbal and nonverbal behaviors of the patient, often positioning in such a way as to form a mirror image and exhibiting the other's exact movements at the same reduced speed several seconds later. In looking at the content of the couple's communication, Rubenstein and Timmins found the partner of the depressed person to take on a caretaker role. Compliant caretakers provided reassurance, explanation, and support in brief conversations focused on the patient's immediate concerns. The aggressive caretaker tried to convince the depressed spouse of the error of his or her ways with forceful lectures and attempts to push the partner out of depression. Either style of caretaking represents a critical stance toward the depression (and the depressed person) and thus tends to perpetuate the cycle.

EARLY MODELS FOR COUPLE-FOCUSED TREATMENT OF DEPRESSION

Marital Cognitive-Behavioral Therapy

As some clinicians have attempted a model of interpersonal transactions involved in the maintenance of depression, others have begun to offer models for couple therapy in the treatment of depression. Neil Jacobson and associates at the University of Washington have developed a model for treating depression that combines marital and cognitive-behavioral therapy (Jacobson, 1984). The protocol developed out of behavioral marital therapy with the addition of cognitive relabeling techniques and problem-solving training, as well as the substitution of parallel for contingent behavior-change contracts. Another addition was troubleshooting, a technique for in-session reenactment of problematic exchanges at home. As the interaction escalates, the therapist stops the "action" to dialogue with each spouse, exploring the cognitions—including automatic thoughts—of one while the other listens.

During the first month of treatment, the depressed partner is seen individually. Thereafter, conjoint marital sessions are alternated with individual sessions for the depressed spouse; the same therapist is used for both. In this model, the explanation for the approach given the couple is not a strong systemic one. The nondepressed spouse is "involved in treatment for depression," the approach is not called marital therapy, the depression is not defined as a marital problem, and the couple's relationship is not the focus of treatment (Jacobson, 1984).

MRI Mood Disorders Center Model

Coyne (1986) presents another strategic model of marital therapy for depression developed at the MRI Mood Disorders Center. The structure used in the model is an integral part of the treatment and is closer to Jacobson's than L'Abate's model, which is described next. First, the partners are interviewed individually, and often are seen individually during the course of therapy. However, treatment focuses on negotiating compatible goals and on marital interactions, particularly the responses of each to changes made by the other. The model is clearly brief therapy—constrained either by an initial 10-session or 12-session limit or by the requirement that certain goals be met if treatment is to continue beyond a specified number of trial sessions.

No guidelines were provided on how decisions are to be made on the balance between individual sessions (with both the depressed and nondepressed partners) and conjoint sessions. There are three foci of treatment in the model—the depression of the identified patient, the response of the nondepressed spouse, and the distressed marital situation. Although not made explicit, the structure of sessions may be determined by the relative need for attention to each of the areas. In any case, the therapeutic approach used for each is strategic. For example, the focus on the depressed partner emphasizes accepting the depression and reframing it as an active, protective strategy to contribute to the marriage, at some cost to the depressed person. Humor and exaggeration are used in homework assignments to make explicit implicit fears of assertiveness and recognition of the nondepressed partner's vulnerabilities and the depressed partner's fear of the greater burdens that would accompany improvement. Assignments are presented in a restraint of change "go slow" format and indirectly educate the partners about the systemic nature of their difficulties.

Similarly, in the focus on the response of the nondepressed spouse, an interactional perspective is taken, restraint of rapid change is used, and ritualized assignments of the problematic responses at set times and in planned situations are given. Examples given, however, suggest more direct explanation of the systemic issues—as in pointing out how the partner's attempts, whether lectures or coercion, to increase the activity of the depressed spouse have had the opposite effect. Similarly, alternating-days assignments in which the degree of involvement of the nondepressed spouse is explicitly varied are given as experiments.

In the third focus—marital turmoil—the couple's inability to negotiate disagreement and solve problems mutually is assumed, but the "direct attack" on these difficulties found in Jacobson's Behavior Marital Therapy (BMT) model is avoided. Instead, the problems are positively connoted by the therapist. Other interventions are also strategic and include the therapist's taking a "one down" position, prescription of marital arguments, restraint of change, and assignments involving planned emotional overreactivity to a behavior of the partner.

Paradoxical Marital Therapy for Depression

Weeks and L'Abate (1982) were the first to discuss the treatment of depression from a paradoxical and systemic perspective. In their book *Paradoxical Psychotherapy*, they devoted half a chapter to the paradoxical treatment of depression. They believed depression must be viewed systemically, which meant it was essential to involve the partner. Their first therapeutic strategy was to reframe the depression from something negative to something positive. They had observed that many patients were depressed because they viewed depression in strictly negative terms.

A positive reframe changed the attitude toward the depression. Second, a systemic reframe was also made that suggested that both partners were involved in the creation or maintenance of the depression. Next, they used a variety of techniques that commonly included prescribing the depression, negative consequences of change, restraint, and prescribing relapse. The case study presented, a couple treated by Weeks in 1978, was the first example in the literature showing the extended treatment of depression from a systemic and paradoxical perspective.

Jessee and L'Abate (1985) describe a systemic model of paradoxical marital treatment for depression. The treatment outlines five sequential stages: (1) positively reframing the depression, (2) prescribing the symptom, (3) asking the marital partner's help in keeping the patient depressed, (4) restraining change toward better marital functioning, and (5) resolving the underlying conflict.

After positively connoting the depression, the therapist next encourages the client to be depressed—in a ritualized way—perhaps during an assigned time period or in a prescribed way. The prescription is intended to either (1) interfere with the pattern of avoiding the depression and instead promote resolution through more fully experiencing it, or (2) lead to response with a "defiant" refusal to be depressed. Both the compliance-based paradox and the defiance-based paradox provide the depressed spouse with an increased sense of control over symptoms that led to a feeling of helplessness. The third stage enlists the spouse in helping keep the depressed partner depressed by doing those things previously identified as depressing and upsetting (paradoxically, helping by not helping).

If the first stages have changed the couple's usual transactions around the depression, new ways of interacting are necessary. The fourth stage of the model uses restraint of change to give direction to emergent behavior. The therapist first evokes memories or potential images of greater intimacy and enjoyment, and then instructs the couple to avoid such situations because the current task is to attend to the depression. The couple's usual response to the directive is to rebel against it and move toward more positive interactions.

It is with the fifth stage that Jessee and L'Abate move beyond a strategic marital treatment mode. If the couple is willing, the deeper relationship conflicts that led to the adaptations that evolved into the depressive cycle are examined. The authors believe the underlying issue for most couples with at least one depressed member is their difficulties in tolerating or creating intimacy, with depression serving as a distance-regulating mechanism in the marriage to reduce anxiety with increased closeness. When the initial stages of marital treatment have alleviated depressive symptoms, the balance of power in the relationship has shifted toward greater equality and conflicts interfering with greater intimacy can be better addressed. Consistent with a systemic view, Jessee and L'Abate note that during this stage depression can reemerge (including in the previously nondepressed partner). This recurrence can then be refocused on as in earlier stages.

THE INTERSYSTEM MODEL

The Intersystem Model of marital therapy (Weeks, 1989; Weeks & Treat, 1992; Weeks & Hof, 1994) can broaden and enrich the models of marital therapy to treat depression offered by Jacobson, Coyne, and L'Abate. Most important, the Intersystem Model is both comprehensive and integrative in its simultaneous consideration of three subsystems: the individual, the interactional, and the intergenerational. In contrast—reflecting their origins in behavior therapy or strategic family therapy—the three models described focus almost exclusively on a single system, the interactional. There are limited exceptions, but these are not well developed or conceptually integrated. For example, Jacobson's model incorporates looking at individual cognitions in the troubleshooting component. Also, Jessee and L'Abate's optional fifth stage—looking at the deeper relationship conflicts that interfere with the couple's developing greater intimacy—suggests consideration of issues outside the interactional focus that is the core of the model.

Recently, Moltz (1993) described an integrative model applied to bipolar disorder that includes biological, psychodynamic, and systemic aspects. Compatible in many ways with the Intersystem Model, his model is founded on the assumption that it is necessary to address each of the dimensions and their interactions in the assessment and treatment of the disorder.

Enriching the Marriage of Marital Therapy and Treatment of Depression: The Model

THE INDIVIDUAL IN COUPLE THERAPY FOR TREATING DEPRESSION

With the first of the three "I's," the Intersystem Model looks at the couple with a depressed member as "a system consisting of two individuals'' (Weeks & Treat, 1992, p. xvii). This focus allows the integration of a wide variety of individual issues as part of marital therapy for depression, in contrast to most systemic models which tend to ignore, or even deny, individual factors, including individual psychopathology and biological vulnerability. In treating a couple with one partner who is depressed, the Intersystem Model would include assessment of individual intrapsychic dynamics, including defense mechanisms and cognitive distortions, as well as family history of depression. Referral of the depressed partner for an evaluation for antidepressant medication or for adjunctive individual therapy would be completely compatible with the Intersystem Model.

Emphasizing the importance of the therapeutic relationship, the model also recognizes the person of the therapist and includes a consideration of countertransference, a view lacking in the other treatment models described. For example, a trainee with a family history of paternal violence seemed ''stuck'' in treating a couple where the wife's depression was met by angry responses by her husband. Videotaped supervision showed the therapist how her own countertransferential withdrawal in the face of male anger led to ineffective treatment.

The model also incorporates, and normalizes, individual factors, such as coexisting physical illness, life-cycle changes, ethnicity, and the impact of socioeconomic issues. While Coyne and colleagues (1991) give an eloquent and reasoned description of the role of contextual factors in depression, the brief treatment model they offer seems to ignore these issues. Certainly life-cycle and contextual issues are integral to understanding depression. Aging, illness, unemployment, infertility, the legacy of racism, the dual-career life style, and the ''empty nest'' are just a few of the contextual issues that can have an impact the couple seen for treatment. In the Intersystem Model, however, these are not merely addressed as pressures or stresses external to the couple. The meaning of each factor to the individual partner and to the relationship may need to be explored in what sometimes becomes a therapy of negotiating new meanings.

INTERACTIONAL THEMES IN THE INTERSYSTEM MODEL

The Intersystem Model also maintains a focus on the interactional system similar to the treatment models noted above. The treatment strategies used can include reframing, enactment, and between-session assignments, as well as strategic approaches, such as prescribing the symptom and restraint of change. "How to" descriptions of these techniques are provided in Weeks and Treat (1992), and specific applications in marital therapy for treating depression are given later in this chapter.

Although the Intersystem Model utilizes strategic techniques, a framework that values the therapeutic relationship and allows flexibility with respect to the length of treatment, the structure of sessions, and the themes addressed creates a treatment model where power differences between the therapist and couple are less integral. With the enrichment of focus on the intergenerational and individual systems, the process itself encourages openness to others' perspectives and greater conjoint agreement on problem definitions and goals—without the degree of therapist direction that exists in the BMT and strategic models.

One contextual theme not focused on in the interactional models for couple therapy for depression and not explicitly addressed by Weeks and Treat (1992) is being more clearly incorporated in the Intersystem Model—gender issues. This focus is particularly important in treating depression as research has shown the importance of the relationship between gender issues, particularly sex roles, in depression in marital couples. For example, Whisman and Jacobson (1989) looked at the relationship between sex roles and depression in women. They found that the marriages of depressed women tended to be characterized by inequitable and unsatisfactorily negotiated marital roles and by the lack of shared decision making, with the wife taking a passive role.

This and other research have shown an association between both stereotyped gender roles and depression and marital dissatisfaction after treatment for distressed couples. Description of the subtle and often taken-for-granted ways in which couple transactions are affected by the larger context of gender beliefs and expectations is difficult. One effort, a study of gender and conflict structure in married couples, reported by Heavey, Coyne, and Christensen (1993), suggests a partial explanation. When discussing problem issues identified by the husband, there was no systematic difference in the roles of the "demander" or "withdrawer" taken by women and men. In contrast, when talking about the problem identified by the woman, a striking pattern of the wife's being more demanding and the husband's being more withdrawing appeared. In examining global marital satisfaction over 12 months, the study showed that the wife's demandingness coupled with the husband's withdrawal was associated with significant decreases in the wife's satisfaction with the marriage, whereas the husband's demandingness and the wife's withdrawal predicted longitudinal increases in the wife's satisfaction. As in other re-search, there was support for the finding that the extent to which a couple reverses the roles typical of gender is predictive of both the wife's and husband's reports of improved relationship quality. The reversal of tradi-tional gender roles in communication roles provides an opportunity to avoid the increased polarization and rigidity that characterize troubled marriages. In addition, a wife may perceive her spouse's demandingness as a sign that he is invested in the relationship.

In the description of both strategic models, the role of gender issues is implied in references to elevating the depressed partner's position in the marital hierarchy, as the partner presenting as depressed is most often the wife. The Intersystem Model, however, now includes explicit assessment of beliefs about gender issues and addresses these, along with other contextual issues, directly with the couple if relevant in the given case. It is particularly common to find unexamined gendered conflict (or an avoidance of conflict that can lead to marital distress) in the areas of finances, household management, decision making, and sex.

Careful attention to the language used by the couple in describing their relationship can often provide an opening for looking at gender issues. For example, one husband stated with high emotional intensity, "She *has* to understand how hard I work and help." The therapist ques-tioned the couple about the meaning and implications of the "has to." The couple's conversation began to focus on communicating their concerns to each other and negotiating as individual choices the support and care they gave each other.

Asking questions of the couple about the unwritten rules underlying their beliefs about gender can also often open these areas for exploration by the couple. "When was it decided it was your job to make decisions about the budget?" "Did your parents make the same choices about who was to take the initiative in their sexual relationship?" "How would things have been different if you had decided that the children needed their father to be home more?"

At times, therapists may also have to ask themselves questions about the language they use and their own assumptions. A useful question at many points in marital therapy is, "How would I be reacting if this statement were being made or this action were being taken by the partner of the opposite gender?"

Carey, an attractive woman in her mid-30s, was referred for individual therapy for acute depression by her family doctor. Five years earlier, she had been referred for individual brief therapy for chronic depression, but did not believe she had been helped. During the first session, Carey revealed intense feelings of guilt and depression about a "one-night stand" with a supervisor in another department during a business trip. She agreed to ask her husband, Jim, to join in marital therapy in an attempt to save her marriage. At the next session, Jim, who appeared to be depressed also, and Carey described a 15-year marriage characterized by conflict avoidance, engagement primarily on issues of running the household and parenting their two children, and little intimacy, including sexual intimacy. Carey had been a homemaker until she began part-time work two years earlier. The marriage was a good example of the wife demand (in this case, complaint)/husband withdraw pattern studied in Heavey, Layne, and Christensen (1993).

It was apparent that Carey had buried her resentment about the traditional gender roles in the marriage and her overfunctioning in the family. Her work—where she was recognized for her considerable talent and creativity in developing personnel training programs—had provided an opportunity for increased assertiveness and confidence in her abilities.

The marital therapy focused on breaking the couple's pattern of conflict avoidance, increasing open communication, and improving joint problem solving. The 10th session focused on choices Carey and Jim needed to make about both their careers and the responsibilities of home and family. Carey's depression had resolved by this point, and she created a "therapeutic moment" in the session when she stated, "I realize now I was depressed all those years because I was always trying to get him to do what I wanted to do myself." The clarity of the insight and the connection with her own experience represented by the statement freed Carey to own her choices—including the decision to remain in her marriage. In turn, Jim was able to respond with more flexibility in conflicts about finances and household management and was thrilled with some of his choices—particularly his greater closeness to their two children. As marital therapy ended, both reported increased marital satisfaction and a new level of intimacy in their relationship.

ADDITION OF AN INTERGENERATIONAL FOCUS

The third "I" of the Intersystem Model, the intergenerational, is a critical focus in treating depression that is also missing in the other models described. The use of the genogram in exploring intergenerational patterns can help to identify the role of unresolved loss in the family history of couples where one partner's presenting complaint is depression. Anniversary reactions, affairs, divorce and separation, trauma (including physical, sexual, and emotional abuse), and loss through death or abandonment can be important issues for both the partner presenting as depressed and for the undepressed partner (who may cope by overfunctioning and repressing or projecting his or her feelings in response to unresolved loss of trauma).

Each partner has a unique history in the family of origin, a history that has shaped the feelings, beliefs, and actions in areas critical to understanding and treating depression—the closeness/distance dance, family scripts about expression of negative feelings, dependence/autonomy conflicts, and resolution of conflict. Increased awareness of the role of family-of-origin issues can also build empathy and understanding and help reduce the rigid blaming and labeling (whether self- or other-focused) often found in maritally distressed couples where one partner is depressed.

The discussion and resolution of these family-of-origin issues are particularly salient for individuals who come from families in which a strong negative message exists about being depressed, namely, that depression was and is unacceptable. Children from these families learn not to show or express depression and come to internalize the belief that normal sadness is bad. They will continue to "fight" feeling sad or depressed throughout their life, using repression, drugs, and their mates to avoid these feelings. In the end, the depression may be overwhelming. Directly addressing the intergenerational messages in therapy, and creating more viable alternatives to the learned patterns of depression–avoidance, can be tremendously freeing for the individual and the couple.

Enriching the "Marriage" of Marital Therapy and Treatment of Depression: Application of the Model

SPECIFIC THERAPEUTIC ISSUES

The applications and techniques of the Intersystem Model described in Weeks and Treat (1992) and Weeks and Hof (1994) are important with all maritally distressed couples, but some issues are particularly critical in marital therapy when one partner is depressed. There is an essential conflict between the despair and hopelessness of depression and the clinical reality that instilling hope is essential in effective therapy. The following approaches are intended to break through the established patterns of dysfunctional interactions and entrenched negative beliefs that are core issues in depression.

Reframing the depression. Reframing is an essential element of all psychotherapy and is discussed in detail in Weeks and Treat (1992). Use of reframing with a couple where one partner is depressed serves several important functions and is integral to establishing a systemic focus. Examples of positive reframing might be, "Depression is your body's natural way of slowing you down to take a look at yourself," or "Depression can be useful; eventually, if you use it right, you may even learn to enjoy it" (Jessee & L'Abate, 1985, p. 1140).

We commonly talk about depression as a friend bringing bad news. You do not send a friend away. You embrace a friend, accept the bad news, and try to change what is not working. Depression is a form of communication, indicating that something is not working. Depression can also be reframed as psychic pain. It is like physical pain in that it tells us when something is wrong. Therefore, rather than flee from the depression, it should be embraced. The idea of embracing the depression then leads into the symptom prescription.

The reframe should also systemically link the depression to the partner. In most cases, the partner does not see the role s/he plays. For example, the therapist might say, "John, you instinctively understood the fact that Mary was sad over the loss of your children going off to college. She could not grieve this loss, so you are grieving for the two of you." This reframe shows the common pattern of one partner "carrying" the depression for the other.

Such a reframe changes from the negative attributions characteristic of depression to positive ones, and from the individual to the couple—a shift particularly important in therapy with a couple usually demoralized by the lack of hope and ability to recognize possibilities that typify the depressed partner's worldview (Weeks & L'Abate, 1982).

Just as important, reframing shifts the nondepressed partner's view of the symptoms. The critical importance of making this shift early in therapy is buttressed by recent research comparing the attributional and affective responses of spouses to depressed and nondepressed wives. Sacco, Dumont, and Dow (1993) found that depressed wives were rated more negatively and that husbands of depressed wives made more dispositional (rather than situational) attributions, and showed more negative affect in reaction to negative events. Depressed wives were rated more negatively both on depression-neutral and depression-related traits. This generalized negative view of the spouse may continue even with symptom improvement. Without therapeutic intervention to help change the nondepressed partner's negative attributions, he may sabotage improvement in the depression. The authors theorize that such a negative schema about the partner might also be easily reactivated by the appearance of transient symptoms of depression and make it extremely difficult to maintain improved functioning after the depressive episode remits.

Shifting to an interpersonal focus. Like an acting out child in a family or an extramarital affair in a marriage, depression can serve as a triangle in the family to stabilize relationships and avoid the risk of change, including the possibility of separation and divorce. Depression or accompanying conflict can maintain the level of emotional distance between the partners, avoiding either the anxiety or greater conflict that might accompany greater closeness or the abandonment of greater separation.

Reframing, previously described, is an important technique in maintaining a systemic focus. Paradoxical techniques, described later, often serve as confusion techniques that at least temporarily unbalance a rigid belief system about depression as an individual problem and create an opening for a systemic focus. Circular questioning, described by Weeks and Treat (1992), can be useful in early problem assessment. Questions such as, "Who notices you're depressed?" or "Who misses your caretaking the most?" or "Was anyone important to you ever depressed in a similar way?" or "Who is best at keeping you going?" can open the session dialogue to increased recognition of the interactional nature of the depression.

Maintaining balance. It is critical in all marital therapy to maintain balance as described by Weeks and Treat (1992). In marital therapy for depression, however, the couple often presents for treatment after one spouse has been given a diagnosis and pharmacological treatment. This focus on the depressed partner makes it more difficult, but no less important, to maintain balance and an interpersonal focus. Initial statements to the depressed partner such as, "This problem looks like yours now, but when it starts to get better, I guarantee we'll see more on his side" can help rebalance the therapy. Similarly, the nonmedicated partner can be told that s/he will be asked to "medicate" him- or herself with therapy assignments later in the treatment to help "cure" his or her part in the marital problems.

Staying concrete. After the initial step of shifting to a positive and systemic frame, it is important throughout the beginning stages of therapy to stay concrete. A characteristic of depressive cognition is global negative thinking—"I never succeed at anything I try," or "My wife is always mad at me.'' And goals tend to be stated in a similar global way—''I want her to be less depressed,'' or ''I want him to stop being mean to me.''

Breaking down these vague global statements is essential. Concrete language creates openings in the depressive schema, enlivens the couple's conversation, and helps create an image of change, making movement toward behavioral goals more likely. Use of concrete language also encourages increased responsibility for change and makes it more difficult to avoid completing an agreed-upon assignment—whether a paradoxical prescription of the symptom or a communication skills exercise.

Perhaps most important are the benefits of concrete language in pointing to the interpersonal context of the depression. ''When he comes home depressed, what do you say?'' or ''When he finds you in bed, what does he do?'' Similarly, having both partners in the session creates a gold mine for the deconstruction of the dysfunctional negative beliefs that are a core element in depression. In individual cognitive therapy, the therapist can help the client examine alternatives to a fixed belief such as, ''When my husband is angry, it shows he doesn't love me.'' With the husband in the room, alternatives become more immediately accessible—''I had a bad day at work and just finished balancing the checkbook,'' or ''I really get angry when I count on you and feel you don't care enough to talk about the problem with me.''

Using paradox. There are ''hopeless teaching cases'' where entrenched beliefs about one partner's depression reduce anxiety in the individual and are maintained by the family system. These difficult cases have often been referred for a variety of approaches and have left many depressed therapists in their wake. Paradoxical techniques such as prescribing the symptom and predicting relapse may be useful in bringing hope to both the couple and the therapist. The following case, which is described in greater detail in Weeks and L'Abate (1985), is a good illustration of the use of paradoxical techniques in chronic depression.

Mark, a 67-year-old man, sought help for his long-standing depression. Mark was retired and he and his wife had two adult sons. Mark's mother had been hospitalized for depression for several weeks after the death of his father when Mark was 22 years of age. One year later, Mark became severely depressed. He was hospitalized for three weeks and treated as an outpatient for two years. A highly successful salesperson, Mark continued to struggle with depression. He had been in and out of treatment with psychiatrists for at least 30 years, had been hospitalized several times, and had received at least 10 electroconvulsive therapy

(ECT) treatments. Two years before beginning marital treatment, he had been hospitalized for one month, treated with ECT, and given more antidepressants.

When Mark came for treatment, he showed the classic signs of a chronic depressive, including lethargy, reduced interest in food and sex, sleep disturbance, and episodes of uncontrollable crying. Mark said that when he became depressed, he started to worry about everything. What he feared most was becoming so depressed he would require another hospitalization.

Asked what he had done to control his depression, Mark repeated his history and said he was currently taking Elavil as needed. He said a psychiatrist many years ago told him the best way to treat depression was to stay busy, so Mark would force himself to stay busy to fight off the depression. It became clear that he could accept no feelings of sadness or depression in himself, believing that the first sign of sadness marked the start of a depressive episode. Sally, his wife, fed into this belief, claiming she could tell when he was "going down" by just looking at him. She said she would try to be sympathetic and encourage him to rest, but she also felt angry when he was depressed. Sally said she almost never felt depressed and only rarely was sad.

Depression had acquired a special significance for this couple. Neither could deal with depression in themselves or each other. When Mark did feel sad, it produced excessive fear and worry in both. They expected it to get worse before it got better.

The initial treatment goal was helping Mark gain control of his depression. Because of the failure to respond to previous treatment and the entrenched beliefs that maintained the couple's interactions about the depression, a paradoxical approach was chosen. The therapists started by asking Mark whether he wanted to get in charge of his depression or let his depression continue to be in charge of him. Mark was perplexed by this question and its implication that being depressed could be controlled. In short, it implied that he made a decision to be depressed.

Mark's depression was next relabeled a blessing in disguise, as some people could not be depressed and they were the ones to really worry about. He was told that everyone gets depressed from time to time, and this helps us know when things are in need of change. Further, depression is a part of living, so that experiencing it makes one a whole person. He had to learn to show his depression the respect and attention it deserved, rather than attempt to avoid it.

Finally, the therapists explained that he would have to learn how to start his depression before he could learn to stop it. By the end of this monologue, Mark looked less depressed but more confused. The therapists continued by instructing Mark to set aside one full hour each morning in which to give in to his depression completely. He was to think all of his worst thoughts and feel as low as he could. In short, a severe depression was prescribed.

Mark accepted the assignment as it was offered, but Sally was afraid he might enter a deep depression. The therapists reversed her concern by telling her they were more afraid he would not be able to depress himself. Sally's role, therefore, was to make sure that Mark had one full hour each morning in which there were no interruptions. The session was ended promptly after the instructions, with Mark looking back to say he might prove the therapists wrong by having a low week.

Mark and Sally returned to the next session with Mark looking much better. He said he was afraid to try the assignment (he called it his meditation time), but did it because the therapists were the doctors. The first couple of days had been difficult. He had no trouble being depressed during his meditation time. By the end of the week, he reported he could not force himself to be depressed for a whole hour. The most significant change was that he had no low during the whole week. He said the past week had been the best in 30 years. Sally was also impressed with his change in mood.

During the next session, the content of Mark's meditation was explored. The reasonable thoughts that depressed him—such as his mother's senility and poor health—were normalized. These and other concerns later in the therapy were labeled as normally depressing thoughts. He was given the same assignment, except he was to reduce the time to 30 minutes a day.

In the next session, Mark stated that his lows were completely gone and he was optimistic—too optimistic—about being able to control his depression. The 30-minute meditation was reassigned, with the prediction that Mark would have a low during the coming week. When he had the low, he was to pay close attention to the moment he started to come out of it and then extend it for 30 more minutes.

Mark proudly announced in the following session that he had experienced no low as predicted. The therapists acted perplexed and then tried to find a low in the past week's events. Mark and Sally were unwilling to buy any of the therapists' views that he really did have a low. They reported an argument during the week and Sally said she could not remember when Mark had been so assertive with her. She verbalized being pleased with her "new husband."

Given that when a depressed partner improves, the relationship often deteriorates, the next strategy was intended to deal with this possibility. The therapists began to point out some of the risks of Mark's becoming too assertive with Sally, suggesting a return to getting depressed rather than angry as one way to protect the relationship. Both acted insulted at the suggestion, but were asked to think about it. Mark's prescribed depression time was cut to 20 minutes a day.

The next session marked several weeks without a low, and there were signs of both individual and marital changes. Asked whether he was really willing to give up a 30-year habit, Mark said he was. He was cautioned about the potential negative consequences of giving up his depression. Asked what the consequences might be, the couple responded that Mark would receive less attention, sympathy, and affection from Sally. The therapists agreed, but warned that this was just the tip of the iceberg.

The therapists remained unconvinced about Mark's giving up the depression completely and prescribed a relapse. He was instructed to select any eight-hour period during the next week in which to act as depressed as possible. He was instructed not to tell Sally that he was faking but to assure her that it was real. He was further told to pay attention to how he triggered this depression, how he maintained it, how he stopped it, and how Sally reacted to him. Sally was, of course, present and was told she should try to guess when he was going to "pull" his depression. She was to respond to Mark just as she would during any real depression. (Neither liked the assignment, as they had a busy week ahead.)

Mark carried out the fake depression as assigned, but reported that it was difficult to pretend to be depressed, as he preferred to be doing other things. He said that he had learned two things from the assignment. He realized how he could use depression to control Sally and express his anger indirectly. The fake depression also allowed him to avoid doing some things he did not want to do, as well as to gain attention and affection from Sally. Not sure whether the depression were real or fake, Sally responded as usual by pampering Mark and later becoming impatient with him. Mark's feedback was used to question the couple again about the wisdom of giving up the depression. Once again they said the depression must go. The prescription to be depressed 20 minutes a day remained intact.

Mark had been in treatment for some time with only one relapse. After the initial sessions, the basic strategy was to predict relapses. With the Christmas holidays approaching, he was told that people prone to depression usually became depressed during the holidays, and the therapists predicted a danger period from December 15 to January 15. His depression period was reduced to 15 minutes a day, but every Monday during the holidays he was to spend an hour considering, as pessimistically as possible, a series of questions about bad things that could happen. Mark defied the prediction by making it through the period without a low.

Stressful life events such as his mother's health, his father's death when Mark was in his early 20s, and a job loss during treatment were discussed in therapy and his appropriate sadness or concerns were labeled "normal depression." He was congratulated on being ready to experience normal depression in the future.

The initial strategy of scheduling Mark's depression was reduced to five minutes a day, and he reported that on some days it was hard to go the full time. It was observed that Mark and Sally were beginning to argue more openly. The therapists predicted a number of fights, framing them as one of the bad side effects of Mark's recovery from depression. Mark and Sally countered that their arguments were good for them. The last sessions were brief. Both were enjoying their retirement and Mark stated that he wanted to continue his five minutes a day of meditation as a way to prevent problems from occurring or to solve problems in advance.

DEALING WITH GUILT INDUCTION AND PASSIVE-AGGRESSIVE BEHAVIOR

In some couples with a depressed partner, session interactions and response to out-of-session assignments will quickly suggest that the couple is unable to express anger directly. The therapy will become as paralyzed as the couple if these problems are not addressed. The righteousness of guilt induction serves to put the other person in the role of being wrong and allows the partner doing the guilt trip to get away with venting anger without owning it. Guilt-inducing behavior can often be confronted by the therapist's highlighting the intentionality and instrumentality of the behavior. "Did that guilt-inducing statement work for you?" "What were you trying to get him to do and did he do it?" Such questions are often followed by a blank stare, and then at least a brief shift in an established way of relating to the partner.

Similar difficulty with expressing anger directly can lead to passive-aggressive communication and such behaviors as forgetting, procrastinating, and not understanding. It is critical that the therapist confront passive-aggressive communication with statements such as, "I don't believe you're saying what you really mean." Passive-aggressive behaviors must also be framed by the therapist as an intentional choice the partner is making. For example, "You often choose to forget to schedule the communication exercise. I wonder if you or your wife have any theories about why the exercise is so difficult for you."

APPLYING AN INTEGRATIVE MODEL: CASE EXAMPLE

Jim and Carla, a middle-class couple in their early 30s, referred themselves for marital therapy with the presenting problem of serious marital conflict. Four weeks earlier, Carla had sought help from her family physician for sleep disturbance, a 10-pound weight loss, and depressed mood. A diagnosis of major depression, single episode was given and an antidepressant prescribed.

In her late teens, Carla had received short-term outpatient therapy for mixed symptoms of anxiety and depression at her college counseling center. Otherwise neither partner had sought help for his or her problems and there was no family history of mental health treatment. With the antidepressant, Carla reported some improvement in sleep, appetite, and the ability to concentrate at her part-time job in a floral shop. However, both partners described the home front as continuing to be a disaster, with Jim's blaming Carla's depression and Carla's blaming Jim's angry attempts to get her to do as much as she had done before the depression. Separation and divorce had been threatened by each—usually in the context of major conflict—and both felt that their six-year-old son and eight-year-old daughter were affected by the depression and conflict.

The current serious blaming and negativity in the relationship were apparent when each was unable to talk about what had initially attracted them to the other 10 years earlier. In this case, the therapist used two reframes at the close of the second session to help break through the negative view each had of the other. Jim's angry lectures and critical diatribes (which had been observed in both sessions) were reframed as needing to encourage Carla to seek help for her depression, since doing something for herself was so difficult for her. Jim was a middle child in a conflict-avoidant family so his anger was described as a caring behavior that made him extremely uncomfortable—and, therefore, represented a sacrifice made for Carla. In turn, Carla's depression was reframed as creating the opportunity for looking at the marital problems that affected the children both cared about. Being depressed was described as a tough thing for Carla to do, as she had always coped by feeling responsible for "trying just one more thing" to make things better (words used by Carla in the first session).

Both partners responded to the reframes with reduced blaming and, on Carla's part, self-blaming. Particularly dramatic was Carla's tearful, "I wanted to make things better, but I just couldn't do it anymore" near the end of the second session. Jim was obviously touched by her response, and the two agreed to negotiate goals at the next session for improving problem-solving and communication skills.

The next five sessions focused on communication exercises and noncontingent contracting in the areas of scheduling "couple time" and renegotiating household and parenting responsibilities. Soon it was apparent that Jim was following through with assignments and saying the right things in sessions, but often failed to carry out commitments he had made. There were always "good" reasons for the lack of follow-through and Carla responded by shutting down and withdrawing, with occasional angry outbursts.

The therapist decided to confront Jim about the anger he seemed able to express only indirectly. Initially denying any anger, Jim acknowledged during the eighth session that he felt he did not have a right to be angry because Carla was obviously trying to change the things that made him angry when they began treatment. He feared a return to their pretherapy battles if he were frank about what he wanted in the marriage. Exploration of his resentment during their history together suggested the birth of their first child as a turning point in the marriage. Jim had grown up as the middle child in a family where parents were busy with their careers and emotionally unavailable. He described being first attracted to Carla because she was emotionally available, a good listener, and able to express her feelings. He experienced the birth of their older daughter 12 years earlier as a loss, for Carla "suddenly didn't have time for me."

As Jim described his hurt and disappointment in the session, Carla was able to reassure him about her desire to increase the level of intimacy in the marriage and to make time for being together outside of the responsibilities of home and children. Over the next three sessions, the couple reported success, with both following through on the agreements they made, and even providing caring bonuses to each other.

Like many distressed couples where one partner is depressed, both had difficulty expressing their anger and negotiating conflict. Each prepared an anger genogram (Weeks & Treat, 1992) and shared their family-of-origin messages about avoiding conflict because "disagreement means rejection." With the insights gained and shared with each other, Jim and Carla worked successfully on structured conflict-resolution exercises that helped them assertively state and then negotiate differences without either experiencing the simmering resentment that had characterized their relationship.

Increasing intimacy in their sexual relationship, however, seemed to be the one area in which they continued to experience serious difficulty. Both partners described the problem as the one area where Carla was still "depressed." She described little interest in sex, frequent shutting down, and "going along" because she knew Jim "needed it." Both wondered whether medication would help, but agreed to an assessment of their sexual history and goals. During this phase of treatment, Carla revealed for the first time a history of sexual abuse without intercourse when she was in the first grade. A neighbor whose son was her older brother's best friend had sexually molested her over a six-month period before her family moved from the development where both families lived. The secret had been shared only with her father when she was in her early teens. Carla's father expressed anger at the neighbor, but what she shared was never again discussed in the family. With the therapist's support, Carla was able to discuss her experience with her husband. Jim not only was angry at the neighbor, but was willing to listen to Carla's ambivalent feelings about the experience and to understand its impact on her feelings about herself and her sexual responses. Over the next three sessions, both partners expanded the anger genogram prepared earlier as the framework for a sexual genogram (Hof & Berman, 1986). Preparing the sexual genogram helped balance the therapy, which had started to focus on Carla's abuse history. Both partners were able to see the negativity about sexual expression and enjoyment in both of their families of origin. Jim was able to see that in many ways Carla's lack of sexual response protected him from fears about sexual desirability and performance.

With the progress that had been made in other areas, the couple was able to use the structured exercises in *The Sexual Healing Journey* (Maltz, 1991) between sessions to change the long-standing problems in their sexual relationship—problems that both failed to report until well into their therapy. Therapy sessions were spaced at two-week intervals for the remainder of the seven-month treatment. At the final session, Jim and Carla said that their presenting problem had been a depressed marriage rather than Carla's depression. They identified indicators that would signal the need for follow-up visits if the depressed marriage came back, but reported satisfaction with their current relationship and family functioning.

CONCLUSION

With the three "I's," the Intersystem Model is clearly both more comprehensive and more flexible as a framework for marital therapy for depression, as illustrated by the marital therapy with Jim and Carla. With the scope of potential thematic content and the variety of clinical strategies available under the model's umbrella, those comfortable with more traditional, less integrative models might question whether depth and clarity are sacrificed for breadth. However, it is the case formulation approach, an integral component of the treatment process in this model, that permits individualized marital treatment for depression within the structure of a unified theoretical and clinical framework. Use of the assessment and treatment plan categories found on the Case Formulation Form provided in Weeks and Treat (1992) and Weeks and Hof (1994) allows the therapy to be structured and focused, yet individually tailored to the couple being treated. Paradoxically, therefore, the most comprehensive model for uniting marital therapy and treatment of depression may also be the most focused in its application to the particular couple looking for help.

REFERENCES

Biglan, A., Hops, H., & Sherman, L. (1988). Coercive family processes and maternal depression. In R. J. McMahon & R. Peter (Eds.), *Marriages and families: Behavioral treatments and processes* (pp. 72–103). New York: Brunner/Mazel.

Brown, G. W., Bifulco, A., Harris, T., & Bridge, L. (1986). Life stress, chronic subclinical symptoms and vulnerability to clinical depression. *Journal of Affective Disorders, 11*, 1– 19.

Brown, G. W., & Harris, T. (1978). *Social origins of depression: A study of psychiatric disorders in women.* New York: Free Press.

Cleary, P. D., & Kessler, R. C. (1982). The estimation and interpretation of modifier effects. *Journal of Health and Social Behavior, 23*, 159–168.

Coyne, J. C. (1986). Strategic marital therapy for depression. In N. S. Jacobson & A. S. Gurman (Eds.), *Clinical handbook of marital therapy* (pp. 495–511). New York: Guilford.

Coyne, J. C., Burchill, S. A. L., & Stiles, W. B. (1991). An interactional perspective on depression. In C. R. Snyder & R. Forsyth (Eds.), *Handbook of social and clinical psychology* (pp. 327–349). New York: Pergamon.

Coyne, J. C., & DeLongis, A. (1986). Going beyond social support: The role of social relationships in adaptation. *Journal of Consulting and Clinical Psychology, 54*, 454–460.

Coyne, J. C., Kessler, R. C., Tal, M., Turnbull, J., Wortman, C., & Greden, J. (1987). Living with a depressed person: Burden and psychological distress. *Journal of Consulting and Clinical Psychology, 55*, 347–352.

Feldman, L. (1976). Depression and marital interaction. *Family Process, 15*, 389–395.

Heavey, C. L., Layne, L., & Christensen, A. (1993). Gender and conflict structure in marital interaction: A replication and extension. *Journal of Consulting and Clinical Psychology, 61*, 16–27.

Hof, L., & Berman, E. (1986). The sexual genogram. *Journal of Marital and Family Therapy, 12*, 39–47.

Hooley, J. M., Orley, J., & Teasdale, J. D. (1986). Levels of expressed emotion and relapse in depressed patients. *British Journal of Psychiatry, 148*, 642–647.

Hooley, J. M., & Teasdale, J. D. (1989). Predictors of relapse in unipolar depressives: Expressed emotion, marital distress, and perceived criticism. *Journal of Abnormal Psychology, 98*, 229–235.

Jacobson, N. S. (1984). Marital therapy and the cognitive-behavioral treatment of depression. *Behavior Therapist, 7*, 143–147.

Jacobson, N. S., Dobson, K., Fruzzetti, A., Schmaling, K. B., & Salusky, S. (1991). Marital therapy as a treatment for depression. *Journal of Consulting and Clinical Psychology, 59*, 547–557.

Jacobson, N. S., Fruzzetti, A. E., Dobson, K., Whisman, M., & Hops, H. (1993). Couple therapy as a treatment for depression: II. The effects of relationship quality and therapy on depressive relapse. *Journal of Consulting and Clinical Psychology, 61*, 516–519.

Jacobson, N. S., Holtzworth-Monroe, A., & Schmaling, K. B. (1989). Marital therapy and spouse involvement in the treatment of depression, agoraphobia, and alcoholism. *Journal of Consulting and Clinical Psychology, 57*, 5–10.

Jessee, E. H., & L'Abate, L. (1985). Paradoxical treatment of depression in married couples. In L. L'Abate (Ed.), *The handbook of family psychology and therapy* (pp. 1128–1151). Homewood, IL: Dorsey Press.

Maltz, W. (1991). *The sexual healing journey*. New York: HarperCollins.

Merikangas, K. R., & Spiker, D. G. (1982). Assortative mating among inpatients with primary affective disorder. *Psychological Medicine, 12*, 753–764.

Moltz, D. (1993). Bipolar disorder and the family: An integrative model. *Family Process, 32*, 409–424.

O'Leary, K. D., & Beach, S. R. H. (1990). Marital therapy: A viable treatment for depression and marital discord. *American Journal of Psychiatry, 147*, 183–186.

Paykel, E. S., Myers, J. K., Dienelt, M. N., Klerman, G. L., Lindenthal, J. A., & Pepper, M. P. (1969). Life events and depression: A controlled study. *Archives of General Psychiatry, 21*, 753–760.

Quinton, D., Rutter, M., & Liddle, C. (1984). Institutional rearing, parenting difficulties and marital support. *Psychological Medicine, 14*, 107–124.

Rounsaville, B. J., Prusoff, B. A., & Weissman, M. M. (1980). The course of marital disputes in depressed women: A 48-month follow-up study. *Comprehensive Psychiatry, 21*, 111–118.

Rounsaville, B. J., Weissman, M. M., Prusoff, B. A., & Herceg-Baron, R. L. (1979). Marital disputes and treatment outcome in depressed women. *Comprehensive Psychiatry, 20*, 483–490.

Rubenstein, D., & Timmins, J. F. (1978). Depressive dyadic and triadic relationships. *Journal of Marriage and Family Counseling, 4*, 13–23.

Sacco, W. P., Dumont, C. P., & Dow, M. G. (1993). Attributional, perceptual, and affective responses to depressed and nondepressed marital partners. *Journal of Consulting and Clinical Psychology, 61*, 1076–1082.

Vaughn, C. E., & Leff, J. P. (1976). The influence of family and social factors on the course of psychiatric illness. *British Journal of Psychiatry, 129*, 125–137.

Weeks, G. R. (Ed.). (1989). *Treating couples: The Intersystem Model of the Marriage Council of Philadelphia*. New York: Brunner/Mazel.

Weeks, G. R., & Hof, L. (Eds.). (1994). *The marital-relationship therapy casebook: Theory and application of the Intersystem Model*. New York: Brunner/Mazel.

Weeks, G. R., & L'Abate, L. (1982). *Paradoxical psychotherapy: Theory and practice with individuals, couples, and families*. New York: Brunner/ Mazel.

Weeks, G. R., & Treat, S. (1992). *Couples in treatment: Techniques and approaches for effective practice*. New York: Brunner/Mazel.

Weissman, M. M. (1987). Advances in psychoepidemiology: Rates and risks for depression. *American Journal of Public Health, 77*, 451.

Whisman, M. A., & Jacobson, N. S. (1989). Depression, marital satisfaction, and marital and personality measures of sex roles. *Journal of Marital and Family Therapy, 15*, 177–186.

6

ADDICTIONS IN MARITAL/ RELATIONSHIP THERAPY

Martha Turner, M.D.

The presence of addictions will inhibit or prohibit the development and experience of healthy, well-functioning relationships. Whether the addiction be to alcohol, drugs, food, sex, spending, debting, gambling, television, or computers, there will be consequences: isolation, shame, secrets, deception, and medical problems. If untreated, the disease of addiction will progress and may even lead to insanity or death. At the least, the relationship between partners will deteriorate to a state in which cold war, overt fighting, gross miscommunication, and diminished intimacy become commonplace.

Simply put, *addictions destroy individuals and relationships*. The destruction is not about weakness, immorality, or malintent, even though observation of behavior might lead one to believe it so; rather, it is about maladaptive coping, low psychic pain tolerance, shame, spiritual bankruptcy, and very negative core beliefs about one's self. The person in an active addiction may swing wildly from the deep pain of self-loathing that usually accompanies it, to a euphoric state, or the perceived normal state that the chosen coping mechanism predictably provides. The addict believes that without this reliable coping tool (substance or experience) s/he will surely die. When survival is at stake, there is little interest in processing, intimacy, or thriving. It is important to understand this lifeline thinking, without judgment, in order to create a safe place for therapy to begin.

Addictions are not limited to the one who indulges. The entire family, like a mobile hanging from the ceiling, is affected. Because of the embarrassment around the behavior, partners and children tend to want to deceive the world so that the family can appear normal. The resulting collusion is powerful, insidious, exclusive, and abusive. Indeed, if couples therapy is stalled, there may be an addiction lurking somewhere. It is grandiose for a therapist to believe s/he can work alone with a couple while an addiction is active. Treatment will almost certainly fail and the therapist will feel inadequate. However, if the addiction is addressed openly, and recovery is made a condition of ongoing treatment, many wonderful things can happen for the individual, the couple, and the family.

FACTS ABOUT ADDICTIONS

The prevalence of addictions will never be calculated accurately because of the secrecy and shame around this disease. It has been estimated that 10–12 percent of the adult population in America is alcoholic. People coming from alcoholic families who never drink are not counted, but they may transmit the disease to their children. There is a genetic component in some cases, as well as the passing on of impaired thinking and affective expression around such things as abuse of substances, sexuality, coping mechanisms, power, and conflict that contributes to the development of addictions. Generally speaking, most addictions are disorders of one of the major feelings: fear, anger, loneliness, depression, happiness, sensuousness/sex, and hunger. Logic around these feelings comes not from the neocortex of the brain but from the more primitive parts of the brain that have to do with survival, safety, and a sense of well-being.

The estimation of sexual addiction in the adult population in America is 6–10 percent, but many think it may be higher. The double life associated with sexual addiction is frequently less obvious than that associated with drug or alcohol abuse. It may be that some people who abstain from sex (known as sexual anorexics) come from families where there has been sexual abuse or addiction. As with some teetotalers, those who abstain or who have severe inhibited sexual desire may transmit a vulnerability to sex addiction. The more we learn about addictions, the earlier the diagnoses can be made, with the result being an increase in percentages greater than we previously thought.

There are huge amounts of abuse in childhood reported from the sexually addicted population. Carnes (1991), in a survey of over 1,000 sex addicts, found that 97 percent were emotionally abused, 81 percent were sexually abused, and 72 percent were physically abused. As a culture, we are just beginning to emerge from denial about child abuse.

There is also much cross-addiction. In the same survey, Carnes (1991) found that 42 percent of sex addicts were also chemically dependent. Of that same group, 38 percent had eating disorders, 28 percent were compulsive workers, 26 percent were compulsive spenders, and 5 percent were compulsive gamblers. Less than 17 percent reported an isolated sexual addiction.

It is also believed that 60 percent of incest occurs in alcoholic homes and that up to 75 percent of chronic relapsers are survivors of childhood trauma. Among the eating disorders, 50 percent of anorexics have addictions in their families of origin and 80 percent of bulimics are chemically dependent. It may be that the numbers of addictions correlate with the amount of abuse any one person has experienced. This strong association between abuse and addictions has contributed to the current pioneer work with trauma survivors and the disorder known as complex posttraumatic stress disorder (PTSD).

We now know that trauma can alter neurochemistry severely and that some addicts can alter their own brain chemistry without the use of external substances (Milkman & Sunderwirth, 1987). Addicted gamblers are among those who can alter their own brain chemistry and 50 percent of them have another addiction. There may well be a genetic component. Hunter (SECAD, 1993) stated that if 100 children are given unlimited time to play Nintendo, they will all develop callouses on their thumbs. At the end of the week, 95 percent of them will walk away, but 5 percent will not be able to. Opportunities for gambling are on the increase— more casinos, more video poker machines, more Lotto games. And out of those new opportunities come an increasing number of addicted or compulsive gamblers, with the estimate being that 50 percent of those new gamblers are women. Video poker is available, socially acceptable, and gets immediate results—three factors known to enhance addictions. Immediate rewards are far more powerful in maintaining an addiction than threats of delayed punishments. In altering their neurotransmitters, gamblers experience delusions of grandeur, an intense belief in their abilities to win, and the euphoria of escape. All are tremendously powerful and potentially destructive.

STYLES OF ADDICTIONS

Milkman and Sunderwirth (1987) associated certain neurotransmitters with various addictions and mental disorders, forming distinct groupings of people (see Figure 6.1). One such group is the arousal seekers. These people dislike boredom and are drawn to adrenalin rushes to escape reality. In this group are the gamblers, as well as the cocaine, amphetamine, sex, work, shoplifting, and crisis addicts. They need to feel powerful in a seemingly hostile world. The manic phase of bipolar illness is also in this category. The result of their excesses can be financial, nutritional, and emotional collapse.

Opposite the stimulus addicts (see Figure 6.1) are those who avoid extra stimulation because they are already in a hyperaroused or anxious state and feel the need to retreat from it. They are attracted to sedating or calming substances or experiences, which include food, alcohol, sleep or pain medications, opiates, shopping, television, computers, and some sexual experiences. They are called the satiation addicts, because the wish is for the relaxed, secure feeling that comes, for example, after a good meal or sexual experience in a healthy committed relationship. Unfortunately, excessive use can put the individual in a near vegetative state that is life-threatening.

The arousal and satiety states seem to be located in the limbic system of the brain, having to do with survival, self-preservation, and well-being, whereas the neocortex deals with fantasy and reality. The neurotransmitters involved in fantasy states are serotonin, norepinephrine, and dopamine (see Figure 6.1). Of interest is the fact that phenylethylamine and indole molecules are the precursors not only to these neurotransmitters, but also to many of the hallucinogens bought on the street. Excessive amounts of these chemicals can lead to drug-induced psychosis or the mental disorder of a brief reactive psychosis or of schizophrenia. The result puts the sufferer out of touch with reality, possibly requiring hospitalization.

Opposite those who seek the fantasy states (see Figure 6.1) are those who like the focused attention of reality. Activities such as rock climbing, skydiving, and flying airplanes would fall into this category. These skills

Figure 6.1   Neurotransmitters, Addictions, and Mental Illness

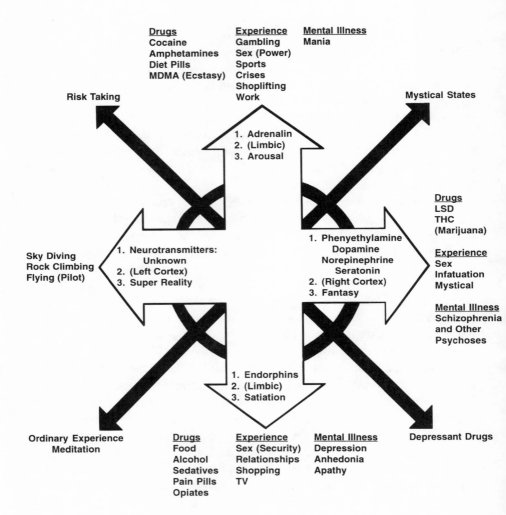

Adapted with the permission of Lexington Books, an imprint of Macmillan Publishing Company, from *Craving for Ecstacy: The Consciousness & Chemistry of Escape* by Harvey B. Milkman and Stanley Sunderwirth. Copyright © 1987 by Lexington Books.

require logical appraisal of one's options and could not tolerate the altered state of awareness that accompany most addictions. One could not successfully engage in this type of activity if one were distracted by such things as the need to feel overly important, powerful, effective, or at one with the cosmos as is prevalent in the fantasy addictions.

CONSEQUENCES OF ADDICTIONS

Much to the disappointment of all people with addictions, there is no steady state of euphoria. Nature always seeks a balance. The extreme in one direction will be followed by an extreme in the other, with the net result (if these extremes occur) of chaos, despair, and desperation. Suicidal feelings and attempts are not uncommon. Alcohol has a diffuse effect on the brain, not only being destructive to tissue but also in dissolving self-esteem and spirituality. There often emerges a compensatory self-centeredness and grandiosity to cover up the damaging effects.

Cocaine depletes dopamine with chronic use by the addict who, paradoxically, wants more and more of the excitement, euphoria, and increased sense of esteem and sexuality that the augmented dopamine provided initially. Thus, increased amounts of the substance are required to give the desired effect. Cocaine abuse can lead to sexual frenzies with indiscriminate behaviors resulting in an increase in sexually transmitted diseases and AIDS.

Stimulant drugs and sex often are combined with disastrous consequences. Corley (SECAD, 1993) states that sex addicts are paying $2 million an hour in 900 numbers for phone sex. Sexually transmitted diseases are escalating as well. Genital herpes, which was relatively rare in the early 1980s, developed into 20 million cases within five years. If 10 percent of adults are sex addicts, AIDS will explode by the end of the century, a potential reality that we cannot ignore. Katner (SECAD, 1993) reports that 45 percent of his new HIV/AIDS cases are women. He also notes that 80 percent of male travelers stopping for sex at the rest stops on the interstate highway system had unprotected sex. Of these, 85 percent were bisexual and 98 percent of their female partners were unaware of these sexual activities. He estimated that there were 1,000 homosexual encounters per month per rest stop, and stated his belief that bigotry and ignorance aid the spread of sexually transmitted diseases.

Carnes (1991) reports the following consequences of sex addictions: near death experiences and AIDS are not uncommon; 40 percent of addicts were left by their spouses; families were impacted profoundly in 70 percent; 36 percent reported grief over abortions, 42 percent had unwanted pregnancies; 57 percent experienced financial crises; 27 percent lost career choices, productivity, or were demoted; 38 percent experienced physical injury as a result of their addiction; 63 percent put themselves at risk for sexually transmitted diseases; and, 58 percent risked arrest through their behavior. Obviously, it is urgent to diagnose and treat addictions wherever possible.

PARTNERS OF ADDICTS

People rarely find each other and marry by accident. Those who team up with people with addictions usually have similar underlying dynamics. Whether one believes in metaphysics, that is, that people come together to complete their development or just think that "birds of a feather flock together," the result is a troubled relationship when an addiction is involved. One can grow personally or one can repeat trauma from the past. In other words, partners of addicts, or codependents, may have had an addicted, chronically ill or otherwise emotionally unavailable parent. Hence, teaming up with another unavailable person is familiar, a repetition compulsion, in which each may desire to get it right this time around, but since the old patterns and skills are so pervasive, the same mistakes are repeated in the new relationship. In other words, both partners may want an open and honest relationship, but may fear that it will become abusive or evolve into something that they cannot handle, thereby leading them to tolerate the distance and participate in the approach/avoidance or rejection/intrusion dance that intimacy disorders create. These relationships are very troubled and incredibly powerful in their dysfunctionality.

Codependents have histories of abuse that parallel addicts. In a study of 289 sex addicts and 99 partners of sex addicts, Carnes (1991) found comparable numbers of characteristics (see Table 6.1).

It needs to be mentioned that some kinds of "abuse" can be unintentional, such as that which is experienced after the death of a parent, an accident, or neglect based in ignorance, that has been badly or ineffectively managed in the family. A child might become overwhelmed, have no help to process what has happened, have little or no source of nurturing, and therefore, be left to her or his own devices to make sense of the experience. In such a situation, whatever the child discovers that works to reduce pain and helplessness is incorporated and becomes a potentially

Table 6.1
Characteristics Reported by Addicts and Coaddicts

	% Addicts	% Coaddicts
Family History		
Disengaged	88	75
Other addicts in family	87	98
Rigid	77	77
Rigid/disengaged	68	63
Abuse History		
Emotional abuse	97	91
Physical abuse	72	71
Sexual abuse	81	81
Emotional History		
Acted against own values	59	59
Emotional exhaustion	79	86
Emotional instability	76	83
Hopelessness and despair	87	87
Living double life	85	63
Loss of life goals	68	61
Loss of self-esteem	91	86
Self-abuse (e.g., cutting or burning)	11	11
Strong fears regarding future	78	80
Strong feelings of loneliness	90	87
Suicide attempts	17	8
Suicidal thoughts/feelings	69	54
Physical Problems		
Extreme weight loss or gain	25	38
Physical exhaustion	58	63
Physical problems (e.g., ulcers, high blood pressure)	25	29
Sleep disturbances	62	70
Consequences		
Financial problems	55	58
Loss of career choice	25	20
Loss of important friends	49	53
Loss of interest in hobbies/activities	65	61
Loss of work productivity	75	54

Table from *Don't call it love: Recovery from sexual addiction* by Patrick J. Carnes, Ph.D. Copyright © 1991 by Patrick J. Carnes, Ph.D. Used by permission of Bantam Books, a division of Bantam Doubleday Dell Publishing Group, Inc.

significant coping mechanism. The normal psychosexual development of the child may have been derailed, and without appropriate help s/he may be "destined" to end up with a chronic illness of codependence, addiction, or other dysfunction.

Mellody (SECAD, 1993), a well-known authority on codependence, describes five characteristics of people coming from a family that was less than nurturing: (1) There is a lack of appropriate self-esteem, making them "other-esteem" oriented. Because of the inconsistencies involved in depending on others to decide one's worth, there are wild swings from grandiosity to worthlessness. (2) Codependents have trouble setting boundaries. They either have no boundaries at all or walls that keep everything out. (3) They have a distorted sense of reality and therefore do not function well as adults. (4) They do not know how to take care of themselves and do so in extremes, mostly neglecting their needs. (5) They do not know how to be moderate. They either "shut down" or are too "uptight." They do not know how to stay in the center and handle their vulnerabilities appropriately. They may even develop addictions of their own to moderate the extremes.

Generally speaking, we can say the following about addicts and codependents: (1) addicts indulge themselves whereas codependents self-sacrifice, (2) they often switch back and forth between indulgence and self-sacrifice, and (3) the addicted/codependent couple is a system that has not yet undergone separation and individuation.

ASSESSMENT

A thorough assessment by the clinician working with the couple is essential to identify the issues and dynamics at work. The assessment framework and process of the Intersystem Model (Weeks, 1989; Weeks & Hof, 1994) in working with couples is extremely thorough and helpful. The clinician looks for individual, interactional, and intergenerational factors contributing to the current symptoms. A genogram of three generations can be very helpful in flushing out addictions. Some of the obvious questions will be about drinking, gambling, eating, overt sexual behavior, financial situations, and diseases. The more subtle questions that may help to reveal secret addictions are marital status (many marriages, never married), unexplained job losses (sexual harassment, stealing, poor attendance secondary to addictions, or poor performance due to preoccupation), or unusual behaviors that stand out in the history. Other clues may be found in exploring chronic illnesses (use of pain pills or sleeping pills, a shift in intimate dyads), the presence of pornography, and people disappearing and not accounting for their time. The clinician should always ask about discipline, abuse, attitudes about sex, enemas, privacy, nudity, dating, children being used as surrogate spouses, sleeping arrangements, financial crises, operations and illnesses in the respective families of origin. The impact of abuse on children will often extend into adulthood. Table 6.2 contains a list of signs and symptoms that are associated with childhood abuse, compiled by the author in over 20 years of working with individuals and couples experiencing addictions and codependence. More recently, Marks (SECAD, 1993), one of the pioneers who is studying complex posttraumatic stress disorder, described a triad of chemical dependency, binge eating, and childhood sexual abuse.

TREATMENT: PRELIMINARY WORK

When the diseases of addiction and codependence are active they must be addressed first. If people are not able to be present because of externally (taking drugs, alcohol) or internally (obsession or fantasy) altered neurotransmitters, they are also not available to work on other issues in therapy. Addicts may be in withdrawal, which is an acutely uncomfortable state characterized by physical discomfort, restlessness, fatigue, anxiety, fear of discovery, anger due to shame and deprivation, and preoccupation with how to get the next fix. Defenses such as denial, projection, rationalization, and intellectualization are prevalent. Codependent partners can have many, if not most, of these same symptoms. Withdrawal from focusing on their addicted partner's behavior can feel like dying from abandonment. They may have intense anxiety and have trouble sleeping and eating. They may take some form of medicating substance, prescribed or not, to cope, and their concentration will often be poor.

All of these factors will get in the way of any open and honest communication. Therefore, as soon as addictions are discovered, the therapist must discuss them openly, with concrete plans regarding how to deal with them. The most life-threatening behaviors must be treated first. For example, chemically dependent people may need to be detoxified or to go through a rehabilitation program to help them understand what they are doing to themselves and take responsibility for it. Sex addicts,

Table 6.2

Constellation of Signs and Symptoms Arising in Adulthood as a Result of Childhood Abuse

Sexual	*Physical*	*Psychological or Emotional*
Compulsive sexual behavior	Weight gain/ compulsive overeating	Low self-esteem
Sexual anorexia	Headaches	Shame and guilt
Paraphilias	Increased blood pressure	Secrets and illusions
Sexual shame	Tachycardia	Depression/isolation
Confusion about sexual identity and norms	Accidents	Suicidal ideation
Sexual preoccupations	Self-mutilation/abuse	Anxiety
Sexual dysfunction	Feel disconnected from body	Abandonment issues
	Chronic illness	Confusion
Spiritual	Endocrine disorders	Self-doubt
Conflict with values	Genitourinary diseases:	Feels inadequate
Feels "less than" others	UTI/frequency	Fear of anger (of self and others)
Not empowered	Interstitial cystitis	Passive/resigned
Spiritually bankrupt	Urethral strictures	Addictions to numb feelings
Unable to relate to God as a loving, caring being	Endometriosis	Dissociation
	Polycystic ovaries	Splits good and bad self
	Hysterectomy	Power needs and deficiencies
Relationships	Elimination problems	Victim mentality or entitlement
Power differential	Hyper-/hyporeactive immune system	Fear of authority figures
Desperate for approval		PTSD:
Vulnerability		Fear of changes (surprises)
No rights or entitled		Not safe
Poor boundaries		Hypervigilant
Avoids/seeks conflicts		Poor quality sleep
Clingy/distancing		Nightmares
Passive/aggressive		Fear of going to sleep
		Panic episodes

(Continued)

Sexual	*Psychological or Emotional*
Exploits or perpetrates others	Spontaneous regressions
Reenacts trauma	Easily overwhelmed
Lack of trust	Unrealistic fears
Overly responsible/irresponsible	Difficulty making decisions
Controlling/chaotic	Extremes in feelings (mood swings)
Sexualizing	
Unable to accept love	Poor memory
Fear of intimacy	Constricted life
Trauma bonded	Intrusive thoughts

especially those using prostitutes, sadomasochistic behaviors, unprotected sex, or other behaviors dangerous to themselves or others, who cannot stop acting out, must go to a treatment facility where this disease is specifically treated. All too often, polyaddicted people have gone to drug and alcohol programs and been told that their sexual behavior will return to normal when they stop drinking or abusing drugs. To their dismay, their sexual addiction escalates and they end up relapsing in their chemical addiction.

The therapist needs to understand and appreciate the insidious, cunning, and baffling nature of addictions. Even if the couple is not forthcoming in admitting addictions, the therapist can glean from the history and genograms a high index of suspicion and begin to confront denial. There may be an unspoken collusion to say nothing about addictive behavior, but it always comes out somewhere. Perhaps a child will be sick or in trouble, acting out the problems of the family. It may be helpful to see the child to get information about what is going on at home. There may be arrests for drunken driving, picking up prostitutes, huge telephone bills from 900 number calls, or credit cards run up to the maximum. Looking for evidence of shame is often a clue to an underlying addiction. If there is a family history of addiction, the therapist can have the couple read books, go to workshops as adult children of addicts, and teach them about the transmission of impaired thinking that is passed down to the next generation. Often, worry about the well-being of their children will help to weaken denial.

When one member of the couple is in denial and the other is not, the therapist may need to do an intervention (Johnson, 1980), which is a special meeting of key people in the addict's life, for the purpose of confronting the addict's denial and facilitating treatment. The one partner who is available can provide information regarding consequences, effects on the family, and the key people in the addict's life. These key people usually are children, employers, close coworkers, close extended family members, and friends. These individuals need to be instructed to itemize very specifically, without attacking, the ways in which the addict's behavior has affected them. For example, they might list broken promises, spoiled activities, abandonments, or inappropriate behavior that was embarrassing to them. Here, the children can have a powerful effect in breaking down denial. It helps to have a reservation secured for treatment in an inpatient facility before the intervention. If that is not possible, the minimum requirement is a definite treatment plan for the addict to follow.

If treatment is refused, there must be consequences that the people participating in the intervention are willing to stand by. For example, at work, the employer may guarantee a demotion or firing from the job unless there is treatment. The spouse may choose to not participate in certain activities, or even to leave the marriage, if treatment is not commenced and continued. The therapist must insist that couples counseling is impossible so long as there is an active addiction. The stance must be firm and unwavering. If the addict still refuses treatment, the therapist may choose to continue working with the partner in the hope that the addict will eventually surrender. If not, the partner will surely need help in detaching and going on with life.

There are a few good programs that have a polyaddiction approach and incorporate family work to help those who are codependent get into treatment. The Meadows in Wickenberg, Arizona, and Sierra-Tucson in Tucson, Arizona, are two prime examples. Del Amo Hospital in Torrence, California is excellent for sexual addiction and has a strong family therapy component. Other addictions are addressed there as well. Finally, for those with disabling PTSD from childhood sexual abuse, there is The Sanctuary, a specialized unit at Northwestern Institute in Fort Washington, Pennsylvania, or River Oaks in New Orleans, Louisiana.

Sometimes one spouse will follow the other into treatment. At times, the codependent partner is so distraught and feeling so unsafe that s/he needs to go first. For example, the betrayal felt by the partner when sex addiction becomes known is very intense and personal. Both partners are in severe shame and pain, sometimes requiring an immediate action, for either party, by the therapist.

Both addicts and partners can benefit enormously from participation in a 12-step program. Each needs his or her own meetings and support systems. Such programs provide a safe place to unload shame, grief, remorse, and anger without judgment or advice coming back at them. They can find unconditional acceptance so that healing can begin. For many, it is the first place they experience a sense of belonging and understanding. A program of attraction rather than coercion, the 12-step meetings draw people out of isolation and into the truth. By sharing secrets, shame is reduced and hope comes into their lives. They learn how to rejoin the human race by hearing what has worked for others. The 12 steps teach them how to trust again, take responsibility for their behavior, work on negative character traits, make amends to those they have harmed (when appropriate), and help others. The program helps them to reduce their egocentricity and return to, or develop, a value system. One cannot experience serenity while operating outside of values that are personally important. Similarly, people cannot work on relationships unless they know who they are, what they want, and have some sense of their partner. These features are absent or woefully lacking when an addiction is raging.

The addict's partner is usually just as impaired, in his or her own style, but hides it better by being the hero or heroine, feeling self-righteous, and being super responsible. Society helps these partners look like the good guys while the addicts look like the bad guys. The truth of the matter is that the partners may be more difficult to treat, insisting that the addict alone must be changed. Partners do this dance because they have forgotten who they are in tending to the needs of the addict. They are afraid of emptiness, abandonment, and loss of social status should they have to make a decision to leave or change. They may even prefer, on some level, that their addicted partners keep relapsing to stay in control and to get support for their own heroic efforts to cope. They thrive on crisis. Yet, security is their balm.

Couples will want to polarize into right and wrong, good and bad behavior, which is an indication of their developmental arrest. The therapist needs to gently and consistently help them move toward parity. The addict will find some relief in the attempt to lessen the policing and shaming often demonstrated by the partner. On the other hand, the partner often will not like having to look inward and may become belligerent or wish to leave treatment. However, if progress is to be made, both have to own their own needs, deficits, and agendas that have contributed to their troubled relationship.

Trauma Bonds

Although not exclusively found among couples where there are addictions, trauma bonds are prevalent in this group and are very powerful. A trauma bond is an adult manifestation of a dilemma experienced in childhood in which a major caretaker was also an abuser. The result is a fusion of love and abuse in the person's life, a fusion that is maintained into adulthood and becomes the primary mode of operating in an intimate relationship.

In a conference entitled "Trauma Bonds," Carnes (1993), a pioneer in the field of sex addiction, described some of the characteristics that help maintain the strength of a trauma bond. One is that the cycles of abuse and pseudoforgiveness are repeated in such a manner that they become rewarding. In other words, the intensity that accompanies the abuse serves to distract the victim from the pain being felt. Here, intensity is often confused with intimacy. The relief of forgiveness provides endorphins and a sense of well-being again. However, what is missing is honesty, the processing of problems, mutuality, care, and vulnerability. Without these capabilities, nothing changes and the cycles are repeated.

Another phenomenon is the feeling of uniqueness, especially on the part of the nonaddicted partner. The partner feels that s/he is the only one who can understand and help the addict, who, by the way, generally accepts the help willingly. This uniqueness flourishes in secrecy and is contributed to by both. The partner is often angry when the silence regarding the collusion is broken and the truth becomes known. There may be other affairs, other sources of money or debt, and other consequences revealed at the time the silence is broken. While the addict needs to share all of his or her shame and details somewhere, in order to heal, too many specifics may result in added injury to the partner, or even contribute to a heightened state of arousal. Especially with sex addiction, the graphic details ought to be saved for a sponsor or other person in the 12-step program who can handle them without being reactively triggered. The partner will feel only more deeply betrayed and have her or his own obsession fueled to bring the addict down in shame. Partners seem never to forget the details, and they continue to use them to beef up their policing endeavors, which keeps them in *their* own disease.

When the abuse cycles endure over time, the couple loses sight of their respective pathologies. This is another way the trauma bond is fortified. As the abusiveness progresses, there is increasing fear, which only enhances this negative type of bonding. The couple may become desperate for the tiny islands of forgiveness and security, and may provoke abuse just to get to the other side. When there has been abuse in early childhood, such that the fear reactions have affected the organic development of the brain, these survivors are more susceptible to trauma bonds. Their neurochemistry is programmed for trauma, that is, there are high norepinephrine outpourings (anticipating abuse), dissociated states, and endorphin surges to reregulate them. These responses contribute to the trauma bond. Extreme responses and reactivity are typical of shame-based people, and most of those who come from addictive and abusive families are shame based. The feelings of defectiveness that are a part of shame are intolerable and drive people into their familiar coping mechanisms.

Another factor that sets up trauma bonds are power differentials. In other words, the greater the power one has, the greater the risk of abusing others, if that power is not used responsibly. The person in power often feels entitled, whereas the one with less power generally sacrifices, all the while looking for ways to reclaim the power. This is common among couples where addictions are present, with the addict overindulging while the codependent starves. In such a situation, resentments develop easily.

Finally, there is the problem of trust. When the ones who are trusted the most are the betrayers, trauma bonds ensue. Children cannot leave their families because they need them. When betrayed and then told to keep secrets, or that the abuse did not occur, several things happen: they try harder, they stop trusting themselves, and they learn to trust people who are untrustworthy or they trust no one. The greater the betrayal of trusted relationships, the more this kind of thinking and belief system is reinforced and tenaciously adhered to. It is easy for a therapist to feel hopeless in this kind of a system. Indeed, the couple often despairs too, wanting the therapist to do something magical to cure them. They will try to make a referee out of the therapist, attempting to make him or her be the arbiter of right and wrong, resulting in resistance to being responsible for, and doing, their own work and, thus, being unable to move forward. The resolution of trauma bonds is discussed in the second phase of the treatment process.

TREATMENT: THE SECOND PHASE

Once the addictions are identified and arrested, and both parties are in treatment of their own, work with the couple can begin in earnest. One can expect resistance from both, as well as unconscious attempts to return to old behavioral patterns because they are so familiar. There will need to be strong ground rules that are basic and conditional for ongoing treatment. The object is to keep the addictions in remission, stop the couple from continuing to abuse each other, and begin to establish clear, firm boundaries. Usually, this is new territory for couples as troubled as those in addictive systems. The use of a timer (and other basic communication skills-building exercises and techniques) to give each equal time to talk without interruption and to be heard by the partner can be very helpful in the beginning to establish effective communication patterns. Because chaos is often the norm, they will need to learn how to establish routines and to value balanced living. It is sad to see how little is known regarding such things as boundaries, effective communication skills, and intimacy, despite high intelligence and advanced education in many cases. On the brighter side, the awareness of severe dysfunction, coupled with a lot of psychic pain, can create avid learners regardless of the level of education. The courage, valor, and willingness can be impressive and touching.

Larsen (SECAD, 1993), who has written books and lectured widely on relationships in recovery, has a practical guide to bring about change, which he employs with couples. The first part is understanding. In order to bring about change, one needs to know what the problem is. Each partner needs to discover behavioral patterns that are problematic. That is, body language, withdrawing, aggression, dismissal, ignoring, or other things that stop the communication process. When this pattern is identified, it needs to be related back to the family of origin, within the context of which it will make sense. Someone else did it "back there" and it did not work there and then either!

The next step is to focus on what will effect change—new behavior and new ways of thinking. These ideas can be created in the therapist's office because the couple will need help discovering or creating what is reasonable and fair for both.

The third step is consistency. Practice is required for anything new to take hold and become effective. Only by repetition of the new behavior will the old become weakened and obsolete. One does not give up a behavior unless something else works better.

Finally, there must be accountability to keep the perspective healthy. By this is meant having a mentor, therapist and/or sponsor, to talk with regularly about the new strategies. No one can out-perform one's self-image or self-definition, but every genuine effort to try new behavior will contribute to improvement. We are all born with needs. None of us, however, is born with the skills to get them met. They must be learned, and this is where therapy and support systems can be extremely helpful.

When the couple is stable, the therapist can begin to help them start to disrupt the trauma bond that they have between them. They would then have the foundation upon which to begin to build trust, honesty, and intimacy. The couple, however, cannot experience a healthier relationship beyond that which both individuals want (some want to be left alone), or go beyond their respective ability and willingness to do the necessary work. This must be noted, discussed, and respected along the way.

According to Carnes (1993), "it takes a system to break a system." As powerful as the trauma bond system is, there needs to be created an equally powerful healthy system to counter it. The therapist can explore what already exists in the couple's life that is healthy and enable them to create ways to enhance it and add to it. When healthy bonds are available, the individual can recognize the discrepancy between them and those that are unhealthy and debilitating. Objectivity is the goal here. Mentors, therapists, sponsors, other recovering people, pastors, coworkers, and community members can contribute to helping a person get out of the unhealthy role and into different behavior. When a victim is able to identify the cycles of abuse, alternatives to the old behaviors will become apparent.

There are some tools that can be used to help the individuals psychologically distance themselves from the intensity that previously has led to abuse. One is to practice detachment by identifying which issues belong to whom and taking them to the respective support groups. For example, if partner A is criticizing partner B for doing a certain activity with friends that B has done often, B may need to step back and look at the situation objectively rather than react out of guilt with a countercriticism. It may be that A is feeling left out and only needs to know when B will return so that they can do something together. Or, it may be that B is doing the activity to avoid abuse from A, but is not saying so. Of course, A must also be willing to look at A's behavior, and if s/he is not being clear or honest in communicating, A must take responsibility.

Another strategy is to use appropriate humor to lighten the perceived severity of the threatening situation. This does not mean to make fun of the partner, but rather to help each other see that the situation is only, for example, a mistake made in cooking (the soufflé took a dive) and not that one was trying to poison the other.

Disengaging by taking a walk, making a call to a sponsor or friend for coaching and perspective, or asking for a time-out can all help interrupt the cycles. If one can see the humanness or vulnerability of the other, as in seeing the sadness or confusion from childhood trauma that led to not trusting and going on the offensive to cover it up, it helps one to not react so quickly. Delays provide a chance to evaluate, marshall resources, and give a better response.

Other strategies for disrupting trauma bonds are to learn to set appropriate boundaries and to identify the roles of the victim, victimizer (or perpetrator), and rescuer. This is not easy, because the roles are dynamic, with partners switching roles often as the need arises. This is about a system and not about fault or blame. The aim is to see and understand what is going on and to help the couple reframe their thinking and perceiving. For example, they may believe that starting and engaging in arguments is a way to get close. They need to be taught how to establish a safe place, with boundaries, where they can be vulnerable to and with each other, and then truly find closeness and intimacy.

The use of metaphors during times that might otherwise escalate into abuse can help people ground themselves so that they can respond appropriately instead of reacting. They need to stay in the present moment in order to participate fully. An example would be to imagine a transparent bell or membrane around themselves to keep out negative energy. Metaphors are transformers for healing. They come to us in dreams and in our creative imagination, giving us tools and symbols with which to work. Dolan's (1991) work can provide the therapist with many interesting and constructive techniques in this area, especially when working with survivors of sexual abuse.

If the tendency is to dissociate under stress, it helps to have a safe place to imagine or to carry a symbol of that safe place in one's pocket.

The symbol might be a photograph, a piece of ribbon or fabric, a phrase on a scrap of paper, or a souvenir that represents a current or positive experience. The use of such evocative devices serves to reduce anxiety by helping the partners return to the here and now. Prayer, too, can help some people stay centered.

Work that focuses on the constructive use of anger can help individuals diffuse tension and protect the relationship. (See Chapters 3 and 4 for a detailed discussion of anger and conflict issues in treatment.) Again, if the situation heats up dangerously, one of the partners can call a time-out in order to use a punching bag or some other nondestructive physical expression of anger. The couple then return, more calmly and with more clarity, to the issue at hand. Often, people need a witness to healthy protesting or expression, someone to simply stand by them, because they may be too afraid of their own anger to release it alone.

Self-hypnosis, both for relaxation and ego-strengthening purposes, has been helpful to many and provides another way to nurture and comfort people by teaching them to draw on their own resources. Audiotapes can be designed and made in the therapeutic session to be practiced at home. Guided imagery, coupled with positive suggestions that are realistic and attainable, can be used toward the realization that they can empower themselves from the inside. (See Dolan [1991] for a variety of techniques building on Eriksonian hypnosis for adult survivors of sexual abuse, and Woolfolk and Lehrer [1984] for a variety of relaxation and hypnosis techniques.)

Adequate food, exercise, and recreation can make the difference during times of stress by providing a structure and routine that may not have been there before. Creative endeavors, community activities, and spiritual/inspirational opportunities help to provide a sense of connectedness to the universe and thereby diminish the isolation that spawns desperation, despair, and regressed behavior. Support systems are essential for healthy living. When there is a push for exclusivity, it may belie another addiction.

The therapist may discover that behind the addiction and codependence there is a complex PTSD, major depression, bipolar disorder, or adult attention-deficit disorder requiring careful psychiatric assessment and medication. If the patient has tried these strategies with a sincere commitment and is still relapsing or remains stuck, there may be a biochemical imbalance that needs to be addressed. The serotonergic antidepressants, lithium or anticonvulsant, have been particularly helpful with compulsive disorders such as the addictions. They can quiet the background sexual static or obsessing, reduce a sense of vulnerability, and help the patient be more available for therapy.

The first line of medications would be those that increase serotonin in the brain. When people are deficient in serotonin, they have difficulty modulating their emotions. They tend to have extreme reactions, feel vulnerable to change and social situations, and have low psychic pain tolerance. Prozac was the first drug to provide relief from such symptoms in large numbers of people. For some it was too strong, interfering with sleep and causing uncomfortable agitation. Zoloft has proved to be gentler, but may cause diminished interest in being sexual or delayed ejaculation, or impair the orgasmic response in other ways. These side effects are reversible upon discontinuance of the medication. There may be headaches from the serotonin surge in the brain and a decrease in appetite for food. Most side effects diminish in the first week or pale in comparison with the benefits. The third drug in this group is Paxil, which is similar in action to Prozac and Zoloft, but has fewer side effects. Sex addicts have been helped specifically by these medications. People who demonstrate depression through anger appreciate the moderating effects of the serotonergic drugs. Instead of flying off the handle, they can pause and think about how they want to respond.

For those with spontaneous mood swings that cause disruption of daily life, lithium may be of significant help. It is inexpensive and flushes out quickly from the system. The disadvantage is that the therapeutic range is close to the toxic level, so that blood level tests must be taken regularly to ensure a safe range. Also, lithium only works in about half of those who take it, and it must be taken three to four times a day as opposed to once a day for the serotonergics.

A backup plan is to use the anticonvulsants. These drugs stabilize cell membranes, which helps to regulate the flow of neurotransmitters. Carbamazepine (Tegretol) and valproic acid (Depakene) are the two most commonly used. In a small percentage of people, Tegretol will depress the bone marrow, but blood tests early on in the treatment process will identify this problem. Valproic acid is contraindicated in people with liver disease. No drugs are free of potentially harmful effects; therefore, they must be prescribed judiciously. But they can also be an enormous help to some people. The hope is that medication can render people more available for treatment, and that, in time, with the help of therapy, new skills, and better self-care, the brain will take back the job of balancing its own chemistry.

Even with the depression or imbalance treated or corrected, there will be grief work that needs to be done. The addict needs to mourn the loss of the addiction(s), as one would an old friend who was always there when needed. The codependent partner needs to mourn the loss of self through "selling out" to others. For both, there likely is sadness over the loss of a healthy childhood. However, the experience of grief is a necessary step in the acceptance of what was, in order to stop investing in the past and to move on. Although mourning is painful, it is also the transformative link to serenity.

TREATMENT: THE THIRD PHASE

Once communication skills are fairly well established, the finer tuning of intimacy can be undertaken. (See Chapter 2 for a detailed discussion of commitment and intimacy issues in treatment, and Chapter 10 for a detailed discussion of the treatment of inhibited sexual desire [ISD], a common sexual dysfunction experienced by those who have been sexually abused as children.) Some alcoholics and drug addicts have never been sexual without being intoxicated. They can feel as awkward as adolescents, not knowing what to do or how to do it. Sensitivity to rejection is very high. The challenge for sex addicts will be to stay present for their partners and not take off into fantasy. They may have split love and lust/passion, so that the spouse is the anchoring partner while the excitement goes to someone outside the marriage. These two aspects will have to be integrated. Sex addicts may want to be sexual more than their partners and may even use sex as a way to act out rather than to express love. The partners may not want to be sexual at all because of the betrayal issues. Or partners may push to be sexual more than they really want to in an effort to keep the sex addict happy. There is not much trust at this level and the emotional equilibrium is very delicate. Neither knows how to say "no" without guilt or fear of impact on the other. It is a bind that must be talked about often.

Incest survivors have their own special problems. They may have been able to be sexual before marriage, but once the commitment was made they shut down (experiencing ISD or sexual aversion) because marriage resembled the trap they were in as children, with no choices. It is critical that they be made aware that they have choices as adults. Free choice must be differentiated from needing to control. So-called body memories frequently emerge for incest survivors. Examples include panic, rage, somatization, dissociation, going numb emotionally, and not wanting to be touched. Much sensitivity is needed in these instances. The survivor may confuse the partner with the perpetrator and will require patience and time to finish healing. There are two excellent books for survivors and their partners, *Incest and Sexuality: A Guide to Understanding and Healing* (Maltz & Holman, 1987) and *The Sexual Healing Journey: A Guide for Survivors of Sexual Abuse* (Maltz, 1991a). Maltz has also created a video for couples' use (Maltz, 1991b), and an excellent article for couples therapists helping patients to deal with the sexual repercussions of incest (Maltz, 1988).

Survivors may feel that they were betrayed by their own bodies, and may have disconnected from them in response. The gentle exercises suggested in Maltz's (1991a) book, as well as deep tissue massage can aid both in releasing body memories and in regaining a sense of and respect for one's body. Safe professional massage can accomplish this when the time is right. Many survivors are astonished that there can be joy in sex instead of dread. They look quite different when their own life force starts to return to them. There is more color and vitality to them and they become more spontaneous and creative.

CONCLUSION

Our culture supports and thrives on immediate gratification, which is the key ingredient of addictions. At the same time, we claim to advocate family values, which are diametrically opposed to addictions. Most would define such values in terms of honest communication, commitment, taking time to solve problems, good and firm boundaries, respect for each other, hard work, and delayed gratification. How do we resolve this dichotomy? First, we have to identify and understand addiction. We must come out of denial to see how ubiquitous it is and what price we are all paying for the consequences: abuse; destruction of families, values, and health; a mentality of blame, irresponsibility, and entitlement. With an awareness of the problems comes a responsibility to do something about them.

In light of the devastating consequences, it is imperative to treat addictions as soon as they are recognized. As enlightened therapists we have the opportunity to have an impact on couples with addiction problems. In understanding the nature and power of the trauma-bonded system, we realize that there must be created an equally powerful healthy system to disrupt the addicted one. Fortunately, there is the 12-step program to help our patients turn their lives around, making their addiction a treatable disorder. We, then, can teach and coach the finer, more spiritual path to intimacy and love. Most people long to be restored to their value system, or to create one that can offer them a fuller life, but they have metaphorically and actually lost their way and do not know how to get back on track. The hope is that once they have been reempowered and reconnected to the fragmented parts of the self, they will have a positive influence on others. They will have become capable of genuine interpersonal intimacy and, thereby, effective agents of change in their own lives and in the broader communities of which they are a part.

REFERENCES

Carnes, P. (1991). *Don't call it love: Recovery from sexual addiction*. New York: Bantam.

Carnes, P. (1993). "Trauma Bonds" Workshop. Philadelphia.

Dolan, Y. M. (1991). *Resolving sexual abuse*. New York: Norton.

Johnson, V. (1980). *I'll quit tomorrow*. New York: Harper & Row.

Maltz, W. (1988). Identifying and treating the sexual repercussions of incest: A couples therapy approach. *Journal of Sex and Marital Therapy, 14* (2), 116–144.

Maltz, W. (1991a). *The sexual healing journey: A guide for survivors of sexual abuse*. New York: Harper & Row.

Maltz, W. (1991b). *Partners in healing*. Eugene, OR: Independent Video Services.

Maltz, W., & Holman, B. (1987). *Incest and sexuality: A guide to understanding and healing*. Lexington, MA: Lexington Books.

Milkman, H., & Sunderwirth, S. (1987). *Craving for ecstacy: The consciousness and chemistry of escape*. Lexington, MA: Lexington Books.

SECAD. (1993). The Southeastern Conference on Alcohol and Drug Abuse, Atlanta, GA. Presentations by R. Hunter, A. Corley, H. Katner, P. Mellody, E. Larsen, and S. Marks.

Weeks, G. R. (Ed.). (1989). *Treating couples: The Intersystem Model of the Marriage Council of Philadelphia*. New York: Brunner/Mazel.

Weeks, G. R., & Hof, L. (Eds.). (1994). *The marital-relationship therapy casebook: Theory and application of the Intersystem Model*. New York: Brunner/Mazel.

Woolfolk, R. J., & Lehrer, P. M. (Eds.). (1984). *Principles and practice of stress management*. New York: Guilford.

7

WORKING THROUGH THE EXTRAMARITAL TRAUMA: AN EXPLORATION OF COMMON THEMES

April Westfall, Ph.D.

Couples presenting for therapy with the problem of sexual infidelity pose difficult challenges for the couple and family therapist. The extramarital affair, as common an occurrence in marriages today as ever, remains enormously troublesome for most couples who must contend with the issue firsthand. The extramarital sexual crisis (Thompson, 1984), triggered by the revelation of a spouse's secret, unsanctioned, sexual involvement with someone outside the marriage, can have a shattering effect on the stability of the marriage as well as on the psychic equilibrium of each of the spouses. The process of recovery, when recovery is possible, typically happens quite slowly. Aftershocks from the crisis may be felt for several months or even years.

Elsewhere (Westfall, 1989), I have written about the perplexing complexities of these cases and present a clinical guide to assist the therapist through the early stages of treatment. I emphasize the importance of careful assessment and delineate several factors to differentiate extramarital sexual (EMS) behavior:

1. Type (heterosexual/homosexual) and level of sexual activity (flirt-ing, petting, intercourse, etc.).
2. Frequency and duration, as well as location, of EMS activities.
3. Number of EMS partners (past and present).
4. Unilateral/bilateral nature of EMS.
5. Degree of secrecy surrounding EMS.
6. Degree of acceptance of and consent for EMS behavior in the marriage by both spouses.
7. Degree of emotional involvement with and commitment to the EMS partner.
8. Relationship of the nonparticipating spouse to the EMS partner.
9. Degree of spouses' emotional involvement with and commitment to each other.
10. Tolerance of EMS behavior within the couple's ethnic community/social group. (Westfall, 1989, p. 168)

Furthermore, the timing of and special circumstances surrounding the revelation of the spouse's sexual infidelity can make the process of recovery more difficult. The extramarital crisis may coincide with other family stresses (for example, a difficult move or loss of job), further depleting the couple's emotional and physical reserves.

Specific suggestions are given for managing the intense emotional reactions following disclosure/discovery of an affair and for offering support to the individual spouses in the face of their different and some-times contradictory needs. For example, grief reactions are quite common during this time, as both spouses report often profound feelings of loss. Still, the spouses are likely to experience these losses in very different ways, causing further misunderstanding. For the participating spouse, the recent decision to give up the affair partner can be quite disturbing, especially when a significant and prolonged attachment has been formed. For the nonparticipating spouse, there is a loss of self-esteem and personal confidence in his or her attractiveness as a mate. S/he is easily threatened by any show of caring for the affair partner by the other spouse, insisting on an immediate cessation of all positive feelings toward that person. Of course, this is an impossible demand, since the participating spouse needs time and support to mourn the loss of the affair partner. At the same time, the nonparticipating spouse needs reassurance that s/he has priority in the emotional life and affections of the marital partner. The therapist, in the role of interpreter, must help the spouses to attain a better under-standing of their different needs during this difficult period and to develop more realistic expectations of each other in the face of their considerable vulnerability. At times, this may call for individual sessions, so that the therapist can offer undivided support to each spouse while, at the same time, encouraging each to consider the emotional needs of and constraints on the other.

Affairs disclosed to the therapist, but not to the other spouse, somewhere in the course of treatment can cause difficult ethical and strategic problems (Karpel, 1980, 1994). Similarly, affairs that continue, with or without the other spouse's knowledge, even as the couple enter into conjoint therapy, can seriously aggravate the crisis and undermine any chance for change in the marriage. Sexual secrets are distinguished by how they are introduced into therapy and by their immediate relevance to the other spouse. The therapist must be careful to avoid entering into a secret alliance with one spouse, compromising his or her ability to behave in a trustworthy and evenhanded manner with both. For example, a currently active, secret extramarital affair, disclosed to the therapist in a private session or conversation at the outset of treatment, is highly relevant to the other spouse. If one spouse refuses either to end the relationship with the extramarital partner or to disclose the affair to the spouse, the therapist has little choice other than to refuse couple therapy at this time. The therapist has greater latitude in handling the disclosure issue when dealing with prior extramarital behavior. S/he can feel more comfortable in leaving disclosure to the client's discretion when the affair ended some time ago and does not appear to have had a lasting impact on the marriage. This is also true when there are rare, isolated instances of extramarital activity, involving little emotional attachment to the affair partner.

Yet, the therapist cannot always accurately assess the impact of an affair on the marriage at the outset of treatment. S/he may choose to begin therapy without insisting on disclosure, but may later call for a more open discussion of the affair with the other spouse, when it appears to pose a sufficient obstacle to therapeutic progress. The therapist needs to proceed cautiously in making a recommendation for or against disclosure of extramarital affairs, carefully weighing the needs of each spouse with his or her own comfort level. There is no simple formula for handling this difficult therapeutic issue; discretion and sound clinical judgment are essential.

In moving through the extramarital crisis, the therapist should observe a gradual change in the emotional tone of the couple's interactions, from the deadly seriousness in the beginning to the spontaneous playfulness and teasing that mark the end of the crisis. An offhand remark or simple reference to someone else's infidelity no longer inflames the spouse's anger as it once would. The couple now feel enough detachment from the unrelenting pain of their particular situation to permit an element of novelty, surprise, and even humor to enter their responses.

Some couples will elect to terminate treatment once the immediate crisis in their marital lives has been reduced to manageable proportions. They are able to view the sexual infidelity, however painful an aberration, as a less serious breach of their marital vows. This is more likely to occur in affairs that are short-lived, that include less emotional involvement, and that are further removed from the couple's social and familial network. For other couples, such a speedy recovery is unthinkable. There is a more serious erosion of trust in the partner, often accompanied by persistent signs of the partner's disloyalty, that make the repair of the relationship more difficult, if not impossible. One or both spouses may feel real ambivalence about continuing the marriage once the affair has ended, and remain in therapy to confront these feelings directly. Others simply want to reach a better understanding as to why the sexual infidelity happened in the first place, so as to prevent a recurrence in the future.

When couples continue in treatment beyond the immediate discovery period and the early part of the crisis, the therapist can be instrumental in shaping the recovery process. Much of the work consists of careful and thorough exploration of certain common themes, which continue to reverberate through their marital lives for some time following the first recognition of the sexual infidelity. Here, the therapist can play a crucial role in restoring trust and rebuilding loyalty ties between the spouses, and in facilitating their search for understanding, if not answers, that can permit forgiveness and healing to occur.

RESTORING TRUST/LESSENING SUSPICION

The precipitous loss of trust in the marital partner that comes with the discovery of his or her affair is felt as a painful blow, leaving both spouses reeling from the force of its destructive impact. This violation of a basic assumption or major tenet of the marital contract can disturb the very foundation of the marital structure. Just as most couples do not enter into prenuptial agreements before they wed, even though fully aware of the prevalence of divorce in America today, most couples also shun open discussion of sexual infidelity, fearing the cynical conclusions that might follow or simply hoping for the best. Unfortunately, this attitude does not permit the couple to take the steps that might improve their chances for success in the area of sexual fidelity, nor does the attitude allow for the early detection of an affair—before things have gotten out of hand emotionally and sexually. Hence, people frequently discount their intuitive sense of the spouse's infidelity again and again, until irrefutable evidence, or the spouse's own confession, requires that it be faced directly.

The person hearing of a spouse's extramarital involvement for the first time can experience a primitive, regressive pull away from his or her normal emotional equilibrium. There are often visceral reactions (e.g., precipitous loss of appetite, heart palpitations, nausea) as the news becomes more fully registered. Whatever sense of safety, stability, and tranquility the spouse has come to expect from the marriage suddenly seems lost. The participating spouse, now held accountable for sexual transgressions and betrayal of the marital vows, can feel equally devastated. The kind of compartmentalization of feeling toward spouse and lover that often occurs in affairs can lead to the denial of destructive consequences for the individual spouse's well-being and for the state of the marriage. Living with the emotional reality of the spouse's extreme distress is in stark contrast to the prior semidelusional state. Now forced to choose between spouse and lover, s/he may also feel confused and deeply uncertain about how to proceed. Both partners know that they have lost something fundamental in their former sense of themselves as a couple, but, at least for the time being, they are unable to find a replacement for what is missing.

During this time of heightened uncertainty and emotional unrest, the therapist must assume a calm but firm control of the sessions. One of the first tasks is to instill hope in the clients through their confidence in the therapist and the therapeutic process, as they so often lack confidence in each other in the beginning (see Chapter 1). The therapist must also help to provide direction for the clients' lives at home in ways that lessen the sometimes unbearable tension felt there. Rageful feelings can suddenly erupt into violence, and the hopelessness and desperation that pervade their lives can make suicide seem like the only recourse. A spouse's ability to function effectively at work or in a parental role may be seriously compromised, so that no area seems untouched by the affair. In this atmosphere of mistrust, the therapist must help the couple to plan their daily schedules and to think about their routine comings and goings in a way that contributes to a feeling of safety for both (having them check in with each other by phone during the day or cautioning them to avoid coming home late from work without prior notification of the spouse). Although this preoccupation with the spouse's whereabouts and the suspicion that comes with any slight deviation from schedule cannot be tolerated for long by either spouse, it does make sense during the immediate discovery period. Willingness to go along with the cumbersome demands in order to reassure his or her still doubting spouse reflects a willingness to sacrifice personal comfort for the sake of the other. This concern for the spouse's well-being can be construed as an important first step toward reestablishing his or her own trustworthiness in the marriage. Moreover, in lengthy affairs that have only recently ended, this period of heightened vigilance by the marital partner may be necessary to ensure the discontinuation of the relationship with the extramarital partner. Framed in this manner, the spouses may be encouraged, even during this dismal time, by the belief that they may still care enough about each other and the marriage to work through the present trauma.

Lying and deception are endemic to affairs, as the husband or wife attempts to conceal the facts of the sexual indiscretions from the spouse. What may begin as only a slight withholding of information—a certain lack of forthrightness—can quickly grow beyond all reasonable bounds. Lies permit the person to continue the marriage and the affair with apparent impunity. Still, for most people, lying is accompanied with often unforeseen consequences, which can have an insidious effect on the marital bond. With the exception of the hardened psychopath, lying does not come easy. In the process, the deceiving spouse becomes emotionally distanced from the partner, as it becomes too difficult to remain intimate with one to whom you are lying. As the negative atmosphere thickens, the husband's or wife's pleasure in the company of the other is gradually eroded as well, seeming to justify the continuation of the affair.

The deceived spouse is likely to feel suspicious of the marital partner prior to the discovery of the infidelity, but discounts the suspicions in order to preserve the desired image of the marriage. In the face of mounting evidence, the spouse will also withdraw emotionally, rather than face his or her worst fears head on. Or the spouse may confront the other, but be met with indignant protestations or humorous dismissals. S/he may be willing to accept the alibis and excuses, even if they do not really fit the facts, as the perceived hold on the spouse grows ever more tenuous. The hold on reality may grow tenuous as well, as s/he begins to suffer a kind of paranoia in relation to the marriage. Others will press their partners more strongly, until the truth is forthcoming, or go about engaging in their own detective work to uncover the necessary, corroborating evidence.

Finally, the truth of the sexual infidelity becomes clear, and both spouses must deal with it. For many, the spouse's habit of lying to them is the worst part of the infidelity, and has the most damaging effect on trust in the partner and in the marriage. "How will I ever be able to believe you again?" and "I don't know you anymore—I feel as if I'm living with a stranger" are typical complaints at this time.

Even though the affair is out in the open, the facts only gradually become known. Given the intense emotional upset and primitive rage experienced by the spouse during the immediate discovery period, it is likely that information will continue to be withheld or distorted in ways that lessen the significance and conceal the full extent of the extramarital involvement. However, once Pandora's box has been opened, the deceived spouse will more easily sense when s/he is being lied to and may go on a scouting mission to unearth all the facts. Consequently, the deceptive spouse may be caught again and again in lies that destroy whatever trust remains between them. For this reason, the therapist should caution the husband or wife to strictly avoid further deception once the affair(s) becomes known. Even though the spouse may be infuriated by new information (hearing that the husband or wife received a phone call from the lover at home or that the person showed up at the office), at least there is the reassurance that s/he is no longer kept in the dark about the important facts. In the long run, this can only help the rebuilding process.

The husband or wife may experience an intense rage that leads to retaliatory behavior, while feeling justified in behaving this way given the sexual betrayal. A few may entertain the thought of, or even enter into, revenge affairs in order to "even the score." These affairs seldom prove satisfying, if this is their only rationale, and only increase the marital rift. The other spouse may experience disbelief at the cruelty exhibited by the vindictive mate and begin to question the spouse's concern for his or her well-being, which may have been in doubt anyway. Some may take refuge in the company of the affair partner once again, in a back-and-forth move that fuels the spouse's rage even more. The therapist must be prepared to confront the destructive behavior, challenging the notion that the sexual infidelity justifies any manner of cruelty. Without siding with the infidel, the therapist might ask how long the spouse plans to punish the husband or wife. Done without sarcasm, the therapist's suggestion that the spouse's vindictive actions might contribute to the ambivalent spouse's attraction to the affair partner can awaken the person to the futility of such vengeance.

Acting in the role of diplomat, the therapist may be able to help the couple to achieve some needed compromise and to make some critical changes, even in these trying times. With both spouses feeling bad about themselves and often behaving badly, interventions that permit the clients to save face (Covelman & Covelman, 1993) are called for, preserving what personal dignity and esteem remains. Moreover, the clients need to be able to acknowledge their mistakes in the marriage without feeling humiliated. Along these lines, therapeutic maneuvers that normalize irrational behaviors, that introduce complexity into narrow definitions of the problem, that achieve balance in the face of the extreme positions the spouses push each other into, and that encourage freer self-exploration in both partners are quite effective with these couples.

With time and considerable patience, many couples will be able to resume a normal life, putting aside the earlier fear and suspicion that are a part of the postdiscovery mistrust. Still, vestiges of mistrust are not uncommon even a year later. In the beginning, attempts to relax with each other or to renew a comfortable level of intimacy are easily disrupted. One or both spouses may feel too frightened by the emotional vulnerability experienced during such times to allow for prolonged closeness. A fight may erupt out of nowhere or one spouse may simply retreat to a safer and more emotionally distant position, bringing such seemingly hopeful moments to a disappointing end. These self-protective but frustrating maneuvers are common enough, and should be presented as such by the therapist. If the couple is able to view these setbacks as something to be worked through while rebuilding trust, they will be better able to endure the attendant frustrations along the way. In time, these interferences should become less frequent, as the partners are able to let down their emotional guard with each other once again. However, there will be occasions that bring forth vivid recollections of the sexual infidelity and cause both spouses to wonder if their life together will ever return to normal.

RECLAIMING LOYALTY TIES/CURTAILING JEALOUSY

Once the sexual infidelity is out in the open, the offending spouse is apt to be barraged with an onslaught of questions concerning the details of the extramarital behavior. The other spouse's need for certain information (the name and/or identity of the extramarital partner, when and where their meetings took place, the extent of their emotional and sexual involvement, etc.) seems reasonable enough. There are cases, however, when repetitive questioning and a seemingly endless demand for ever more details go beyond reason. Obsession characterizes the jealous response and sets it apart from other common emotional states.

In the beginning, the therapist needs to take charge of the couple's discussions of the spouse's extramarital behavior in the face of obsessive jealousy. If left alone, the spouse may become the prosecuting attorney, interrogating the partner with an array of insinuating queries that leave little room for nondefensive replies. Furthermore, the husband or wife may ask for details about the partner's activities that s/he is not prepared to handle emotionally, worsening an already precarious situation. This is especially true in cases involving compulsive and indiscriminate sexual behavior by the spouse, where discussing the details of the sexual escapades can be humiliating for both spouses. In these cases, the therapist should conduct a more careful examination of the spouse's extramarital activities in individual sessions without the presence of the other spouse to constrain the line of questioning.

By contrast, the extramaritally involved spouse may question the need for any serious discussion of the affair once the outside relationship has ended. For this person, it seems that delving into the hurtful details of the past will only drive a wedge between them, delaying their getting on with their lives. Here, the therapist should support the spouse in the need to know, as the confusion and misunderstanding surrounding the partner's extramarital activities make it impossible to think clearly about, and to decide on, a future together. In addition, the husband or wife may have rather hastily and impulsively ended the affair in the face of the spouse's overwhelming protests, without really thinking much about his or her own desires. Such a decision can be easily reversed if not examined more carefully and without some consideration of the spouse's emotional attachment to the affair partner.

The jealous spouse can be encouraged to keep a journal during this time, writing down thoughts and questions s/he might want to ask the spouse, while refraining from open discussion of the matter outside the therapy sessions. With these ideas on paper, the person may be able to get a better hold on his or her ruminative thinking. S/he should be asked to think carefully about the questions s/he wishes to ask the partner. Why is s/he asking the question? What kind of answer is expected? How will the information help resolve feelings concerning the partner's infidelity? Slowing down the process and creating a thoughtful pause in this line of questioning can help the jealous spouse avoid material that would only result in needless torture.

In session, the therapist reframes the spouse's questions in a more useful way for the couple. The therapist can follow up with questions and comments that enlarge the couple's understanding as to why the affair happened and what kept it going once it started. In so doing, s/he moves them away from the destructive polarization that occurs when the couple view themselves as villain and victim. In addition, the therapist is better able to challenge the fairly unrealistic expectations that the involved spouse may harbor concerning continued contact with the affair partner once the sexual relationship has ended. The therapist can calmly present this challenge from a more detached position than that of the threatened spouse.

One who has been involved in a lengthy affair often engages in an idealization of the affair partner. This partner is viewed in an isolated context, where the two are focused intently on each other, often in a highly charged sexual and emotional state. Removed from the normal humdrum of daily life, the affair partner appears more interesting, more sexually attuned, and more understanding than the marital partner. Additionally, the spouse is risking a great deal to be with the lover, which further reinforces this person's special worth.

The jealous spouse may sense this specialness and confront the spouse with his or her worst fears—"Did you like being with your lover more than you liked being with me?" The therapist can reframe the spouse's question in a way that gets at the heart of the question, but without the painful rejection implicit in the spouse's plea. For example, "How were you different when in the company of the affair partner?" or, "What did you like about yourself in this situation?"

Long-term marriages can sometimes lead to a rigidity and inflexibility of thinking and behavior that stifle change and growth in the individual spouses. A kind of inertia sets in over time. The kind person grows weaker from the neglect of self; the controlling person becomes weary of the responsibility entailed in this role; the peacemaker suffers from internalized anger never resolved. Many affairs start as an effort to break away from these limiting aspects of the marriage, even if unrecognized as such by the involved spouse. The affair partner, even if unremarkable, is valued for his or her difference from the spouse. This difference, even if more illusory than real, can permit the person to experiment with new ways of being in relationship, often long overdue. Once the couple realize what has been missing in the marriage, they can begin to consider corrective action, although it is not an easy prospect even with this new insight. At the very least, the magical thinking that can lead the spouse to imbue the affair partner with incredible powers and to imagine that all things are possible in the company of the lover has been called into question.

When the husband or wife begins to describe the affair partner to the spouse, the effect is to bring the person down to size, including flaws and limitations, once open to the unflattering perusal of the other spouse. The therapist should discourage the malicious trashing of the affair partner by the jealous spouse, as this will only make the other come to his or her defense. Not to defend the affair partner would feel disloyal when that person was there when needed. Still, the active discussion by the spouses of the affair seems to draw them closer together—difficult as it can be—while moving the affair partner to a more distant position from the marriage. Whereas before the husband or wife chose to confide to the affair partner the intimate details of the marriage, now the reverse occurs. In fact, those who adamantly refuse to discuss their affairs may still be trying to preserve an attachment to the lover. In turn, the spouse may realize that the partner's loyalty remains with the other person and be consumed by jealousy. In this instance, the therapist should not be afraid to question the spouse as to whether the affair has really ended.

Not infrequently, other friends or family members are implicated in the spouse's infidelity, intensifying feelings of shame and personal injury. When it is a close family friend or relative of the other spouse who becomes a lover, the feeling of betrayal is even greater. The couple's relationship with this person may be so impaired by the sexual infidelity and disloyalty that it becomes impossible for it to continue. Or, if it is to continue, as often happens when the lover is a family member, it will do so only in a perfunctory and emotionally empty way.

Given the damaging effect of such sexual intrigues, why do they happen as often as they do? More often than not, they take place because the person simply happens to be there, spending time with the husband and wife in a way that leads to an increasing emotional intimacy and a deepening bond with one spouse. Sometimes the connection grows out of a change in the nature of the relationship between the spouses and with the friend or relative, with one spouse moving to a more emotionally distant position from both. The pair may unwittingly draw closer together, feeling the loss of the same important person. In other instances, the affair may grow out of a longstanding rivalry between the friend or relative and the husband or wife in a power play to gain the upper hand. The spouse may have an even harder time dealing with the disloyalty of the marital partner who has sided with this important rival. At other times, the spouse senses that the competition is really a personal one with the friend or relative and almost ignores the role of the other spouse in the betrayal.

To a lesser degree, the husband or wife is apt to feel a similar disloyalty on the part of friends or family members to whom the spouse has confided the affair and then sworn to secrecy. S/he may read into the friend's or relative's continued silence a tacit approval of the spouse's behavior, which is interpreted as aiding and abetting that spouse. Even when the friend or family member has harshly criticized or shunned contact with the participating spouse—perhaps even going so far as to break the news to the other spouse—the relationship with the couple is still likely to be scarred.

The nonparticipating spouse is often embarrassed by the simple fact that the friend or family member has been privy to such intimate and unseemly details of his or her marital life. The participating spouse is likely to suffer from his or her own feelings of betrayal, seeing the friend or relative as siding against him or her at a critical time. Here some education by the therapist as to the inevitable discomfort and loyalty conflicts experienced by anyone drawn into the awareness context of secrets (Karpel, 1980) can be helpful. The couple may be better able to appreciate the dilemmas and limited options for action available to friends and family. A balance must be found. It is unwise for the couple to attempt to rectify the situation with others before the ties to each other are stronger. On the other hand, the couple should not postpone contact for too long, if they hope to restore the former bonds. Encouraging the couple to plan meetings carefully in the beginning (e.g., how long they will stay, how they might deal with certain questions) can ease the way, lessening the embarrassment of all concerned.

A still more difficult and potentially damaging situation occurs when the couple's children are drawn into the secrecy surrounding the affair. A child may have accidentally discovered something that inadvertently revealed the parent's infidelity or the parent may have openly shared the secret with the child. Either way, the child is bound to feel a conflict of loyalty that can cause great stress and can jeopardize the relationship with both parents. If one child knows of a parent's affair and the other siblings do not, s/he may become isolated from the sibling group. These situations require the utmost care and delicate handling by the therapist.

It is often helpful to do some family work with the child, the other siblings, and the parents. In these sessions, the therapist can carefully assess the child's emotional state, looking for evidence of continued stress and/or depression. The important work can be done with the parents to restore the proper generational hierarchy and with the other siblings to repair any damage done to the child's relationship with them. These sessions can also be viewed as preventive, helping the child to come to some reasonable understanding of the parent's behavior so that undue anxiety doesn't develop in later adult relationships concerning the possibility of sexual infidelity. In witnessing the parents' becoming more honest in reckoning with the issues, the child may become more confident about his or her own prospects for an honest, trusting bond someday.

SEARCHING FOR UNDERSTANDING/ REDUCING UNCERTAINTY

Once the couple have been able to return some measure of calmness to their marital lives, they can begin to explore more carefully the question of why the sexual infidelity happened. Although this question is often raised at the beginning of therapy, these early discussions of the issue are not likely to yield much useful information. During this time of heightened emotionality and marital discord, neither husband nor wife is able to think rationally about such causative factors. As stated before, the extramaritally involved spouse wants to minimize the importance of his or her actions and, consequently, tries to deny meaning. Although some affairs may fall into the category of the accidental (Pittman, 1989), in that they simply happen without much prior thought or deeper motivation, many more do not. Moreover, even these so-called accidental affairs occur within a context of time and place that before had inhibited their formation, suggesting the need for some attention to these contextual aspects. Sometimes the involved spouse will point to weaknesses in the marriage or personal deficits in the other spouse to explain his or her actions when confronted by the enraged partner. These explanations, so quickly and defensively offered, may or may not point to real issues in need of further exploration. Finally, even though unrelenting in the initial questioning of the other spouse, the noninvolved spouse is likely to be closed-minded and unreceptive to the spouse's answers. In the beginning, the husband or wife feels that any support for the partner's explanations may seem to justify and excuse the wrongful behavior, which the spouse is not yet ready to do. Consequently, the partner's efforts to account for the extramarital behavior is apt to fall on deaf ears, frustrating them both.

In recent years, several books (Brown, 1991; Lawson, 1988; Moultrup, 1990; Pittman, 1989) have been written dealing with the issue of why extramarital sex so frequently happens. These writings underscore the importance of shared understanding to a successful resolution of the crisis, at least among clinical couples. If trust is to be restored in the marriage and loyalty ties between spouses renewed, there must be a foundation built on greater insight into the more personal meanings of the infidelity.

In his recent book on conjoint therapy, Charny (1992) introduces his own classification scheme for affairs. Here the author creatively ties together the motivational factors for the affair-er and affair-ee into a single set of dynamic concepts. For example, certain affairs point to a lack of commitment to the specialness and sacredness of marriage; a hedonistic pleasure-seeking is the prime motivation for the affair. In one such type, the affair-er believes that an affair is necessary in order to create variety in life and that boredom is inevitable in any long-term relationship; the affair-ee feels unable to provide the necessary fun and stimulation in the spouse's life and does not feel entitled to limit the spouse's enjoyment. Charny's idea of looking at the interlocking dynamics of the couple is a most interesting one.

Of special note in this literature is the work of Glass and Wright (1977, 1985, 1988, 1992), who are to be commended for their efforts to bring the normative findings of empirical research to the attention of clinicians. Their studies have expanded our knowledge of the relationship between extramarital attitudes and behavior, yielding important information as to gender differences in the justifications offered by men and women. Their findings are supportive of the conventional wisdom that men more easily separate sex and love, whereas women believe that sex and love go together—creating perpetual confusion and misunderstanding between the sexes in their different ways of interpreting their affairs.

Just as the Intersystem Model (Weeks, 1989, 1994) of therapy calls for a multilevel assessment of both intrapsychic and relational dynamics, the therapist's approach to the more specific issue of extramarital sex calls for a multilevel assessment of both individually and interpersonally oriented concepts and techniques. This model permits the sexual infidelity to be understood in its full complexity, organized here at the *individual*, the *dyadic*, and the *family system* levels of understanding. The explanatory concepts presented here are not meant to be an exhaustive list of motivating factors, but are included because of their frequent implication in extramarital sexual relations. These explanatory concepts should not be construed as mutually exclusive; more often than not, an extramarital relationship draws significance from multiple sources. Concepts from one explanatory level interact with and qualify the concepts of another level, changing the meaning of both. For example, the effect that a couple's gender-role confusion—an issue at the dyadic level—will have on the marriage will change dramatically as they move into a parental role—a life-cycle issue at the family system level.

Using this model, the therapist works diligently with the couple to reconcile their disagreement over the affair(s), to find and to create together some consensual truths (Smith, 1991) from each of their separate stories. To achieve this end, the therapist must be able to assume different positions, flexibly moving from sidelines coach to impartial negotiator to strong advocate, as the situation demands.

Individual Level

At this level of explanation, the therapist studies the situation whereby individual biological, psychodynamic, and developmental factors impinge on the marital relationship in such a way as to increase the likelihood of extramarital relations.

ADULT DEVELOPMENTAL CRISIS

Certain writers (Berman, Miller, Vines, & Lief, 1977; Vines, 1979) have incorporated the available knowledge on adult development into a theory of marital conflict. According to their thesis, adult development consists of various age-related stages interrupted by periods of transition, characterized by feelings of restlessness and the need for reevaluation of the life structure. At such times, formerly tolerable problems in the marriage are suddenly perceived as intolerable, thereby unbalancing the couple relationship in a critical way and causing more serious conflict. During these transition-phase periods, a husband or wife is prone to entering into extramarital relations or to entertaining fantasies thereof, which offer the alluring prospect of a new and different lifestyle and/or mate.

Marriages entered into during or just prior to a prolonged period of professional education and training, by at least one spouse, are especially vulnerable to this phenomenon. During much of his or her young adult life, the spouse rather single-mindedly focuses on career goals. Often, the overall quality and growth of the marital relationship have suffered in the face of career aspirations too physically and emotionally exhausting to allow for competing distractions at home. A pattern of habitual avoidance of conflict, as well as more positive forms of stimulation, evolves over time. Coincidentally, the critical point in the marriage often comes with an important event in the professional life of the spouse (for example, graduation from law school, completion of residency training), with the spouse typically in the late 20s or early 30s. With partial attainment of his/her professional goals, the husband or wife relaxes enough to begin to examine other life issues. When s/he focuses on the marital relationship once again, it seems to pale in comparison with the more challenging and tangibly rewarding work or study environment. At this point, the prospect of a new partner, often drawn from the more interesting arena of work/study, seems like the easiest remedy to a stale marriage.

When affectional ties are attenuated and there are no children to make the couple hesitate, they may move rather hastily to dissolve the marriage. In other cases, the couple will enter therapy at the behest of one spouse, still hoping that the marriage can be saved and seeking a positive resolution to the extramarital crisis. The therapist must help the couple to distinguish their longstanding problems and conflicts from the general restlessness and need for change that are a part of this transition-phase process. When their individual capacities for self-reflection are good and there are sufficient flexibility and willingness to consider change on the part of both partners, the chances of marital survival are more favorable.

Marriages growing out of an adolescent or early adult romance are similarly vulnerable to later feelings of restlessness during transition periods. The couple meet, fall in love, and make the commitment to marry prior to their having seriously dated anyone else. In certain regions of America, in rural settings almost everywhere, and in neighborhood communities with strong religious traditions, such limited relationship experience prior to betrothal is often the norm. Those reared in an urban environment and/or raised in a more secular tradition typically seek out sexual and romantic experience before attempting to choose a lifetime partner. Consequently, the couple who move from a community supportive of their early marriage to an urban, secular one will often undergo some rather dramatic shifts in their attitude toward their relationship over time. What was believed to be an acceptable life choice in the first setting may be viewed as insufficient and unduly confining in the new one. One member of the couple may bristle as s/he now confronts what seems like a lost opportunity to have lived more freely for a time.

Although some individuals are able to accept this loss with only mild regret, others view it as a serious omission in their lives. These persons may insist on no less than an actual physical separation from their spouse, even if their present affair is short-lived, to determine if they really want to remain married after all. Some spouses will agree to a trial separation, rather than insisting on an immediate resolution of the crisis, when their own sentiments are close to those of the partner. Others feel hurt and suffer a greater sense of personal rejection by their partners' yearnings. They may be in a very different place emotionally (e.g., ready to start a family or build a home together) and are unwilling to have their plans derailed by their partners' frustrating indecisiveness. Sometimes the therapist is able to achieve a compromise, permitting the spouses to hold off any final action for a limited period as they think through their options more carefully. Frequently, the spouse will choose to return home to the marital partner after only a brief episode of living apart. Having lived on his or her own for a short while, the spouse comes to realize the difference between the fantasy and the stark reality of being single, at least as it is played out during this phase of life.

Middle adulthood extends from about 40 to 60 years old. The mid-life transition (Levinson, 1978), typically reaching its peak sometime in the mid-40s, is a time of possible developmental advance as well as great threat to the self. Major issues to be dealt with during this important transition period include: (1) the aging of the body and the increased awareness of one's mortality; (2) the realignment of important relationships with friends, children, parents, and spouse; (3) an altered sense of time, now construed in terms of time left; (4) the move into a mentoring role with younger colleagues and the next generation; and (5) the integration of more feminine qualities in men and more masculine traits in women. With so much to be accomplished, this transition tends to be a tumultuous time for many individuals. When there is great turmoil, it will undoubtedly cause great disturbance in the person's marital relationship as well, and hence the frequent reference to the mid-life crisis as the bane of the good marriage.

In particular, marriages tend to be affected most dramatically by coming to terms with the aging of the body. According to Colarusso and Nemiroff (1981), there is a normative conflict between a denial of the aging process and an acceptance of the inevitable decline in youthful vigor, especially sexual vitality. This conflict can cause some persons to attempt a magical repair of their body image, including actual attempts at bodily repair (for example, dyeing hair, having plastic surgery) or a search for a new, younger sexual partner to replace the visibly aging spouse. Although not so inclined to seek out younger men, given the cultural constraints on their doing so, women may still look to an affair partner to validate their sexual attractiveness or to experience the heightened sexual excitement that such intrigue offers. Obviously, these sexual escapades can wreak havoc with marriages, considering the increased vulnerability of the spouses during this period. According to the authors, the successful working through of the crisis brought on by these adult bodily changes can eventually result in a less conflicted sexuality, permitting a continued enjoyment of, and deepening sexual intimacy with, the marital partner. In their view, the person's appreciation and valuing of longstanding relationships, as compared with the youthful gratifications of body and more casual sex, is the hallmark of the integrated, authentic self at mid-life.

PSYCHIATRIC DISTURBANCE

Sexual infidelity happens too frequently to be considered the result of emotional disturbance alone. Psychiatrists and other mental health professionals have erred in construing extramarital sexual behavior in far too limited terms. In doing so, they have failed to consider important relational dynamics of the couple and family or the embeddedness of such behavior in a sociocultural context of values.

Nevertheless, there are certain instances in which extramarital behavior seems indicative of a major psychopathological disorder in at least one spouse. Sexual acting out is a common feature of chronic alcoholism, in which a temporary loss of control and lowering of inhibitions accompany the use of alcohol. Other commonly abused drugs that can produce a similar effect include the amphetamines, the barbiturates, and cocaine. Cocaine abuse, in particular, can lead to frenzied and indiscriminate sexual behavior, putting abuser and spouse at risk for sexually transmitted disease and AIDS (see Chapter 6).

In the last decade, considerable attention has been focused on compulsive sexual behavior that resembles the substance abuse disorders in its addictive quality. In his two books dealing with this subject, Carnes (1983, 1991) describes a constellation of factors comprising the syndrome (for example, preoccupation with thoughts of sex, ritualized sexual activities, risk taking) and outlines the important elements of its treatment (for example, breaking through the person's denial, interrupting the addictive cycle, addressing the codependency of the partner). Although such an addiction can assume many different forms (for example, exhibitionism, voyeurism), a history of repeated extramarital affairs, particularly when they seem to have operated outside the person's conscious control, can point to the presence of sexual addiction.

Apart from the various substance use disorders and other addictive behaviors, extramarital sexual behavior is sometimes associated with disturbances of mood. Hoping that a new and exciting sexual partner will provide escape from a dismal emotional state, the husband or wife may begin an affair in an effort to ward off a serious depression. Less frequently, the extramarital behavior is a result of psychotic decompensation: impaired judgment may follow an acute manic episode or schizophrenic reaction. For example, the father of a respected member of the clergy was reported to have suddenly begun making sexual overtures to several parishioners, both male and female. This happened immediately before his psychiatric hospitalization with a diagnosis of bipolar disorder. Finally, adults with attention deficit disorder (ADD) (Hallowell & Ratey, 1994) may turn to outside sex as a form of intense stimulation to help them focus. When the extramarital episode occurs secondarily to a major psychiatric disorder, treatment of the person should follow accepted therapeutic practices for the primary disorder, including the use of pharmacological intervention when indicated. Steps taken to help the couple cope with the extramarital activity should be applied in conjunction with these other therapeutic measures.

In earlier decades, it was common for psychiatrists to consider sexual infidelity the result of a personality disorder or of the neurotic conflicts of one spouse. These labels were often applied indiscriminately to the point of diagnostic meaninglessness. Still, individuals with severe personality disorders frequently demonstrate little regard for their spouses' feelings in pursuing a narrow range of self-interested behavior. Moreover, hypersexuality (Goldberg, 1987), often prompting the husband or wife to seek sex elsewhere, is a common feature of certain personality disorders, namely, the sociopathic, histrionic, narcissistic, and borderline disorders. Similarly, certain individuals are unable to sustain an intimate relationship with their marital partners without triggering anxiety due to unresolved neurotic conflicts (Strean, 1980). One way of defending against this anxiety is to engage repeatedly in extramarital relations. Obviously, this behavior is seldom compatible with the stable functioning of the couple and is sure to cause additional distress for the individual and spouse.

SEXUAL ORIENTATION ISSUES

Shifts in a husband's or wife's attraction to same-sex individuals, accompanied by an increase in fantasies involving homoerotic encounters, can lead to a greater desire to act on these urges. (To be sure, a similar shift in an individual's attraction to persons of the opposite sex can jeopardize a commitment to a sexually exclusive gay or lesbian relationship.) Sometimes this change is indicative of the person's willingness to accept his or her basic homosexual orientation. Such acceptance may have come about only after years or even decades of personal struggle with sexuality. Even though there is far more tolerance of a gay or lesbian lifestyle today than a generation ago, there still exist widespread discrimination and sometimes blatant condemnation of this way of life. The fact that AIDS first made its appearance in this country in the gay male population and, to this day, is still often mistakenly thought of as a "gay man's disease" has only worsened the situation. The desire to adopt a more "normal" lifestyle, to become a parent and to live within the protective confines of a family, and, finally, to avoid the disappointment of, and the rejection by, one's parents or religious community can be quite strong. With these influences can come a denial of one's sexual preference, if not a deliberate effort to contain and to rework it into the more acceptable heterosexual orientation.

Not surprisingly, given the strong desire to be accepted, the person is frequently able to engage in sexual behaviors with the spouse over the course of several years. Sexual relations in these marriages are often described as tolerable, but not particularly pleasurable or associated with much sexual excitement. In some instances, the spouse knew of the partner's same-sex proclivities prior to their marriage. S/he may have joined the partner in the belief that such homoerotic feelings and experiences were a passing phase of adolescence—a natural part of an earlier period of sexual experimentation—that would end with the person's entering into a more mature, heterosexual relationship.

Others seem to fall into the category of true bisexuality, feeling a strong sexual attraction to, and enjoyment with, partners of both sexes. Although a vow was taken at the time of the marriage to remain sexually faithful, the desire to participate in social and sexual activities with gay or lesbian individuals may increase over the years. These shifts in feelings can challenge the original pledge of sexual fidelity. Others enter into marriage with little or no intention of ever confining their sexuality to an exclusive heterosexual orientation. Instead, they choose to live out their bisexuality in occasional homosexual liaisons that are kept secret from their spouses.

Although such shifts in sexual feelings and the desire to act on one's sexual attraction to same-sex persons can happen at any point in the marriage, an especially vulnerable time occurs as the couple's children near the age of puberty and during the remainder of their adolescent years. As the children begin to deal with emergent sexuality, the parent's own sexuality and steadfast allegiance to a heterosexual lifestyle are called into question once again. These doubts can become even more pronounced as the children prepare to leave home for the first time and as the couple reach the end of their child-rearing years. With the central reason for choosing a heterosexual lifestyle and conventional marriage now removed, one partner may seriously question the original commitment to the spouse and the future viability of the marriage. S/he will sometimes enter into a sexual liaison with a same-sex partner at this time, hoping to test the strength of the homosexual preference before making a definitive decision to leave the marriage. Depending on the outcome of this period of sexual experimentation, the person may make a renewed commitment to the marital partner or take steps to end the marriage.

Generally speaking, when the spouse has been informed of the partner's same-sex proclivities early on in the relationship, s/he can cope better with the partner's later extramarital activities. The sense of betrayal associated with the infidelity is less intense if the spouse views the partner's homoerotic leanings as less subject to personal control, and if the spouse was aware of the partner's struggle with this issue all along. Yet, even in this instance, s/he is apt to be worried when considering the implications of the spouse's extramarital behavior for their future together. Furthermore, this spouse (usually the wife) may feel more intense anxiety than usual, if not outright panic, concerning the possible transmission of the AIDS virus.

Spouses who have only recently learned of their partners' homosexual orientation, through the discovery of an extramarital relationship, are likely to be angry over their partners' earlier decision to withhold such intimate information from them. The spouse may now protest that the marriage has been a sham and that s/he would never have married the other if the confusion about sexual orientation had been brought out into the open. The spouse may have sensed that something was awry, feeling a lack of strong sexual desire from the partner, but lacked the necessary information to assess the problem accurately or to take corrective action. The person may have even blamed her- or himself for the partner's lack of sexual interest and, in the process, harbored considerable doubt about her or his sexual appeal. The spouse may now become enraged that the partner allowed such self-doubt to fester, rather than disclose the truth.

Other spouses are more understanding, even of their partners' reluctance to confide in them, and search for a way to permit the marriage to continue. The person may genuinely and deeply love the partner and the family life they have created together, even in the absence of a more fulfilling sexual relationship. Others have had their own share of sexual conflicts, apart from those of their spouse, so that their expectations for sexual fulfillment were quite limited to begin with. Some couples will consider some type of open marital arrangement, in order to accommodate a spouse's increased desire for a gay or lesbian relationship. If the sexual component of the marriage has never been a vital part of their sense of themselves as a couple, such an arrangement may seem preferable to ending their partnership. Even more so, the spouse may feel indebted to this person who agreed to marry him or her in spite of homosexual inclinations. Consequently, the spouse may experience considerable guilt over the decision to leave the marital partner to pursue a gay or lesbian lifestyle, while the partner is still adamantly opposed to a divorce.

However the couple choose to accommodate to their situation, the arrangements tend to be highly unstable, with both spouses continually revising their thinking about what are realistic compromises for them. It can take several years for these couples to work out an arrangement acceptable to both, and there are apt to be many casualties along the way. In these intensely conflicted circumstances, it is critical that the therapist not be too quick to judge what might be a suitable arrangement for the particular couple. Nor should the therapist hastily move the couple in a specific direction—toward either a renewed commitment to the marriage or a more openly gay or lesbian lifestyle—in order to satisfy his or her own need for a less ambiguous conclusion to their dilemma.

MAJOR MEDICAL ILLNESS

When one spouse has been diagnosed as having a serious physical malady, it can have an impact on the couple system that results in an extramarital affair. This behavior is more likely to happen with illnesses that first make their appearance early in the life of the couple. Sickness comes at a time when both still think of themselves as healthy and robust, catching them off guard and unprepared to deal with such grave matters. Suddenly, the afflicted spouse finds that s/he is forced to confront the specter of mortality for the first time.

In some cases, there is considerable distress accompanying the first recognition and medical diagnosis of the disease. Even if there is a complete remission of symptoms, the couple is left with continued anxiety concerning the probable course of the disease. When the anxiety is neither acknowledged nor discussed openly by the couple, there is a greater likelihood of its precipitating a marital crisis. One spouse may make a sudden move toward separation or enter into a seemingly unrelated extramarital liaison.

It is possible for either spouse to engage in extramarital activity as a diversionary tactic to escape the tensions caused by illness. Not surprisingly, the medically affected spouse can become self-centered and completely preoccupied with personal needs; furthermore, this person may become resentful of the other spouse and his or her continued vitality. Not wanting to burden the weakened spouse with less compelling needs, the well spouse will turn elsewhere for emotional consolation and physical comfort. Alternatively, the medically affected spouse may seek out an extramarital relationship in a misguided attempt to exercise some control over the disease and its impact. At such times, extramarital activity functions in the manner of a preemptive strike: fearing that the well partner will flee from the marriage, the other hastens to make the first move to leave. Marriages in which the couple's prior relationship style has been characterized by a rigid division of roles into overfunctioning and underfunctioning spouse (Kerr, 1981) are jeopardized by an illness that threatens a reversal of customary roles.

Therapy with the couple must help them to begin to examine the emotional impact on each spouse of the medical illness. This would include an exploration of the spouse's extramarital behavior in terms of its escape value from the medical trauma, when this connection seems probable. The couple must deal more directly with their fears concerning their common future, if they are to develop the necessary resources to cope with the assaultive impact of the illness. In some cases, the treatment of the disease may have required surgical procedures or other medical interventions that have been disfiguring, causing the person (and possibly the marital partner) to view him- or herself as less physically attractive. In addition, in cases in which sexual dysfunction is likely to be a prominent feature of the disorder or its treatment (e.g., diabetes, multiple sclerosis), the therapist should help the couple to identify the sexual difficulties, and to consider effective means to deal with them.

The following case is illustrative of many of the common dynamics experienced by these couples. The couple, both in their early 40s and together for 10 years, first consulted me asking for help in dealing with the husband's recent disclosure of an affair. In the first interview, they related a grueling series of events over the last five years, since the wife's initial diagnosis of ovarian cancer while still in her mid-30s. The wife spoke of the shock she experienced after the initial series of medical treatments that left her physically scarred, infertile, and prematurely menopausal, as well as almost continuously anxious when thinking about her slim chances of survival. When she had recovered sufficiently to consider resuming sexual relations, she broke into tears when confronted with continued physical discomfort and, for the first time, a complete lack of sexual desire for her husband. After a few aborted attempts at lovemaking that ended in a similarly discouraging way, they stopped trying altogether. Within the year, the husband, as could be predicted, began an affair with a colleague at work who had been an important source of emotional support through his ordeal.

Even when the medical crisis occurs later in life—at a time that seems less out of step with normal expectancies—the couple may still be caught off guard. If the prognosis is poor, including a shorter life expectancy or a marked decline in physical vitality, the partners may look back at previous decisions and commitments with added scrutiny. In marriages with little affection or deep emotional satisfaction that may have continued only for reasons of convenience, the partners may now regret the earlier decision to remain together. The spouse who is ill may be even more fearful of separation, in the face of an uncertain medical condition. Still, s/he may long for a freer and more satisfying emotional and sexual connection to some other person before it is too late. There may be a push to pursue relations with someone who is desired/admired, yet kept at a safe distance, so as not to prove fatal to the marital bond. Eventually, the spouse's affair is brought out into the open and the couple may seek therapeutic assistance to cope with it. In this instance, the therapist must help the couple to address their longstanding problems with emotional and/or sexual intimacy and their individual rigidities and reluctance to change, even in the face of the added stress and anxiety brought on by the illness.

Dyadic Level

At this level, the focus is on the spousal relationship, with its special needs and tensions, as the couple struggle with the therapist to make some sense of the affair.

INFERTILITY PROBLEMS

Infertility affects approximately 12 percent of couples. As such, it represents a special kind of medical disability, profoundly affecting the individual lives of those it touches and threatening the important needs and goals of the couple (Mahlstedt, 1985, 1987). Because its consequences are so critical to the overall functioning and quality of life of the couple, it is included in this classification as a potential factor at the dyadic level of understanding. The process of diagnosing and treating infertility tends to be an excruciatingly difficult one for most couples. It can create conflict in formerly stable marriages and exacerbate once tolerable problems to an uncomfortable level. Much of the couple's individual privacy and independence are sacrificed to the medical regime prescribed by the physician. After a while, their infertility becomes an all-consuming focus. Other important, but unrelated, needs and goals are neglected in the process. Sometimes the course of treatment can extend over several years, severely taxing even the best of marriages.

Men and women tend to cope with the stress of infertility in different ways. Husbands, more often than not, will minimize their own distress while concerning themselves with that of their partners. Wives are more likely to want to talk about the hardship of the infertility ordeal. A vicious cycle may develop. The wife complains with greater intensity in order to involve her husband. The husband, feeling powerless to alleviate his wife's unhappiness, stops listening and withdraws to a more distant position. At a time when they need each other more than ever, they are unable to offer essential comfort.

Most couples report lowered levels of sexual satisfaction during this time. An act that once gave pleasure becomes associated with the pain of infertility. Moreover, the failure to conceive threatens one's sexual identity, since producing a child is regarded as the natural outcome of a healthy sex life. The medical workups to which the couple must submit are invasive and demand performance. Treatment frequently requires the couple to have sexual intercourse on schedule, making it a mechanical exercise to be performed whether or not there is desire. In addition, physical discomfort resulting from surgery can interfere with sexual enjoyment. The problems surrounding infertility can lead to serious sexual dysfunction in either partner, which in turn can cause additional problems for the couple and interrupt the medical treatment routine.

Given such a difficult emotional and sexual climate, that either spouse should seek refuge elsewhere seems almost expected. An affair can provide a refreshing experience, free of the debilitating issues around infertility. An element of spontaneity and pleasure can once again enter into the experience of sex. At a deeper, unconscious level, the spouse may also hope that this liaison with the outside partner will confirm his or her fertility. I have worked with two couples after the supposedly infertile wives had become pregnant in the course of an affair. In both cases, the affair was preceded by a prolonged period of failing to conceive with the spouse. In another instance, the husband of the infertile couple went so far as to speak of his fantasy of impregnating his girlfriend, who was then supposed to give up the baby to him and his wife to rear. The unlikely prospect of this really happening did not deter this line of thinking. After almost 10 years of grappling unsatisfactorily with infertility problems, it seemed a fittingly absurd resolution to their unfortunate predicament.

The emotional impact of the affair on the couple, once known, can be quite traumatic. The extramarital crisis comes at a time when their emotional resources are badly depleted and their viability as a normal couple is called into serious question. Additionally, abandonment fears, which are quite common among infertile couples, are aggravated by the fact of the affair. In working with couples in such precarious circumstances, the therapist must take special care to manage the heightened tensions during the crisis. The feelings of loss and betrayal are expected to be even more intense than usual. Moreover, just because the couple have been so thoroughly probed and examined with regard to the medical aspects of their infertility, the therapist should not assume that they have received professional assistance with the emotional components of the problem. Such assistance, although becoming more common, is still seldom offered to infertile couples. Consequently, the therapist must help the couple begin to explore the problem of coping with infertility apart from the more immediate issue of dealing with the extramarital crisis. Most couples will fail to make a connection between the two areas of difficulties. Therefore, the therapist should proceed cautiously in suggesting the possibility of such a link. With time, the therapist may be able gradually to move the couple beyond the current extramarital crisis to work more directly with the infertility problem.

TRIANGLE OF LOVE

Sternberg (1986, 1987) has put forth a tripartite theory of love, which explores the specific nature of love and its various forms in different relationships:

> According to the theory, love has three components: (a) *intimacy*, which encompasses the feelings of closeness, connectedness, and bondedness one experiences in loving relationships; (b) *passion*, which encompasses the drives that lead to romance, physical attraction, and sexual consummation; and (c) *decision/commitment*, which encompasses, in the short term, the decision that one loves another, and in the long term, the commitment to maintain that love.
>
> In general, the intimacy component might be viewed as largely, but not exclusively, deriving from emotional investment in the relationship; the passion component as deriving largely, although not exclusively, from motivational involvement in the relationship; and the decision/commitment component as deriving largely, although not exclusively, from cognitive decision in and commitment to the relationship. From one point of view, the intimacy component might be viewed as a "warm" one, the passion component as a "hot" one, and the decision/commitment component as a "cold" one. (Sternberg, 1986, p. 119)

The three components of love have somewhat different properties. The intimacy and decision/commitment components appear to be relatively stable in close relationships, whereas the passion component tends to be unstable—waxing and waning in an unpredictable way. Similarly, one has some measure of control over the feelings involved in the intimacy component and even more over those associated with the decision/commitment component; however, the drives and motivational states that compose the passion component function largely outside one's conscious control. In addition, the three components are weighted differently in short-term and long-term relationships. In the short-term variety, the passion component is in the ascendancy, while the intimacy component is only moderately operative, and the decision/commitment component is hardly in evidence at all. In long-term relationships, the intimacy and decision/commitment components tend to predominate, with the passion component playing a lesser role and declining over time.

According to Sternberg, the amount of love one experiences depends on the absolute strengths of the three components, whereas the kind of love one experiences depends on their relative strengths. In general, one is likely to experience greater relationship satisfaction when the ideal for that relationship corresponds more closely to the actual relationship in terms of the absolute and relative weights of the three components. Likewise, the greater the discordance between parties as to the preferred balance of the components, the greater will be the relationship disharmony.

When one partner desires a greater degree of involvement of the passion and/or intimacy component, s/he may attempt to satisfy this desire through an extramarital relationship. When the outside involvement consists of passionate arousal alone, one is in a state of infatuated love. When the connection between lovers goes beyond physical attraction and arousal to include an emotional bond, romantic love is the outcome. Unless there is considerable commitment to the outside partner and that relationship in a way that competes with and threatens the commitment to the marital partner, these love relationships need not undermine the long-term viability of the marriage. Indeed, the extramarital relationship may even have a stabilizing influence on the marriage, lessening tensions that might otherwise develop at the emotional and arousal levels of involvement. For example, some couples cannot feel an emotional connection without becoming fused, the spouses in these marriages lacking a basic sense of personal boundaries and independence of self. These couples tend to retreat from shared intimacy, because of the threat to their experience of themselves as separate, autonomous beings. At other moments, the spouses may assume opposing positions—with one spouse actively pursuing closeness and the other maintaining distance—in an elaborate and ever changing intimacy dance.

An affair serves as a mechanism for increasing the emotional distance between the two spouses as one spouse becomes involved with a third party. Although a fairly common vehicle for regulating the emotional distance–closeness in the marriage, and sometimes useful as such, an affair has the potential to cause confusion and chaos. Sometimes the spouse will draw erroneous conclusions about the meaning of his or her partner's affair—assuming that the marital commitment has been jeopardized—and take steps toward divorce. Moreover, while the presence of the outside partner can act to reduce tensions in the marriage, there is little opportunity for real growth between marital partners in these tension-filled areas as long as the affair persists.

Therapeutic work with these couples should seek out the source of the marital tension. How do the husband and wife view the marital relationship in terms of the relative balance of the three love components? How has the balance shifted over time? What is the most desirable balance according to each spouse? Does the perceived lack in the marital relationship involve the intimacy and/or passion components? How do the spouses think of and define intimacy? And, finally, is there agreement in their preferred styles of intimacy?

Once the nature of the dissatisfaction has been clarified, the therapist can begin to work with the couple to remedy the problem. In this regard, the work of Schaefer and Olson (1981) is of value in expanding our conceptions of intimacy, in distinguishing different domains of intimate sharing (e.g., emotional, social, intellectual, sexual, and recreational). Couples are likely to feel more compatible when they are similar in their needs for certain degrees and kinds of intimacy. The self-report instrument developed by Schaefer and Olson, the Personal Assessment of Intimacy in Relationships (PAIR), can be used clinically to help couples gain a more objective understanding of their differences. The questionnaire takes into account both how the spouses perceive the relationship now and how they would like it to be, promoting self-disclosure and open discussion of these important issues in the therapy sessions.

In addition, steps taken to introduce variation and novelty into their routinized lives together are called for when one spouse complains of a lack of passion in the marriage. The suggestions of those working in the area of marital and sexual enrichment (Hof & Miller, 1981; L'Abate & Weinstein, 1987; Stuart, 1980; Treat, 1987; Weeks & Treat, 1992) are especially useful. Although the couple cannot expect to achieve the same kind of passionate arousal associated with falling in love in marriages of several years, much can be done to enliven their shared experience.

GENDER-ROLE CONFLICT AND CONFUSION

Sexual attraction, as it flows back and forth between husband and wife, is inextricably tied to the issue of gender role, which exerts an influence largely outside the couple's conscious awareness. According to Rubin

(1983), our earliest developmental experiences within the family lay the foundation for our gender roles, and our cultural commandments about masculinity and femininity support and reinforce these early experiences. Traditionally, the developmental tasks confronting a boy and a girl have been quite different, resulting in quite different core personality structures for each. Still, Rubin argues, these different developmental tasks, and the psychological differences that follow from them, are not inherent in human nature; instead, they are the product of a social world. Consequently, psyche and society form a reciprocal relationship, interacting in a complex and dynamic way to form our gender roles.

We live in a time of radical change in the way men and women are asked to conduct themselves and their relationships: new roles and new rules of behavior are the norm in today's world. Many of these recent changes in family life are the result of complicated social forces, including a changing economy and shifting demographics, which have produced the burgeoning numbers of women now in our work force. With radical change comes insecurity in our personal lives and relationships, and contradictions within and between our ideals and behavior confront us everywhere. To quote Rubin (1983), "Thus it is that some people will speak words of change without living it, and others will live in changed ways without acknowledging it" (p. 214). Where economic need is the prime motivation for change, as is the case in working-class families and, increasingly, in middle-class families, consciousness and attitudinal change tend to trail behind behavioral change. Where ideology creates the desire for change, as often occurs in upper-middle-class and professional families, behavioral change tends to fall behind important shifts in beliefs and attitudes.

Nowhere is this more evident than in the increasingly common dual-career marriage, where the role prescriptions for husband and wife permit much more latitude than in a conventional type of marriage. A marriage of two professionals can be mutually advantageous. Such a marriage can provide opportunities for sharing ideas, offer support and encouragement, and promote economic gain. There are, however, also elements of strain associated with this way of life. When partners are highly competitive with each other, the success of one spouse may trigger reactions of envy, depression, or antagonism in the other. These reactions are usually more intense and more disruptive to the marital relationship when it is the wife who has attained greater professional stature. The contractual theory of Sager (1976) can shed some light on this frequently encountered phenomenon among dual-career couples. Central to his thinking is the notion that each partner brings to the marriage an unwritten contract consisting of a set of expectations and promises, both conscious and unconscious. At a conscious level, each spouse may openly encourage the other's professional growth. Yet, one or both may harbor unconscious contractual expectations that demand more traditional role relations, harkening back to one's childhood experience and the marriage of one's parents. This conflict at the conscious and unconscious levels of the contract can produce inconsistent behavior and cause misunderstanding.

When couples meet and become involved during the period of their academic and professional training, there is likely to be a more radical shift in the balance of power between them as they begin to launch their careers. Sexual attraction is an elusive quality, quite sensitive to these shifts in power between spouses. On several occasions, I have treated couples with inhibited sexual desire on the part of one or both spouses that seemed to follow a change in their relative status: one spouse begins to earn substantially more than the other or becomes the first to receive academic tenure. While they are adjusting to this change, they each may begin to feel anxious, fearful, and ill at ease in the presence of the other. Without thinking much about it, one spouse may begin to spend more time and to speak more freely with someone other than the spouse. Feeling more comfortable in the company of this other person, the spouse can become drawn to this individual in a way that increases the risk of an extramarital affair.

There is also a dramatic rise in the demands on the dual-career couple, and on the two-income couple, more generally, with the arrival of the first child. Both spouses are apt to feel consumed with work both inside and outside the home, with very little time remaining for leisure activities. Few are prepared to make the difficult compromises required on both domestic and work fronts in order to juggle multiple roles. Understandably enough, the marital relationship is likely to suffer under the strain. Both partners feel depleted of the necessary emotional and physical reserves that might permit them to give freely to each other. Sexual difficulties in the form of a lack of interest in sex are especially common during this time. Again, this can lead one spouse to begin an extramarital relationship, responding to the loss of emotional and physical intimacy in the marriage and hoping to discover a simpler, more pleasure-oriented bond once more. Indeed, this can happen notwithstanding the time and energy that such an endeavor would seem to require!

Certain other events can produce major power imbalances in the marriage and can strain the couple's ability to accommodate to these changes in gender-role expectations. An unexpected job loss—through firing, lay-off, or the down-sizing of a company—seriously jeopardizes the financial well-being of the family. The impact on the couple is apt to be quite different if it is the husband, rather than the wife, who is unable to work. This difference cannot be explained solely by the fact that men, on average, still earn substantially more income than women, so that the financial impact on the family of his unemployment will be greater. Even today, unemployment for the man is regarded as more personally disabling, as a more serious blow to self-esteem. For both husband and wife, it is viewed as a serious gender-role failure, an interruption of his "breadwinner" function. Even when the decline and eventual end to productive work is voluntary, as in the case of planned retirement, the loss of personal gratification that comes with productive and fulfilling work can be devastating for some men. At the same time, they may experience a loss of respect from their wives, who regard their constant presence at home as a nuisance and disruptive to their own endeavors. It is not difficult to understand why some men might begin an extramarital affair as an ego-bolstering maneuver at this stage of their lives.

Family System Level

At this level, our attention shifts to the larger family system, to the more specific nuclear family unit at any given moment and to the evolution of the extended kinship system cross-generationally. Here, the meaning of the affair becomes embedded in an intricate and increasingly complex web of family relationships.

FAMILY LIFE CYCLE

In the late 1960s, stress researchers (Holmes & Rahe, 1967) first became aware of certain difficulties in adaptation brought on with the entry or departure of family members into or from the system. They soon realized that they were dealing with normal, expectable, life-stage crises—a crisis of accession when a new member joined the family, and a crisis of dismemberment when a member was lost to, or departed from, the group. Family structures are under pressure to change at these transition points and there is no avoiding the inevitable stress and disruption that herald the eventual transformation of the system. Just as symptoms in one or more family members tend to cluster around these nodal points in the family life cycle, so does the occurrence of extramarital behavior by either spouse. Its presence indicates that the couple/family is having difficulty negotiating change at these critical points.

Becoming a parent can influence the couple's sexual attitudes and practices, as well as the more general balance of emotional closeness and distance between them (Bradt, 1989). Even before the birth of the child, the couple must contend with the fact of the wife's pregnancy, which not only distorts the physical form of her body in quite dramatic ways, but also causes hormonal changes that affect her sexual interest and appetite. Apart from these anatomical and physical alterations, the husband and wife bring their own emotional reactivity to the situation. Men often report considerable change in their erotic feelings toward their wives, who are now experienced as ''mothers'' in the full symbolic sense of that word. Women are especially sensitive to their physical appeal during pregnancy; a concern with disfigurement can diminish sexual interest considerably. For couples who are emotionally fused, the birth of the child can be quite threatening. Typically, the infant forms a close, emotional bond with one parent, usually the mother, and the other parent occupies a more distant, outside position. The traditional separation of parenting functions along gender lines portrays the ''good father'' acting as a good provider in economic terms and the ''good mother'' forming an intense, exclusive bond with the infant. Although this division of roles is no longer so strictly prescribed—coparenting by both sexes is the ideal today, at least among middle-class couples—it does continue to exist. Extramarital liaisons on the part of either spouse become more likely at this time, as each reacts to the change in the balance of closeness and distance between them.

A particularly critical period for most families occurs with the first departure of young-adult children from the parental home, the so-called launching stage (McCullough & Rutenberg, 1989) of the family life cycle. Some parents are able to view this time as one of fruition and completion, one that will afford them an opportunity to explore new roles. For others, it is associated with feelings of emptiness and loss, leading to a further disruption of existing family ties. One response to the emotional vacuum in the family might be to pursue an extramarital relationship. This is more likely to occur when the departing child has occupied an important position in the balance of the parents' marriage or has maintained close affectional ties with either parent.

There is often a need to reinvest in the marriage and to challenge some of the basic tenets of the role relationship between husband and wife at this time. Women, according to our cultural myths, are expected to undergo a profound and lasting change in personality as the children leave home. Phrases such as the "empty nest syndrome" warn us of the dangers of this life-cycle transition for mothers. On the positive side, women frequently respond to the demand to let go of children by turning to more self-oriented endeavors (e.g., returning to school or starting a new job or business). Men, more often than not, are left to themselves to cope with the loss, which in our culture is typically minimized for fathers. Still, the almost overnight departure of a beloved daughter can leave a painful void in the father's life. Rather hastily, the father may attempt to fill this void by entering into an extramarital relationship with a much younger woman. Such behavior at this time is understandable, given that men often overly sexualize their emotional experiences. Yet, we often misread this phenomenon, which is commonly viewed as a problem with the aging process, in a way that limits our vision and fails to take into account the system imbalance as it relates to the affair.

At the same time that they are adjusting to the departure of their grown children, the middle generation must contend with the changing relationship to their own parents (see Chapter 8). A number of changes can be expected from this older generation, including retirement, physical disability, increased dependency, and eventual death. Sometimes the middle generation must serve as caretakers for their parents. This may require a parent to move into an adult child's home or the child to make frequent trips to the aging parent's home. This can further upset the already tenuous balance in the couple/family system, making it more vulnerable to the possibility of extramarital relations by either spouse.

DEATH IN THE FAMILY

Death is one kind of life-cycle event that has the potential power to cause enormous upheaval. Several factors combine to determine the degree of upset to the larger family system (Brown, 1989), including the following: (1) the timing of the death, (2) the type and specific nature of the death, (3) the openness of the family system, and (4) the importance of the dying member to the family group. A death that occurs out of phase with the normative course of the family life cycle is, generally speaking, more disruptive. When the death occurs unexpectedly, the family typically reacts with shock. There is no time to achieve a better resolution of relationship difficulties or to say final good-byes. The openness of a relationship system refers to the degree to which persons are able to communicate freely to each other their thoughts, feelings, and fantasies. It is contingent on the ability of the person to remain nonreactive to the emotionality of others in the system. Still, not all deaths are equally important to the family as a whole. A family member's significance must be understood in terms of his or her functional and emotional role in the group.

Bowen (1976) first described the *emotional shock wave* as "a network of underground 'after shocks' of serious life events that can occur anywhere in the extended family system in the months or years following serious emotional events in a family" (p. 339). Such a shock wave typically happens after the death or threatened death of an important family member. It operates on an underground level, reflecting an underlying emotional dependence among family members that is denied by all. Symptoms of a shock wave can be emotional, physical, or social— and can affect any member throughout the family system. An extramarital liaison, especially when it occurs for the first time in a marriage, is one common symptom. Family members tend to deny any connection between symptoms and the death that preceded them. Bowen ascribed this to the human tendency to deny emotional dependence, especially when the degree of interdependence is considerable.

Certain deaths are likely to be followed by a shock wave, whereas others are more emotionally neutral and can be handled through the usual grief and mourning. The death of a parent when the children are young is especially traumatic, interfering with the important parental functions of breadwinner and nurturing caretaker at a critical stage in the life cycle. The death of a child can upset the family equilibrium for years. The impact of the child's death on the marital relationship, in particular, can be devastating, with separation and divorce estimated to be high in such cases. The death of a grandparent who has functioned as the head of the clan can generate a series of underground disturbances.

Families seldom enter treatment in response to an earlier death. More commonly, the couple will seek therapeutic help in dealing with an extramarital affair that only much later is understood to be a part of the emotional-shock-wave phenomenon. The couple will fail to make any connection between the current extramarital crisis and the earlier death, which may not even be mentioned. And unless the therapist is in the habit of doing a genogram or life-event chronology as part of the routine assessment of the couple or family, this critical event is likely to go unnoticed. Once it is brought out, the therapist must proceed cautiously in suggesting a possible connection between the events. The hope is to achieve a gradual opening up of the family emotional system. If the issue is pushed too soon, it may only increase resistance and jeopardize the therapeutic relationship.

ANXIETY-BASED CONCERNS ABOUT MARITAL SURVIVAL

Several important figures in the family therapy field (e.g., Bowen, Framo, and Boszormenyi-Nagy) have adopted a more historically oriented approach to their subject. Central to their thinking is the study of the process by which symptoms are passed from one generation to the next in families. Bowen (1978) described the process by which anxiety in the family group tends to cluster around a particular person or issue and be transmitted across generations. Briefly, the presence of systems-generated anxiety is broadly attributable to two variables, the level of differentiation of family members and the degree of stress in the overall family system. The kind of anxiety-binding mechanisms that a family uses will determine what type of symptom will appear and where. Over the years, Bowen and his followers (Guerin & Pendagast, 1976; McGoldrick & Gerson, 1985; Wachtel, 1982) have developed specific tools, the family genogram and life-events chronology, for gathering information along those lines. These tools have been used extensively in both research and clinical work with families. More recently, Hof and Berman (1986) have adapted the use of the family genogram to their therapeutic work with sexually dysfunctional couples in a most creative way; Berman (1993) has extended this adaptation to take into account our gender-role legacies.

Whenever the husband or the wife comes from a family in which sexual infidelity has been a problem, there is a greater likelihood that the couple will be concerned about the possibility of an affair in their own marriage. This anxiety-based concern may or may not eventuate in actual extramarital sexual behavior. Still, the couple live with a real fear of sexual infidelity. This fear undermines their basic trust and confidence in the marriage. Should an affair occur, the anxiety from the family history of infidelities will intensify and complicate their reactions. This residual anxiety can prolong the period needed for recovery or render recovery impossible. For example, a spouse may react to a single night's sexual indiscretion with a level of rage that exceeds that of those who have endured philandering behavior throughout the marriage.

Other events in the extended family history of either spouse can give rise to fears concerning the possible dissolution of the marriage. In particular, when one has experienced the earlier separation or divorce of his or her parents, there is more likely to be tension and anxiety about the possible breakup of his or her own marriage. At a time in the couple's marriage that often coincides with that of the first separation of the spouse's parents, this systems-based anxiety can escalate to dangerous levels. To defend against this anxiety, the person may engage in an extramarital affair and, in so doing, bring about his or her worst fears.

A family history of parental abandonment can have profound and lasting consequences for the adult survivor and his or her relationships. Apart from the immediate effects that a parent's desertion of the family has on the child (e.g., loss of financial and emotional resources, debilitating impact on the other parent), as s/he moves into adulthood there will undoubtedly be difficulties in establishing and maintaining an intimate and trusting bond with another individual. The lack of belief in the possibility of a trustworthy relationship may cause the person to behave in ways that actually destroy that possibility in the marriage (repeatedly lying, breaking confidences, engaging in extramarital affairs). And without the existence of a foundation for trust, should the partner become involved in an extramarital affair, the already vulnerable spouse's feelings of personal injury and victimization may be so intense that recovery is improbable.

The same kind of denial of family interdependence observed in relation to the emotional shock wave operates with respect to intergenerationally transmitted anxiety in general. Again, the therapist should proceed cautiously in exploring the possibility of cross-generational connections. The family genogram and its various adaptations are valuable tools for beginning the exploratory process—informative, yet not too threatening, if used properly. Bowen (1978; Kerr & Bowen, 1988) has elaborated elsewhere his procedures—too lengthy to be considered here—for achieving a more differentiated self in relation to the family emotional field.

INCEST AND OTHER CHILDHOOD SEXUAL TRAUMAS

Given the significant number of persons who are sexually victimized as children, the couple therapist must be prepared to recognize and to treat the sexual intimacy concerns of these adult survivors and their partners. Maltz (1988, 1991) described in detail the more common repercussions of childhood incest on the adult survivor's sexual functioning, including fear and avoidance of sexual contact, conditioned negative responses to sex, flashbacks to the earlier abuse, and mind–body dissociations. According to the author, the partners of the survivors are themselves victims of the earlier abuse, experiencing their own array of sexual symptoms and general confusion in attempting to cope with the frequently perplexing demands of the survivor. In addition, noncontact sexual experiences (i.e., being subjected to sexually explicit overtures and discussions, intrusive and emotionally overwhelming to the child) can have consequences on adult sexual functioning similar to those of more overt childhood traumas. In these circumstances, the sexual innocence of the child is destroyed, as is his or her trust in the adult family members to offer protection. When these less obviously exploitative behaviors are considered in conjunction with the more narrowly defined incestuous behaviors (estimated by Maltz [1988] to be a part of the childhood experience of one in six females and one in 10 males), the magnitude of the problem becomes alarmingly apparent.

Extramarital relations are not uncommon in the marriages of these adult survivors. Although a general disinterest and withdrawal from physical touch and sexual contact is more typical, a significant number of incest survivors engage in compulsive sexual behavior, sometimes in dangerous, high-risk situations (see Chapter 6). Such acting-out behavior on the part of the adult survivor tends to replicate the earlier traumatic experience, with its associated feelings of shame and its high emotional intensity.

For others, the decision to begin an affair is made more deliberately, following a prolonged effort, which eventually failed, to enjoy sexual relations with the marital partner. In some cases, it represents a last resort by the survivor to recapture some former sense of him- or herself as a functional sexual being. This person may even have enjoyed sex with the spouse earlier in their relationship, but lost this feeling of enjoyment as they became more seriously involved with each other. The inability successfully to integrate sexual feeling with a deepening emotional intimacy and commitment is a common and frustrating consequence of childhood sexual abuse. This fact is frequently misunderstood by the survivor and the spouse, who mistakenly view the survivor's diminished sexual pleasure as indicative of a failure of their marital relationship. Consequently, the obvious solution to the problem seems to be a new sexual partner.

At other times, it is the survivor's spouse who seeks out an extramarital relationship, longing for a feeling of sexual intimacy once more and no longer willing to settle for the sorry state of affairs at home. The husband or wife may have the tacit approval, if not the wholehearted blessing, of the survivor spouse. The survivor may feel a temporary sense of relief, no longer pressured to perform sexually and no longer riddled with guilt for continually disappointing his or her partner.

When these couples enter treatment with the problem of sexual infidelity, the betrayal of their marital vows is typically handled in one of two extreme ways. There can be an almost complete denial or minimization of the sexual betrayal, with the survivor's numbed response seeming to parallel that of the earlier way of coping with the childhood betrayal. The absence of a strong emotional response may be misconstrued by the survivor's spouse as a lack of real caring. In contrast to this flattened affect, there can also be an intensification of the usual anger and upset that surrounds such occurrences to almost unbearable levels. The survivor may even prefer to run away from the situation and the spouse, rather than face the fact of having again been betrayed.

The therapist must help the couple to understand how the present infidelity is tied to the earlier childhood trauma, when such a connection seems likely from the particular circumstances. Some survivors will have done little previous work to address the childhood sexual abuse and its aftereffects and may require some additional individual therapeutic work to heal the incest wound (Courtois, 1988). They may have shared almost no information with their spouses concerning their abusive history. Consequently, their spouses are likely to be upset with the notion of additional secrets to contend with along with the secrecy surrounding the extramarital affair. Other survivors will have much more understanding concerning the legacies of childhood sexual abuse, but still be unable to make the connection between the earlier trauma and the marital infidelity. As noted before, couples who have experienced an earlier period of more satisfactory sexual relations often have difficulty understanding how there can be delayed effects from the childhood abuse that hamper their capacity for sexual enjoyment at a much later time in their relationship.

Maltz (1988, 1991) has developed a highly effective model for treating the sexual problems of adult incest survivors and their partners that consists of a dynamic combination of incest resolution therapy, sex therapy, and couples therapy. Her model calls for the initial education of the couple concerning the dynamics of childhood sexual abuse, the modification and reduction of sexual trauma patterns carried over into the couple's sexual behavior, and, finally, their replacement with newly created sexual experiences that are satisfying to both partners. This is delicate and often painstakingly slow work, requiring the most measured response by the therapist and careful attunement to the special needs of these couples. The therapist must remain steadfastly calm in the face of the dramatic swings toward and away from the treatment goals. Such composure is needed to gain the couple's cooperation with the assigned tasks, so that the treatment can eventually move to a successful outcome.

OFFERING FORGIVENESS/ REMOVING THE OBSTACLES TO HEALING

Forgiveness is possible only after the couple have reached a consensus in their understanding of the sexual infidelity, including the important facts of the matter, the personal motivations of the participating spouse, and the emotional and relational consequences for all concerned. With such understanding comes the hope that the couple will have achieved a firmer control of this issue and of their marital life in general. With understanding comes forgiveness, and with forgiveness comes hope for the eventual healing of the couple relationship.

By now, the couple should have already discussed and reached some agreement about the important facts of the spouse's extramarital activities. Most, if not all, of the necessary details should have been disclosed, so that there is little danger of the nonparticipating spouse's being surprised and hurt once again by new revelations. Most important, the participating spouse is now fully aware of the personal injury experienced by the partner because of the critical breach of trust, having witnessed the partner's intense pain and emotional upset during this crisis. In addition, the damage to the spousal relationship, eroding the affectional ties and loyalty to the spouse in the face of continued deception, is now clearly understood. This is in stark contrast to his or her earlier stance, feeling baffled by and failing to comprehend the depth of the partner's distress, or simply feeling too ashamed and guilty to accept responsibility for his or her actions. With greater insight into the personal motivations for the sexual infidelity and into the consequences for the partner and for the marriage, the husband or wife is able to offer a more heartfelt apology to the spouse. The other spouse is able to sense the sincerity—or its lack—in the partner's apology, evoking a corresponding willingness—or unwillingness—to grant forgiveness.

Forgiveness also demands that both spouses will have gained a fuller understanding of the complex meanings of the sexual infidelity as related to their individual selves and its place in the couple and larger family context. With such understanding, the betrayed spouse can begin to feel some compassion for the personal weakness and emotional vulnerability of the partner. The sexual betrayal can also be placed in the context of other personal injuries that the couple have, unwittingly or knowingly, inflicted on each other: the unrealistic expectations and impossible demands the couple make on the marriage at the outset, the frequent misunderstandings that result from their differences, all the unfinished business from their childhoods, and the simple stresses of life that can deplete their personal resources so that there is less to offer each other. All of these factors can damage the marital relationship, making it difficult for the couple to behave lovingly and fairly. Thus the sexual infidelity takes its place among other relational infidelities in the marriage, no longer regarded as the unpardonable sin it was felt to be in the early stages of treatment.

Of course, there are couples who are not able to put the sexual infidelity behind them so that the marriage can continue in a vital and healthy manner. Perhaps the extramarital affair—or pattern of repeated affairs—continued for too long and with too many attendant lies for the spouse to ever really trust again. In other cases, the spouse's ability to trust was obviously impaired even on entering the marriage in a way that could not tolerate such a serious breach of the vows. Some couples are unable to agree on the desirability of sexual exclusivity in the future relationship, even after protracted deliberation over the matter. Others will discover a basic incompatibility of needs and goals in the course of therapy, dividing them further. Even when reconciliation is not possible and the couple eventually choose to separate, the need for forgiveness, to whatever degree it can be given, is still there. Forgiveness will dissipate feelings of guilt and bitterness, allowing each to go on with his or her separate life.

"To forgive and forget"—or so the saying goes. This maxim joins these ideas together in our thinking. However, forgetting, which seems impossible to do anyway, is not to be encouraged, insofar as it is the remembrance of the infidelity, of the ensuing crisis, and of the process of working through the issues by both spouses that will help prevent a recurrence. Although couples who have experienced this trauma may never again feel the sense of security they felt earlier in the marriage, they need not live in a state of perpetual anxiety, waiting for the next affair to happen. For those couples who remain in treatment long enough to permit a better understanding of the reasons for the sexual infidelity, the value of an affair as a way of bypassing individual and interpersonal issues in their lives is greatly reduced. An affair is now clearly recognized as an ineffective solution to problems that are better handled in other ways that do not destroy the trust base of the marriage. Moreover, the couple should have acquired the necessary skills to address whatever problems may arise in the future with confidence. Although not forgotten, the memory of the sexual infidelity should begin to fade, there to be recalled if necessary, but no longer ever present as a disruptive and destructive force.

Nearing the end of treatment, couples will often seize upon a particular metaphor or look to some kind of ritualized experience to mark the end of the extramarital ordeal. Not infrequently, couples will want to celebrate the jealous spouse's release from the obsessive concern about the facts of the infidelity in some way. This can take the form of a ritualized destroying of the evidence, with the couple together burning or burying the earlier confiscated letters, restaurant and hotel receipts, or whatever other incriminating documents still exist. Some spouses will not be able to let go of the evidence entirely, instead choosing to hand over the materials to the therapist, so that these things are no longer there to torment them. Other couples will create a metaphor that both captures the essence of and commemorates the end to the harrowing events of this period. Such metaphors can bring some emotional distance and an element of levity to the seriousness of the situation. After several months of therapy, one couple related a humorous story of how the husband had purchased almost a dozen pairs of shoes that were a whole size smaller than his actual size during the year and a half of his affair. They could now speak of "that crazy time that he didn't even know his own shoe size" when referring to the confusion that characterized the husband's mental state, laughing a little at his disorientation. Their trip to the neighborhood thrift shop with the barely used shoes marked the husband's return to his senses.

According to Imber-Black and Roberts (1992), an important aspect of rituals is their ability to hold and to give expression to the many contradictions of our lives. Contrary to popular thought, celebrations can also contain one's loss and grief, allowing healing to occur. The use of religious rituals and traditions can be an effective part of the healing process; yet, out of shame or guilt, they are often passed over. If the therapist appreciates and respects these possibilities for healing, s/he can help those who are religiously and spiritually inclined to access this potentially helpful resource (see Chapter 1).

I witnessed one of the more poignant examples of this with a couple who, nearing the end of therapy, were planning a twentieth wedding anniversary with a religious ceremony and a reciting of their marital vows. This couple, both Italian Catholics now in their early 40s, had hastily married in a civil ceremony in their late teens when the wife became pregnant. Up until that time, the wife, who had been raised as a devout Catholic, had been actively involved in church affairs, along with the rest of her family. Because of her noticeably pregnant condition at the time of the marriage, their priest, who had known the wife since childhood, refused to perform the religious ceremony. The husband's affair, decades later, brought back the old feelings of shame and embarrassment that had marred their original marriage. As the couple worked to recover from the fairly intense upset brought on by the sexual infidelity, there was a similar reworking of the older trauma, allowing them to reach a new closure on this painful event. The couple could now feel a real legitimacy to their union that had been denied to them earlier. Through the religious ceremony marking their twentieth anniversary, the couple were able to give new meaning to both the older trauma and the newer trauma, enabling them to feel whole and connected to each other, their families, and their spiritual traditions once again.

CONCLUSION

In the beginning stages of treatment, both spouses feel extremely insecure, as they confront the devastating consequences of this serious betrayal of their marital vows. Living with the ensuing suspiciousness and lack of trust can be unbearable. The process of rebuilding trust is quite slow, interrupted by frequent setbacks, requiring enormous patience on the part of the couple and calm perseverance from their therapist. Similarly, the nonparticipating spouse can be consumed with jealous rage in the beginning, rage that infiltrates all aspects of his or her thinking and blocks out more reasonable responses to the marital crisis. Loyalty ties between the couple and other affected family members and friends cannot be restored without the combined efforts of both spouses.

Next, and perhaps most important to the eventual growth of the couple, is a search for meaning through the infidelity. As they struggle to come to terms with this painful occurrence, they may achieve a deeper understanding of themselves and their interlocking needs in the process. With understanding can come a willingness to forgive both the self and the marital partner—something impossible to even imagine earlier. Finally, with forgiveness can come a more complete healing of the marital rift, so that the couple eventually are able to put the extramarital trauma behind them. Of course, there will be couples who are unable to achieve such healing. However, even these couples need to reach some level of forgiveness, if they are to end the marriage without prolonged acrimony, residual bitterness, and continued guilt.

One thing is surely true: sexual infidelity will continue to happen with some regularity, and it is, perhaps, as natural a part of being human as is our desire to pair-bond and to form monogamous relationships. This is the provocative and intriguing proposal put forth by Helen Fisher (1992), an anthropologist, who recently wrote a book about the mating behavior of our human species. Viewed from an evolutionary perspective, extramarital sexual behavior makes good sense, with clear and ample genetic payoffs and rooted in the behavior of our primitive ancestors over our four-million-year history. Fisher's explanations of extramarital relations have an evolutionary honesty about them that makes attempts to cast such behavior in more personal and psychological terms seem like unnecessary obfuscation. Yet, just as extramarital behavior can be understood as a natural and inevitable part of being human, so is the inevitable disturbance to our relationships and our psychic well-being that accompanies this behavior. As Fisher (1992) sums up our plight:

> But the human animal seems cursed with a contradiction of spirit. We search for true love, find him or her, and settle in. Then, when the spell begins to fade, the mind begins to wander. (p. 97)

Perhaps it is this "contradiction of spirit" that we, as therapists, confront in our work with the problem of sexual infidelity, and in our efforts to find a way to help these couples recover from what, for them, remains a very personal trauma.

REFERENCES

Berman, E. (1993, November). *Questions for a gender genogram*. Paper presented at the annual Treating Couples Conference, sponsored by Marriage Council, Philadelphia, PA.

Berman, E. M., Miller, W. R., Vines, N., & Lief, H. I. (1977). The age 30 crisis and the 7-year-itch. *Journal of Sex and Marital Therapy, 3*, 197–204.

Bowen, M. (1976). Family reaction to death. In P. J. Guerin, Jr. (Ed.), *Family therapy: Theory and practice* (pp. 335– 348). New York: Gardner.

Bowen, M. (1978). *Family therapy in clinical practice*. New York: Jason Aronson.

Bradt, J. O. (1989). Becoming parents: Families with young children. In B. Carter & M. McGoldrick (Eds.), *The changing family life cycle* (2nd ed., pp. 235–254). Needham Heights, MA: Allyn & Bacon.

Brown, E. M. (1991). *Patterns of infidelity and their treatment*. New York: Brunner/Mazel.

Brown, F. H. (1989). The impact of death and serious illness on the family life cycle. In B. Carter & M. McGoldrick (Eds.), *The changing family life cycle* (2nd ed., pp. 457– 482). Needham Heights, MA: Allyn & Bacon.

Carnes, P. J. (1983). *Out of the shadows*. Minneapolis: CompCare.

Carnes, P. (1991). *Don't call it love: Recovery from sexual addiction*. New York: Bantam.

Charny, I. W. (1992). *Existential/dialectical marital therapy*. New York: Brunner/Mazel.

Colarusso, C., & Nemiroff, R. (1981). *Adult development*. New York: Plenum.

Courtois, C. (1988). *Healing the incest wound*. New York: Norton.

Covelman, K. W., & Covelman, S. (1993). Saving face: A neglected dynamic in couples and family therapy. *Family Journal, 1*, 331–336.

Fisher, H. (1992). *Anatomy of love*. New York: Norton.

Glass, S. P., & Wright, T. L. (1977). The relationship of extramarital sex, length of marriage, and sex differences on marital satisfaction and romanticism: Athanasiou's data reanalyzed. *Journal of Marriage and the Family, 39*, 691–703.

Glass, S. P., & Wright, T. L. (1985). Sex differences in type of extramarital involvement and marital dissatisfaction. *Sex Roles, 12*, 1101–1120.

Glass, S. P., & Wright, T. L. (1988). Clinical implications of research on extramarital involvement. In R. Brown & J. Field (Eds.), *Treatment of sexual problems in individual and couples therapy* (pp. 301–346). New York: PMA.

Glass, S. P., & Wright, T. L. (1992). Justifications for extramarital relationships: The association between attitudes, behaviors, and gender. *Journal of Sex Research, 29*, 361–387.

Goldberg, M. (1987). Understanding hypersexuality in men and women. In G. R. Weeks & L. Hof (Eds.), *Integrating sex and marital therapy: A clinical guide* (pp. 202–220). New York: Brunner/Mazel.

Guerin, P. J., Jr., & Pendagast, E. G. (1976). Evaluation of family system and genogram. In P. J. Guerin, Jr. (Ed.), *Family therapy: Theory and practice* (pp. 450–464). New York: Gardner.

Hallowell, E. M., & Ratey, J. J. (1994). *Driven to distraction*. New York: Pantheon.

Hof, L., & Berman, E. M. (1986). The sexual genogram. *Journal of Marital and Family Therapy*, *12*, 39–47.

Hof, L., & Miller, W. (1981). *Marriage enrichment: Philosophy, process, and program*. Bowie, MD: Brady.

Holmes, T. H., & Rahe, R. H. (1967). The social readjustment rating scale. *Journal of Psychosomatic Research*, *2*, 213–218.

Imber-Black, E., & Roberts, J. (1992). *Rituals for our times*. New York: HarperCollins.

Karpel, M. A. (1980). Family secrets. *Family Process*, *19*, 295– 306.

Karpel, M. A. (1994). *Evaluating couples*. New York: Norton.

Kerr, M. E. (1981). Family systems theory and therapy. In A. S. Gurman & D. P. Kniskern (Eds.), *Handbook of family therapy* (pp. 226–264). New York: Brunner/Mazel.

Kerr, M. E., & Bowen, M. (1988). *Family evaluation*. New York: Norton.

L'Abate, L., & Weinstein, S. E. (1987). *Structured enrichment programs for couples and families*. New York: Brunner/Mazel.

Lawson, A. (1988). *Adultery: An analysis of love and betrayal*. New York: Basic Books.

Levinson, D. J. (1978). *The seasons of a man's life*. New York: Knopf.

Mahlstedt, P. P. (1985). The psychological component of infertility. *Fertility and Sterility*, *43*, 335–346.

Mahlstedt, P. P. (1987). The crisis of infertility: An opportunity for growth. In G. R. Weeks & L. Hof (Eds.), *Integrating sex and marital therapy: A clinical guide* (pp. 121–148). New York: Brunner/Mazel.

Maltz, W. (1988). Identifying and treating the sexual repercussions of incest: A couples therapy approach. *Journal of Sex and Marital Therapy*, *14*, 116–144.

Maltz, W. (1991). *The sexual healing journey*. New York: HarperCollins.

McCullough, P., & Rutenberg, S. (1989). Launching children and moving on. In B. Carter & M. McGoldrick (Eds.), *The changing family life cycle* (2nd ed., pp. 285–309). Needham Heights, MA: Allyn & Bacon.

McGoldrick, M., & Gerson, R. (1985). *Genograms in family assessment*. New York: Norton.

Moultrup. D. J. (1990). *Husbands, wives, and lovers*. New York: Guilford.

Pittman, F. (1989). *Private lies: Infidelity and the betrayal of intimacy*. New York: Norton.

Rubin, L. B. (1983). *Intimate strangers: Men and women together*. New York: Harper & Row.

Sager, C. J. (1976). *Marriage contracts and couple therapy*. New York: Brunner/ Mazel.

Schaefer, M., & Olson, D. (1981). Assessing intimacy: The PAIR inventory. *Journal of Marital and Family Therapy*, *7*, 47–60.

Smith, T. E. (1991). Lie to me no more: Believable stories and marital affairs. *Family Process*, *30*, 215–225.

Sternberg, R. J. (1986). A triangular theory of love. *Psychological Review*, *93*, 119–135.

Sternberg, R. J. (1987). *The triangle of love: Intimacy, passion, commitment.* New York: Basic Books.

Strean, H. S. (1980). *The extramarital affair.* New York: Free Press.

Stuart, R. (1980). *Helping couples change: A social learning approach to marital therapy.* New York: Guilford.

Thompson, A. P. (1984). Extramarital sexual crisis: Common themes and therapy implications. *Journal of Sex and Marital Therapy*, *10*, 239–254.

Treat, S. R. (1987). Enhancing a couple's sexual relationship. In G. R. Weeks & L. Hof (Eds.), *Integrating sex and marital therapy: A clinical guide* (pp. 57–81). New York: Brunner/Mazel.

Vines, N. R. (1979). Adult unfolding and marital conflict. *Journal of Marital and Family Therapy*, *5*, 5–14.

Wachtel, E. F. (1982). The family psyche over three generations: The genogram revisited. *Journal of Marital and Family Therapy*, *8*, 335–343.

Weeks, G. R. (Ed.). (1989). *Treating couples: The Intersystem Model of the Marriage Council of Philadelphia.* New York: Brunner/Mazel.

Weeks, G. R. (1994). The Intersystem Model: An integrative approach to treatment. In G. R. Weeks & L. Hof (Eds.), *The marital-relationship therapy casebook: Theory and application of the Intersystem Model* (pp. 3–34). New York: Brunner/Mazel.

Weeks, G. R., & Treat, S. (1992). *Couples in treatment: Techniques and approaches for effective practice.* New York: Brunner/Mazel.

Westfall, A. (1989). Extramarital sex: The treatment of the couple. In G. R. Weeks (Ed.), *Treating couples: The Intersystem Model of the Marriage Council of Philadelphia* (pp. 163–190). New York: Brunner/Mazel.

8

MARITAL ADJUSTMENT TO LIFE CHANGES ASSOCIATED WITH AGING

Paul R. Sachs, Ph.D.

"To enter the country of age is a new experience, different from what you supposed it to be. Nobody, man or woman, knows the country until he has lived in it and has taken out his citizenship papers'' (Cowley, 1980, pp. 2–3). As Malcolm Cowley eloquently suggests, aging is foreign to people. The lack of familiarity with the nature and problems of aging is reflected in the literature on couples and couples therapy. The earlier stages of marital relationships—courtship, marriage, childbearing, and launching—have been well described in terms of characteristics of the couple at these stages and treatment interventions for problems faced during these times. Less well understood are the adjustments marital couples must make later in life.

The relative lack of attention to the older couple is due, in part, to misunderstandings about aging among professionals and the general public. In some societies, old age has been associated with vision and wisdom, and older adults have been honored accordingly (de Beauvoir, 1973). In contemporary American society, however, old age is often associated with intellectual and physical decline, and great effort is expended to deny the impact of aging (Friedan, 1993).

Psychological work with older adults may be unpopular with professionals because of the perceived difficulties that the older person presents. Garfield (1978) cites Freud as a source of the notion that the older person's rigidity makes that person less suitable for psychological treatment. Moreover, the intimate interactions with older adults that occur in psychological treatment may be threatening to professionals because engaging in such work forces them to confront their own vulnerability and mortality (Poggi & Berland, 1985; Zivian et al., 1992).

In fact, however, the older adult has assets that facilitate rather than detract from the ability to benefit from psychological intervention. The older adult's maturity and experience provide a valuable context for understanding his or her own support of the marital relationship and a circle of family and friends. They are often less pressured by the financial and time constraints of work and childbearing, allowing more time to enjoy each other's company and to reflect on life's accomplishments (Monte, 1989).

Careful attention to the needs of the older couple is important for both practical and theoretical reasons. Adults over 65 years of age constitute the largest growing segment of the United States population, and those over 85 years of age are the fastest growing segment among the aged (Geographic Profile, 1993). In 1990, older adults made up about 13 percent of the United States population, up from 11 percent in 1980 (Crispell & Frey, 1993). By 2030, it is estimated that approximately one in five Americans will be over 65 years of age (Crichton, 1987).

Given these numbers, it is clear that the psychological problems of older adults and elderly couples will be an increasingly common focus for clinicians. Effective assessment and treatment approaches for the older couple are needed now and will be in more demand in the future. Furthermore, by carefully delineating the tasks and problems of an older couple, professionals can gain a more complete developmental perspective of a couple's relationship. They may be better able to prepare younger couples for old age, perhaps preventing the psychological distress that couples often experience as they age.

In discussing the tasks faced by younger couples, a distinction has been suggested between the normative life changes that occur to families and systemic trauma as the result of "unpredictable life events" (Nichols & Everett, 1986, p. 187). For the older couple, however, this distinction may be impractical. Many changes that would be designated as traumatic for the younger couple (disease, disability, death of a partner) are normative for an older couple. This distinction underscores the need to consider life events in the context of the full life span.

Theoretically, a rationale for a special approach to older couples can be found in the work of existential psychologists who have pointed out the importance of a future orientation in psychological counseling. May (1958) states, "Personality can be understood only as we see it on a trajectory toward its future; a man can understand himself only as he projects himself forward . . . the person is always becoming, always emerging into the future" (p. 69). For those fortunate enough, the future into which they will emerge is old age. By understanding this future and the dilemmas that it presents (Vandenberg, 1991), we may arrive at a clearer understanding of the development of personality and close relationships earlier in life.

TASKS OF OLD AGE

An essential goal of old age is to achieve integrity. This achievement involves "the acceptance of one's own and only life cycle and of the people who have become significant to it as something that had to be and that, by necessity, permitted of no substitutions. It thus means a new different love of one's parents, free of the wish that they should have been different, and an acceptance of the fact that one's life is one's own responsibility" (Erikson, 1980, p. 104).

Under the rubric of integrity, Erikson discusses the importance of the reconciliation for the older person and the changed relationship with one's parents. These developmental tasks can be viewed in a marital context and in an individual context. Because many older adults have lived longer as part of a marital relationship than as unattached individuals, it could be argued that the older person's identity and life tasks are better understood in terms of the relationship with his or her partner than in terms of individual concerns. Thus, the integrity of an older person will depend on the ability to achieve reconciliation in marital life and with the chosen partner in addition to individual life.

It is proposed here that the achievement of integrity for the older couple involves several tasks: managing loss without destabilizing the relationship; identifying and transmitting a meaningful legacy; and taking responsibility for the past, present, and future of the couple's relationship. By examining how the older couple manages these tasks the clinician can develop a better understanding of the couple's situation and how best to help them. In this chapter, the couple's ability to accomplish these tasks is illustrated with respect to particular problems: retirement of one partner, the caregiving for the parent of one spouse, and caring for an impaired spouse.

PRESENTING PROBLEMS

Retirement

Earlier phases of life are characterized by various rites of passage (graduation, marriage, birth of children). Retirement is one of the only rites of passage for the adult entering old age (Rosow, 1977; Walsh, 1980). For present purposes, retirement is defined as a period of time during which the individual, who had been working full-time, shifts to less than full-time employment and derives at least part of his or her income from retirement pensions (Riker & Myers, 1990).

Retirement presents the older adult with a significant role change. Work, which had been a principal life role for decades, becomes secondary to roles in the family or community. The individual is challenged to see his or her identity as separate from job or profession. Although retirement is often viewed negatively, as a sign of one's inability to maintain full-time employment or to compete in the workplace, it may actually serve a very positive purpose of providing a structured method by which to disengage socially and vocationally (Streib & Schweider, 1971). The individual is able to save face or maintain self-respect by withdrawing from potentially difficult or embarrassing social and vocational situations. The rites of retirement serve as means of accomplishing and affirming this disengagement.

At retirement, the individual must also review his or her financial status and search for effective substitute activities to maintain physical and intellectual stimulation. In this regard, community involvement is not simply a convenient substitute for a job; the retired worker has experience and assets that may be used by community organizations.

IMPACT ON THE COUPLE

Retirement also affects the couple's identity. The couple's roles, particularly in the single earner household, are defined in large part by their responsibilities at the workplace and at home. Indeed, one of the tasks of a younger couple is to establish adequate boundaries between partners, and between the couple and others (Nichols, 1988). Work roles are a focus of, and a means of, accomplishing this boundary task.

After retirement, however, the separateness of roles is less clear. The working individual faces the loss of job, vocational role, and identity. The nonworking partner confronts the loss of independence as the result of having the other partner around more often. In the case of a dual-career couple, both partners face the identity confusion associated with retirement. Without the challenge of work activities and the circle of social contacts from the workplace, couples may feel socially isolated. They have more time together and turn to each other for more social and intellectual stimulation.

The retired worker reflects on what s/he has accomplished at work over the years. The couple seeks to understand the contributions that each partner made to the accomplishments of the working partner. The couple seeks to reconcile itself to the changes that retirement brings, seeing them as part of the course of life, accepting the decisions that were made earlier in life, and making decisions that are right for the couple now rather than living life acording to past standards. Indeed, it has been noted that, "couples who plan for the changes in their relationship prior to retirement make better and faster adjustments than those who fail to plan" (Riker & Myers, 1990, p. 91). In addition, the couple tries to communicate its legacy to a new generation. The legacy may be concrete (financial support) or psychological (guidance or values passed on to others).

Mr. and Mrs. AB, a couple in their 60s who have been married for 45 years, sought counseling for assistance with problems associated with Mr. AB's business. Mr. AB was planning his retirement. He had established and built up his own sales agency and had decided to sell it. About 20 years ago he had taken on a younger associate in the hope of training him in the operation of the agency. This younger partner became part-owner in the business. But over the years Mr. AB had become disappointed in his partner. The younger man had shown less enthusiasm and ingenuity than Mr. AB had anticipated. As a result, rather than gradually diminishing his time at work, Mr. AB found he had to spend more time to assure that the business would run properly. Reluctantly, he was thinking about selling his business to a larger firm. This decision would, in effect, end the sales company as he knew it. He wanted to pass on the company to his younger associate, but he felt that the wisest business decision would be to sell it to an established firm.

In the past year, Mrs. AB had to discontinue her work as a medical records administrator in a hospital because of a work-related injury. She had originally been encouraged by her husband to seek work after their children were raised, and she had held this position for about 20 years. She was close to retirement herself when she became disabled by her injury.

The couple's two daughters had never expressed a particular interest in the business, nor had they been encouraged to become involved in it. Mr. and Mrs. AB had planned to move, after the sale of the business, to a warmer climate. Now this move had been delayed. Currently, they felt depressed and unhappy together at a time when they thought they should be enjoying each other's company. Mr. AB had lost much sleep over his business decision. Mrs. AB was concerned about her husband's distress and was angry that he was being pulled back into work. Now she also felt uncertain about how to support her husband in his decision. In the past she had supported him in his work, respected his independence, and deferred to his decisions.

COMMENT

Mr. and Mrs. AB's situation illustrates some important themes. Both individuals were facing the loss of their jobs and the important roles and responsibilities that accompanied those jobs. For Mr. AB in particular, as the founder of his business, the loss was both tangible and symbolic. One of the difficult adjustments that Mr. AB faced was how to come to terms with his legacy, knowing that he might not be able to pass it on to a new generation.

The marital relationship appears to have been a positive, traditionally structured one in the past. Now, however, it was strained because it was expected to accomplish new tasks. The couple had more time together and now they looked to each other to make up for the losses they were experiencing as they left the workplace. Mr. AB was angry at himself for having chosen the younger partner. Mrs. AB needed to reconcile her inability to work and her limited ability to help her husband through his business dilemma.

Treatment focussed on highlighting these problems. The couple were asked to discuss what they had accomplished in their work and personal lives, emphasizing accomplishments rather than regrets. They were also asked to look toward the future in terms of what they hoped to accomplish in the next 10 years. They were able to become excited about their plans to move. They had located a retirement home and had begun to sort through their accumulated belongings in anticipation of moving.

Mr. AB thought about staying involved with business and passing on his legacy of knowledge to others. Both he and his wife were also able to express in counseling some of the positive feelings they had toward each other and how these feelings helped them accomplish things at work and as a family.

Caregiving to Parents

An adult child's responsibility for the care of an aging parent is an increasingly common and publicly discussed situation (Mace & Rabins, 1981; Stone, Cafferata, & Sangl, 1987). Brody (1985, 1990) notes that although parent caregiving is a common life task, particularly for women, it is not strictly speaking a developmental stage. The age span during which individuals have parent caregiving responsibilities is wide, ranging from childbearing years to postretirement years.

The cognitive and physical decline in one's parents creates practical problems, including managing their daily activities, safety, financial security, and decisions about institutional placement. The impaired parent may show inconsistent, demanding, or confused behavior depending on the nature of the impairment. The parents' sense of self-esteem, derived in large part from being self-sufficient, is reduced as they become the recipients of care. The adult child may need to take increasing control of important decisions in the parents' life.

The changed relationship between the parent and child and the anticipation of the end of that relationship in the death of the parent is a difficult psychological adjustment that underlies the practical difficulties of caregiving. It is common to speak of the change in the parent and child relationship in later years as a role reversal, with the adult child caring for the infantile parent. This characterization oversimplifies the parent/child relationship over time and ignores the impact that memories of the relationship have on the present and future nature of the relationship (Brody, 1990; Walsh, 1980).

IMPACT ON THE COUPLE

The strain on the couple when a parent requires care is derived from several sources. A sense of loss may be experienced by the partners, with each feeling the impact differently, based on the relationship with the parent or in-law, or based on the sex of the partners. One partner may have a closer emotional bond with the ill parent and experience the distress more intensely. The woman, customarily the parent caregiver, may have a greater burden to manage the parent or in-law, thereby taxing her physically. The spouse who is the child of the impaired parent may have the emotional burden of being custodian to a parent's legacy, in terms of managing the parent's household, and psychologically, in terms of what to retain of the parent's memory and past accomplishments.

These individual differences may strain the marital relationship because they affect the degree to which partners can understand and support each other in the caregiving situation. Other aspects of their relationship as a couple may be compromised by these responsibilities. Over the course of establishing their relationship, one task for the couple was differentiation from their families of origin (Nichols, 1988). Parent caregiving involves, to varying degrees, a reversal of this differentiation. The balance that the couple was able to establish by its separation from parents is disrupted by the new situation, which brings the couple into closer contact with them. It can be particularly stressful if the aging parent must move into an adult child's household.

Mr. CD is a 64-year-old man, the middle of three sons. His father died suddenly and recently of a heart attack and his mother now lives alone. She has had chronic pain from arthritis that has worsened in recent years. She manages slowly and independently at home, but is dependent on assistance for mobility outside of the home.

Mr. CD has been married for 40 years and has two sons and six grandchildren; one of the sons lives nearby, the other out of town. Mr. CD's brothers are not married. He describes them as having had difficulties with drug and alcohol abuse. Although they live nearby, they have always been somewhat estranged from their parents.

In contrast, Mr. CD has always taken an active role in maintaining his relationship with his parents. As a truck driver he was on the road often, and his wife has developed a close, caring relationship with her in-laws. Mrs. CD works part-time as a store clerk and visited the parents often, providing for their daily needs and assisting in caring for the mother with her increasing physical disability. There is also a visiting nurse's aide who assists the mother with bathing and hygiene activities twice a week.

Over the past several months since his father's death, Mr. CD and his wife have experienced tension in their marital relationship and family life. They have reported increased arguments and less enjoyable time with each other including reduced sexual intimacy. The focus of much of this tension appears to be the caregiving situation with the mother.

Since the father's death, Mr. and Mrs. CD feel that the mother has become more demanding and unreasonable. Though she has recognized physical limitations, they believe that she is not motivated to do more for herself and prefers to call them frequently to handle simple matters. Mrs. CD has felt angry and burdened by the care of her mother-in-law, yet she also acknowledges the need for this care. Mrs. CD also spends time with her own parents, who live independently, but for whom she provides assistance with shopping, particularly during the winter. She would like Mr. CD to do more for his mother or to consider placing her in a nursing care facility.

Mr. CD is obligated by his work responsibilities. He feels he has already taken off much time from work because of his mother's needs and is fearful that taking more time would jeopardize his job security and the benefits that accompany it. He is very close to retirement and would prefer not to retire early because this would affect the pension he is qualified to receive. He is, however, reluctant to agree to place his mother in a nursing home. The task of moving his mother from the home she and his father have lived in for many years is overwhelming to him. His mother does not want to move, and he feels that such a placement would represent an abandonment of his mother.

In addition to his concerns and frustrations about his mother's behavior, Mr. CD has also expressed grief over his father's death. He describes his father as having been more level-headed about his problems and as having tended to keep his mother's behavior in line to shield the family from the extremes of her moods. Now, without his father present, his mother's behavior has been more upsetting for him and his wife.

COMMENT

Mr. and Mrs. CD's ability to handle their own relationship, its responsibilities and enjoyable times, is limited by the caregiving they are providing. Though they agree on the need for caregiving, they are differentially affected by the task based on the nature of their relationship with the mother and their availability to provide care.

In treatment, the couple ventilated their feelings of frustration about their losses and the difficult decisions they faced. Mr. CD spoke of his father and his previously more amicable relationship with his mother; Mrs. CD spoke of her prior relationship with her mother-in-law and of her time with her husband. Specific behavioral suggestions were given to them regarding how to handle the mother's demanding behavior and setting up schedules that would give Mrs. CD in particular greater freedom and flexibility.

Mr. and Mrs. CD were also encouraged to include the two sons and their families in the care of the mother. The couple stated that they shielded their children from the problem because the sons had families of their own. With further discussion it was revealed that both Mr. and Mrs. CD had too often felt pulled into their own parents' problems in the past and had been resentful of this. As a result, they tried to avoid this problem with their own children. The sons were included in a treatment session and a plan that included the sons in the care of the mother/ grandmother was worked out.

Mr. CD also discussed at length his difficulties about deciding to move his mother to a nursing home. He had many memories of his parents' house and did not feel ready to go through all of his father's memorabilia. He feared that pushing his mother to do so would only upset her more. With time, he was able to approach this task more readily. His wife was able to express support rather than frustration when she saw that he was making steps toward a decision.

Treating adult couples in their reactions to an impaired older adult presents the therapist with a real-life opportunity to incorporate family-of-origin therapeutic work (Framo, 1981). The needs of the impaired older parent bring the adult couples into direct contact with the parent on a regular basis. Past difficulties in the parent-child relationship can intensify through this contact, but likewise it can present an opportunity for therapeutic resolution of these problems.

Impairment of One Partner

Marriage is a commitment expected to endure through both sickness and health. However, the illness or disability of one partner can put a tremendous strain on that commitment.

Couples usually wish to die together. This preference is related in part to the desire not to suffer oneself nor to see the partner suffer. The person does not wish to be a burden to the partner and does not want to be left alone. Men and women may differ in their concerns, given that both are aware that women are more likely than men to experience the death of a spouse.

Older adults are generally more aware of illness and disability than younger adults. Most have experienced the deaths of close family members and the illness or impairment of themselves or close family and friends by the time they reach old age. The impairment of a marital partner represents a loss. The person's behaviors or capabilities change.

In the case of illness, the change may be sudden. Greater awareness, however, does not necessarily translate into a smooth adjustment.

IMPACT ON THE COUPLE

The impairment of one or both partners in a relationship requires a transfer of dependence on to each other and other family members, resulting in a drastic shift in the balance of power in the family. Reduced physical and cognitive capacities in the person may result in a decreased ability to comment on problems in the relationship or to leave the stressful situation (Herr & Weakland, 1979). The couple must manage to salvage something from their relationship and mourn the loss of what they are unable to accomplish or attain.

One's accomplishments in life encompass physical and cognitive achievements. The older person with an impairment may not be capable of telling others about him or herself, which puts the partner in a position of having to keep the legacy of the other person alive. This task is complex, involving decisions about what and what not to retain about that person's past.

The older couple must reconcile their past relationship with their current relationship. Because the impaired person's medical status may change, a longer view of the relationship may be necessary—that is, one that recognizes that the couple could not face the challenges of the present were it not for what they built together in the past. Reconciliation also involves the acceptance of new ways of interacting, of changes in power and control, in values, and in communication style, as well as of the new roles for the children who assist in care of the impaired spouse.

Mrs. EF is a 68-year-old woman, married for 45 years. Her husband, age 70, fractured a hip in a fall, which resulted in a hospital and rehabilitation center stay of about three weeks. He returned home able to walk with a cane, but he needed assistance for stairs, and handrails were put into the bathroom for support.

Prior to the fall, Mr. and Mrs. EF had been well with no history of any severe medical problems. They had been working part-time in their youngest son's business, though they had thought about retiring and moving south where many of their siblings lived. Mr. EF was an active man with many interests. The couple had a wide social circle and were involved in a number of community organizations. They had three children, and the youngest son lived with them and actively helped his father.

Since Mr. EF's fall, he had become more cautious about moving about. Correspondingly, Mrs. EF had become more solicitous of her husband. Not only would she help him up and down the stairs, she would also fetch things for him. She would wake up in the middle of the night to assist him going to the bathroom, despite being advised by the physical therapist that these activities were within his capabilities.

Mrs. EF had cut back on her work and many of her community and social activities because she wanted to be home with her husband. She would go out for brief periods when she knew that her son was at home. The son had become resentful of this arrangement. Although he was willing to help his parents, he also felt a responsibility for managing the business and believed his mother was insensitive to his needs in this area. The physical therapist had suggested the couple see a psychotherapist for help with their relationship and how they handled Mr. EF's condition.

Mrs. EF acknowledged that the change in routine was a burden to her, but she stated that she was fearful that Mr. EF would fall again. She believed that her feelings of regret would be so overwhelming if he fell again, and she could have prevented it, that it was worth inconveniencing herself to help him. She also admitted, however, that her relationship with her husband had become dissatisfying despite her feelings of obligation to him.

Mr. EF had appeared to become more passive in the relationship. He readily accepted the assistance given to him and had become less active in his home exercise program. He had also lost interest in many activities and spoke about how he wished he had more time to spend with his wife. At the same time, he became tearful when stating that he felt he had become a burden to her.

COMMENT

Both Mr. and Mrs. EF were upset about the loss they had experienced. Perhaps more important than Mr. EF's loss of physical mobility and independence was the couple's loss of security. Mrs. EF's concern about her husband's stability when walking had an existential quality to it, reflecting her anxiety that she might lose him and lose the balance in her life. Mr. EF, his limitations and vulnerability exposed to him by his injury, appeared reluctant to reenter work and social situations, and to face the challenges that would accompany such reentry.

Treatment for the couple focused on helping them to identify and talk about their anxiety. This discussion often led them to reflect on how they felt about being old, a state that they never seemed to feel before because of their active life. In addition, treatment focused on concrete goals of Mrs. EF pulling back from her involvement with Mr.

EF and, simultaneously, encouraging him to make less overt and indirect demands on her for assistance. The couple were focused on how Mr. EF's independence could not be facilitated without a complementary change in Mrs. EF. The couple were also encouraged to spend more time together in positive interactions not concerned with a caregiving situation.

In this case, as compared to that of Mr. and Mrs. CD, it was felt that the son should be less involved in the couple's interactions. By relying on her son to be available when she was not, Mrs. EF avoided, or was rescued from, facing her own feelings about her limitations and her husband's capabilities. Therefore, in one treatment session that included the son, it was agreed that he would be available to the parents on a set schedule. At other times, Mr. and Mrs. EF would have to make other arrangements for caring for Mr. EF or take the chance that Mr. EF could manage on his own.

TREATMENT CONSIDERATIONS

General Goals

The overall goal of treatment with the older couple is to facilitate their ability to master the tasks of aging described earlier. Within this framework, four general goals have been identified with respect to treatment with older adults in general (cf. also Kuypers & Bengston, 1983). They can be modified for use with older couples specifically.

1. *Creating a feeling of mastery and control.* Changes with age may occur from within the person, in terms of capabilities, or from outside the person, in the form of environmental stressors (Lieberman & Tobin, 1983). Older adults often feel a loss of control in response to such changes along with a sense of vulnerability or helplessness. Psychological treatment will be beneficial insofar as it is able to help a person create or recognize a feeling of mastery and control. This feeling is not necessarily created through an improvement in cognitive or physical capabilities, or environmental circumstances. Rather, it develops through a realistic appraisal of the environment and one's capabilities and limitations. The individual can then distinguish between what s/he can accomplish and what s/he cannot. For example, Mrs. CD was able to avoid frustration by ignoring some of her mother-in-law's demanding behaviors and to gain control by interacting with her in more selective ways, taking more time for herself, and getting others to assist her in caregiving.

For the older couple, mastery may be found in their ability to manage roles, to make choices in their activities, to support each other, and to have spheres of activity in which they feel satisfaction and accomplishment. For example, Mr. and Mrs. CD developed more mastery as a couple of the caregiving situation by learning some methods of managing the mother's behavior and by taking proactive, rather than reactive, roles in planning for their own life activities as well as the mother's long-term living situation.

2. *Reduce dependency.* As noted earlier, the older person's self-esteem is closely tied to self-sufficiency. When the person becomes dependent on others, feelings of insecurity and loss of control may be experienced. Increasing the person's feeling of independence or confidence will improve emotional status.

The efforts to reduce one partner's feelings of dependency must be considered differently in the context of the couple. A healthy couple relationship is based on power shared through complementary roles and responsibilities (Beavers, 1985). Reducing one partner's dependency will be a positive outcome for the couple only if the other partner is able to accept and manage this change. Therefore, it may be more accurate to speak about helping the couple to manage their interdependence in a balanced manner.

3. *Reduce negative labeling.* Since many prevailing images of the elderly are negative, older people often incorporate these attitudes into a negative view of themselves. Thus, Mr. AB was critical of himself for seeming to have missed his goals in work and having to retire. Psychological treatment should promote the recognition and avoidance of these negative self-images and labels.

For the couple, negative images are reflected in the tendency for partners to blame each other, particularly for behaviors that are associated with aging, such as slowness or memory loss. Rather than seeing difficulties as resulting from troubled marital interaction, one partner may blame the other, and the other may accept the role of scapegoat. These couples may present to treatment with one partner identified as the problem, and with the stated goal of resolving this problem in isolation, in order to set the marriage straight again. Treatment goals, therefore, are to help the couple to recognize this labeling and blaming, and to appreciate each partner's contribution to the couple's functioning.

4. *Maintaining identity.* The changes that the older person experiences, and the feeling that life is slipping out of control, lead to an anxiety about one's identity. Rather than feeling that s/he is being transformed

into another person entirely, the person needs reassurance that his or her identity remains intact. Reviewing the past and allowing for reminiscence as a way of incorporating the past into the present and future are methods of accomplishing this goal.

The couple may be helped to recognize the connection between their individual identities and their identity as a couple. This goal may be reached by focusing on the manner in which they accomplish tasks as partners and reviewing how their partnership has led to their accomplishments. For example, Mr. and Mrs. AB were able to reflect on their individual work accomplishments and to recognize how the support of their spouse was critical to these accomplishments. With this recognition, the couple was able to focus more positively and actively on working together for postretirement life.

Specific Techniques

In addition to these general treatment goals, some specific techniques may be utilized in treatment with the older couple (Kuypers & Bengston, 1983).

1. *Clarify the distressing event.* The presenting problems of the older couple may be upsetting because they are poorly defined or because they are taken out of context. Thus, one of the goals of treatment would be to define the problems and to place them in their proper context. For example, some of the marital difficulties that occur as the result of retirement may not necessarily indicate a problem inherent in the relationship. Rather, the couple must adjust slowly, sometimes fitfully, to the retirement period. Likewise, in the case of a parent or partner with an impairment, it may be helpful to discuss with the couple what are normal, expected reactions to someone with a disability and what are reactions that indicate a more deep-seated problem.

2. *Suggest roles.* The couple will function more effectively if the partners are able to maintain stability and clarity in their roles despite the changes in roles brought on by age. Thus, the couple that has difficulty managing the increased time together after a spouse's retirement may need to work on maintaining some separation from each other by structuring separate activities in the home or community. In the case of caregiving to the spouse, it is common to feel as though the unimpaired spouse is parent to the impaired spouse. These couples may need to discuss ways in which they can relate to each other as equals despite one spouse's

limitations. Similarly, the couple may benefit from clarification of the roles of other family members who may be involved in the caregiving scenario.

3. *Mobilize external supports.* The older couple may feel isolated from the family and the community. Treatment can be beneficial to them in examining family and community resources and discussing frankly how to utilize such resources. Negative attitudes and feelings of loss of control may interfere with the older couple's ability to take advantage of the resources that exist. For example, it is common to find that one or two members of the extended family are available as supports for the couple, but have not been contacted because of fears of creating dependency or losing face. The treatment session can be a forum for discussing the costs and benefits of asking for help.

4. *Set goals.* Setting goals is important in any treatment modality. With respect to the difficulties presented by older couples, both long- and short-term goals are important. Short term goals should be designed to maximize a quick feeling of success within a period of a few months. The feeling of accomplishment derived from attaining these goals will be satisfying to the older couple.

Long-term goals may relate to practical or more existential issues. For example, a short term goal might be managing the emerging dependency of one partner on the other. The longer term issue, however, might concern how the partners feel about their vulnerability, age, and competence, and how these attitudes will affect their lifestyle.

5. *Avoid old issues, mobilize strengths.* Reminiscence is an important activity for the older couple. On the other hand, therapeutic treatment will stagnate if the couple spends too much time reviewing old issues that have been discussed at length, perhaps in previous professional settings. These issues, which represent weak spots in the relationship, can be avoided by focussing the couple on their areas of strength, where their relationship is satisfactory or exemplary, and sharing positive feelings (Beavers, 1985). Sometimes, the old problems can be redefined in terms of aging. For example, a retired spouse may be asked to reflect on the reasons behind seeking or maintaining a particular career. The goal of this discussion is not to review regrets about past career choices, but rather to see how the same goals or needs can be fulfilled now, in the present retirement circumstances. For example, Mr. and Mrs. EF revealed long-term differences about how to manage their youngest son, who was still living with them and whom they helped out in his business. These issues obviously affected the interaction between family members around

Mr. EF's injury. A focus on these issues, however, would have distracted the family from the chance to make short-term improvements in their interactions. The therapeutic focus was therefore on the dependency between Mr. and Mrs. EF.

Technical Considerations

Therapeutic focus. Beavers (1985) describes the healthy couple as functioning primarily in the present. To be sure, the couple's current problems are usually the reason for their involvement in psychological treatment in the first place. The therapist's focus with an older couple, however, must be balanced among past, present, and future.

As mentioned, reminiscence can be a valuable therapeutic activity for the older couple. The couple is also aware of the future and the anticipation of death or problems associated with older age. Rather than avoiding these issues, it is very valuable for the therapist to bring them into the discussion. In so doing, the therapist can validate the older person's ideas and demonstrate the positive impact of understanding rather than denying such fears.

Therapist's role. As noted earlier, older adults may be viewed as unsuitable for psychotherapy. The rigidity of old age may be conceived as rendering them unlikely to achieve substantive behavior changes. The older adult's cognitive style of reflecting on the past or tangential details can seem unrewarding for the professional accustomed to short-term, insight oriented treatment with a younger population.

Psychotherapeutic work with the older couple forces the professional to confront issues such as decline, deterioration, and death. There is a real possibility that at least one member of the older couple will die during the course of treatment. Moreover, psychotherapeutic work with the older adult can activate the therapist's feelings about relationships with parents and parental figures. The therapist may become emotionally distant or overinvolved with the couple in an attempt to minimize the pain of aging for the couple and the therapist.

Being aware of the obstacles to psychological treatment for the older couple is one step toward appropriate intervention with them. The therapist can benefit from reflecting on past relationships with older adults and what was positive and negative about those relationships.

Within the treatment situation, the therapist should be attuned to the role that the older couple may transfer onto the therapist. This role may be a useful tool in therapeutic work. For example, the male therapist for Mr. and Mrs. AB often felt like a son to the couple. This role allowed the therapist to form an alliance with Mr. AB in discussions about Mr. AB's disappointments with work. It was perceived that Mr. AB was able to talk more openly to the male therapist because of this perceived alliance.

FUTURE CONSIDERATIONS

Several demographic changes suggest that psychotherapeutic work with older couples may change in the future. The greater number of dual-career couples in the current workforce suggests that couples at retirement will face more complex adjustments. Both partners will be adapting to the loss of work identities and seeking to find satisfaction through other roles.

As our anticipated life span increases, more and more older people will provide caregiving to parents. The strain on the older couple caring for very old parents is different from that on younger couples. Moreover, generational changes in social values, divorces and second marriages, and living arrangements among multigenerational families may affect the feelings of obligation and connection among family members. These changes will have an impact on who should provide care and how much of a psychological burden these individuals will feel the caregiving to be.

Clinical research and treatment would be beneficial in identifying what characteristics of younger couples will facilitate their ability to manage the tasks of old age. Such information would be valuable for the development of programs aimed as prevention of some of the psychological distress that is faced by older couples.

REFERENCES

Beavers, W. R. (1985). *Successful marriage: A family system approach to couples therapy*. New York: Norton.

Brody, E. M. (1985). Parent care as a normative family stress. *The Gerontologist*, 25, 19–29.

Brody, E. M. (1990). *Women in the middle: Their parent care years*. New York: Springer.

Crichton, J. (1987). *Age care sourcebook: A resource guide for the aging and their families.* New York: Simon & Schuster.

Crispell, D., & Frey, W. H. (1993). Special report: American maturity. *American Demographics, 15*, 31–38, 40–42.

Cowley, M. (1980). *The view from 80.* New York: Viking.

de Beauvoir, S. (1973). *The coming of age.* New York: Warner.

Erikson, E. (1980). *Identity and the life cycle.* New York: Norton.

Framo, J. L. (1981). Family of origin as a therapeutic resource for adults in marital and family therapy: You can and should go home again. In R. J. Green & J. L. Framo (Eds.), *Family therapy: Major contributions* (pp. 343–373). New York: International Universities Press.

Friedan, B. (1993). *The fountain of age.* New York: Simon & Schuster.

Garfield, S. L. (1978). Research on client variables in psychotherapy. In S. L. Garfield & A. E. Bergin (Eds.), *Handbook of psychotherapy and behavior change: An empirical analysis* (2nd ed., pp. 191–232). New York: Wiley.

Geographic profile of the aged. (1993, Jan.-Mar.). *Statistical Bulletin*, pp. 2–9.

Herr, J. J., & Weakland, J. H. (1979). Communication within family systems: Growing older within and with the double bind. In P. K. Ragan (Ed.), *Aging parents* (pp. 144–153). Los Angeles: University of Southern California Press.

Kuypers, J. A., & Bengston, V. L. (1983). Toward competence in the older family. In T. H. Brubaker (Ed.), *Family relations in later life* (pp. 211–228). Beverly Hills, CA: Sage.

Lieberman, M. A., & Tobin, S. S. (1983). *The experience of old age: Stress, coping and survival.* New York: Basic Books.

Mace, N. L., & Rabins, P. V. (1981). *The 36-hour day: A family guide for persons with Alzheimer's disease, related dementing illnesses and memory loss in later life.* Baltimore: Johns Hopkins University Press.

May, R. (1958). Contributions of existential psychotherapy. In R. May, E. Angel, & H. F. Ellenberger (Eds.), *Existence: A new dimension in psychiatry and psychology* (pp. 37–91). New York: Simon & Schuster.

Monte, E. P. (1989). The relationship life-cycle. In G. R. Weeks (Ed.), *Treating couples: The Intersystem Model of the Marriage Council of Philadelphia* (pp. 287–316). New York: Brunner/Mazel.

Nichols, W. C. (1988). *Marital therapy: An integrative approach.* New York: Guilford.

Nichols, W. C, & Everett, C. A. (1986). *Systemic family therapy: An integrative approach.* New York: Guilford.

Poggi, R. G., & Berland, D. I. (1985). Therapists' reactions to the elderly. *The Gerontologist, 25*, 508–512.

Riker, H. C., & Myers, J. E. (1990). *Retirement counseling: A practical guide for action.* New York: Hemisphere.

Rosow, I. (1977). *Socialization in old age*. Berkeley: University of California Press.

Stone, R., Cafferata, G. L., & Sangl, J. (1987). Caregivers of the frail elderly: A national profile. *The Gerontologist, 27*, 616–626.

Streib, G. F., & Schweider, C. J. (1971). *Retirement in American society: Impact and process*. Ithaca, NY: Cornell University Press.

Vandenberg, B. (1991). Is epistemology enough?: An existential consideration of development. *American Psychologist, 46*, 1278–1286.

Walsh, F. (1980). The family in later life. In E. A. Carter & M. McGoldrick (Eds.), *The family life cycle: A framework for family therapy* (pp. 197–217). New York: Gardner.

Zivian, M. T., Larsen, W., Knox, V. J., Gekoski, W. L., & Hatchette, V. (1992). Psychotherapy for the elderly: Psychotherapists' preferences. *Psychotherapy, 29*, 668–674.

9

INHIBITED SEXUAL DESIRE

Gerald R. Weeks, Ph.D.

Inhibited sexual desire (ISD) is one of the most common problems with which couples present for treatment, and yet our experience has been that it is also one of the most underdiagnosed and undertreated of problems. Many therapists operate on the assumption that once the problems in the relationship have moved toward resolution and relationship satisfaction, sex will somehow improve by itself. The belief, often mistaken, is that there is a direct relationship between increased couple satisfaction and increased sexual desire. Moreover, when desire does not return, many couple therapists are ill equipped to deal with ISD because training in sex therapy for couple therapists has traditionally been weak. ISD is also a relatively recently defined disorder, and it does not respond to the usual methods of traditional sex therapy. Hence, the effective treatment of this disorder requires specialized knowledge as well as strategies, techniques, methods, and treatment.

Masters and Johnson (1970) did not recognize ISD in their classification of sexual disorders. The closest they came to identifying the disorder was in the use of the term "sexual avoidance." In 1979, Helen Singer Kaplan published a landmark text entitled *Disorders of Sexual Desire*. This book represented the first attempt to provide a comprehensive understanding of the classification, etiology, and treatment of ISD. Kaplan was also instrumental in getting this disorder included in the revised third edition of the *Diagnostic and Statistical Manual of Mental Disorders* (DSM-III-R) (American Psychiatric Association, 1987).

In DSM-IV (1994), ISD is referred to as hypoactive sexual desire (p. 496). It is defined as "persistently or recurrently deficient (or absent) sexual fantasies and desire for sexual activity. The judgment of deficiency or absence is made by the clinician, taking into account factors that affect sexual functioning, such as age and the context of the person's life" (p. 498). This diagnosis should only be made when the occurrence of the symptom is not exclusively during the course of another Axis I disorder, such as another sexual dysfunction or depression. DSM-IV also included sexual arousal disorders for both males and females, which should not be confused with hypoactive sexual desire disorder. The arousal disorders have a physical component, such as the failure to lubricate for women and the failure to achieve an erection for men. In this chapter we will use the term ISD rather "hypoactive sexual desire" because ISD has been used in the literature to date and is commonly known to clinicians.

Kaplan's (1979) original definition and classification are still among the most clinically useful in the literature. She defined ISD as the active, rapid, suppression of sexual desire. Each term in the definition is critical to the understanding of ISD.

First, Kaplan postulates that the lack of desire results from an active mental process. This mechanism is the opposite of what happens during sexual excitation or arousal. Second, the process may be rapid. Some individuals with ISD do experience desire, if only occasionally. These individuals may go from experiencing sexual desire to a loss of that desire in the matter of an instant. They use such metaphors as a switch being turned off. Third, ISD involves a suppression of desire. The individual with ISD loses most, if not all, sexual interest.

Kaplan could have extended her definition to state that desire is also repressed. In the classical use of repression, the person is unaware of the fact that s/he is repressing; it is an unconscious process. There are some individuals with ISD who have no desire to feel desire. They are totally turned off and are disinterested in any treatment to restore desire. Most clients, however, want to feel desire again and try to will it to reappear. This attempt fails because something is operating unconsciously to keep them from feeling desire.

Kaplan (1979) also uses a classification scheme similar to that developed by Masters and Johnson (1970). The term "primary ISD" is used to denote the individual who had never experienced sexual desire; secondary ISD referrs to the individual who had experienced desire at one time but no longer does. In addition, she coined the term "global ISD" for those individuals who lacked desire for every potential sexual partner, and "situational ISD" for those who could respond with desire to at least one partner or in some situations, but would fail to respond with desire to the established partner or in some situations. In DSM-IV, the term "primary ISD" has been replaced by "lifelong ISD, "secondary ISD" by "acquired ISD," and "global ISD" by "generalized ISD."

It should be noted that Kaplan defines ISD within an intrapsychic framework, although she recognizes interpersonal factors in its etiology. A few years later, ISD was reconceptualized in strictly interactional terms by Zilbergeld and Ellison (1982). They based their definition on discrepancies in desire between partners: "It is not that one person has too much desire and another too little on an absolute scale; it is rather a discrepancy in two people's styles or interest" (p. 68).

Both definitions have merit, the individual and the interactional. In most of the cases of ISD that the editors have treated, two discrepancies exist—one within the individual and another in the couple. As we noted, most clients want to feel more desire, and hence they feel an internal discrepancy. The partners also experience a discrepancy that has become exacerbated due to the disorder. The partner with ISD feels pressure from both within and without, and the other partner often feels frustrated and becomes preoccupied with the desire for increasing the frequency of sex.

ISD is a disorder that is intriguing from several perspectives, one of which is philosophical. The questions often arise, "What is sexual desire?" and "How much desire is too much and how much is too little?" These questions are asked by both clinicians and clients. Leiblum and Rosen (1988a) attempt to answer these questions in the introduction to their volume on ISD. They define sexual desire as a subjective feeling state that could be triggered internally or externally, and may or may not result in sexual activity. The answer to how much is normal pits those thinkers who are more instinctively inclined against those who are more environmentally inclined.

It is our contention that sexual desire is an inherently normal state for those persons free of biologically based difficulties. We find this view useful in our clinical work. The word inherently does not refer to instinctive factors, but to those factors in the person's biological and psychological (learned behaviors) makeup and the cultural influences on their sexual fantasies, expectations, and rituals. Sexual desire and performance are complex behaviors. At this time, more is known about sexual performance than about desire. For example, crosscultural studies of primitive societies have revealed a myriad of fascinating patterns, from those encouraging frequent sex to those in which there is little sexual activity (Hyde, 1979).

Unfortunately, these studies examined only sexual behavior, not desire. Desire has been much more difficult to define and measure operationally.

INCIDENCE OF ISD

The difficulty in defining and measuring ISD has hampered efforts to assess just how common a problem it is. Not all those with ISD seek treatment. (Of course, this is also true of all other disorders.) In the case of ISD, it may have to do with embarrassment, or with the idea that therapy for such a problem is not possible. How common might this problem be in the nonclinical population? Several studies have attempted to answer this question.

Frank, Anderson, and Rubinstein (1978) were interested in the sexual functioning of couples as part of a larger study done on couples relationships. They were able to recruit 100 couples who said their marriages were "working." These couples were not randomly selected, but were self-selected, white, and highly educated, and many were professionals or businesspeople. Eighty percent of the couples in the survey stated that their marriages were "happy" to "very happy." These demographics might suggest that these couples would be relatively free of sexual complaints, and yet 40 percent of the men had an erectile or ejaculatory problem and 63 percent of the women had an arousal or orgasmic problem.

These statistics reflect a surprisingly high frequency of major sexual problems. When the researchers examined minor problems or difficulties, the percentages soared to 50 percent for men and 77 percent for women. Because this study was conducted before the identification of ISD, this disorder was not directly examined. However, under the heading of minor difficulties or problems there were two headings that are pertinent: 16 percent of men and 35 percent of women reported feeling sexual disinterest, and 28 percent of men and 10 percent of women felt "turned off." Unlike some of the other sexual disorders, these two problems were correlated with decreased marital satisfaction. One way to interpret this finding is that a partner who believes that the problem is out of his or her control does not blame or personalize as much as when the partner believes that the problem is something over which he or she has control. In our experience, one partner generally believes the other partner has control over the desire for sex and when s/he wants sex. This perception leads to the belief that the ISD partner is deliberately withholding feelings, and, in turn, behavior. The issue will be elaborated later as a treatment issue.

Bahr and Weeks (1989) replicated the study by Frank et al. (1978) using a sample of 90 gay couples (male couples), and found that 20 percent of the men reported feeling disinterest and 9 percent reported feeling turned off. These statistics are similar to those reported for the heterosexual men. Additionally, sexual disinterest and feeling turned off were significantly related to the level of sexual satisfaction.

Several surveys have shown that ISD is common among couples presenting for therapy. Two surveys were conducted at the Marriage Council of Philadelphia. In the first, 20 percent of male clients and 37 percent of female clients reported ISD, and in the second survey, 14 percent of men and 31 percent of women reported ISD (Lief, 1977, 1985). LoPiccolo (1980) reviewed 37 cases treated at the Stony Brook Sex Therapy Center. He found 63 percent of men and 37 percent of women reporting low sexual desire when presenting as a couple. Schover and LoPiccolo (1982) reanalyzed data from 1974–1981 at the Stony Brook center and found that among 152 couples, 38 percent of husbands and 49 percent of wives complained of low desire. Additionally, 18 percent of women but none of the men reported sexual aversion (revulsion to sex). In a more recent survey conducted by LoPiccolo (LoPiccolo & Friedman, 1988), the incidence of low-desire cases was 55 percent. These statistics were gathered in 1981 and 1982. The latter survey showed that 55 percent of the cases involved low male desire. In the 1974–1976 survey, low desire was reported in the women 70 percent of the time.

Among our own cases at PENN Council, we have noted an increase in the number of men presenting with this disorder. Apparently, it is either becoming more common in men or more commonly recognized by the clients and their therapists. On the other hand, Rosen, Leiblum, and Hall (1987) surveyed clients in their sex therapy clinic and found that twice as many women as men presented with ISD, although many men who came to therapy with erectile dysfunction also showed a lack of desire. These researchers also noted that men with ISD tended to be older, to feel more marital distress, and required more sessions than their female counterparts. This finding suggests that men with ISD may be more disturbed than women. The reader who is interested in more statistics on incidence should consult Leiblum and Rosen's (1988b) book.

ETIOLOGY

In his introduction to the first integrated etiological model of IDS (Weeks, 1987), the major theories regarding the etiology of this disorder were reviewed. Since that publication, there has been an explosion of theories regarding the etiology of ISD. The most comprehensive collection of these theories can be found in the volume by Leiblum and Rosen (1988b). The theories presented in their book encompass the full range of orientations (for example, biological, cognitive, analytic, systems, scripting). It is noteworthy that each theorist views the etiology from within the limits of her or his theoretical perspective. The exception to this theoretical purity is Lazarus (1988). He uses a multimodal approach that takes into account a multiplicity of factors in both etiology and treatment. The reader interested in an in-depth understanding from one of these specific theoretical perspectives should consult Leiblum and Rosen's book. However, for a comprehensive or integrated perspective, the reader should find the following material sufficient to understand and treat the problem.

An Integrated Etiological Model

The model used in this chapter is consistent with the Intersystem Model developed by Weeks (1989, 1994). One of the strengths of this approach lies in its provision of a structure that helps to sort out the various causes of a disorder and then puts strategies for therapy into a workable plan. The literature suggests that ISD is a multifactorial disorder, rarely caused by a single factor, but by a number of factors working synergistically. Understanding ISD using the Intersystem Model requires examining the factors that contribute to the disorder within the context of the individual, interactional, and intergenerational systems of the client. The factors listed next were derived from the literature and from our own experience in treating many cases. Some of the factors could have appeared under different headings or under two headings, depending on one's definition or interpretation. An effort has been made to identify the most common factors.

INDIVIDUAL FACTORS

Biological/medical functioning. A lack of sexual desire may result from depressed levels of hormones. Segraves (1988a) reviewed the literature on the relationship between hormones and libido. This area of research is relatively new and has been called behavioral endocrinology.

The hormone that has received the most attention is androgen. In men, the research suggests that androgen replacement therapy may be warranted when low levels of testosterone lead to lowered desire. Androgen has not been investigated extensively with respect to women. However, a recent article by Kaplan and Owen (1993) describes the female androgen deficiency syndrome.

Although the relationship between these hormones and desire is not simply one of cause and effect, some evidence does exist showing that replacement therapy may facilitate desire for some patients.

Another possible factor in insufficient desire is the use of medication. Currently, research shows that many medications may interfere with sexual desire and with sexual functioning. Segraves (1988b) has provided a comprehensive review of those drugs that are known or suspected to affect desire. He lists antihypertensive, psychiatric, anticonvulsant, and other prescribed drugs that decrease libido. The psychiatric drugs he listed included Thorazine, Mellaril, Navane, Prolixin, Haldol, Valium, Tranxene, Anafranil, Elavil, Tofranil, Vivactyl, Xanax, Asendin, Nardil, and Eskalith. Additional information on drug influences may be found in Kaplan's (1979, 1983) volumes, and a more recent critical review by Rosen (1991) examines the effects of alcohol and drugs on sexual response.

Loss of health, whether real or imagined, may lead to a loss of desire. A partner who is having health difficulties may be experiencing significant fear and anxiety. Often it is not the health difficulty itself, but the perception of that difficulty that is most important. A minor problem may be exaggerated and become the object of obsessive concern. Not only might the person fear losing health, but s/he might become worried about death and dying. The clinician must assess both the physical status of the individual and the person's perception of his or her health and what it means. Fear and anxiety are often incompatible with feelings of desire. Individuals with ongoing health concerns often become depressed as well.

Age may also be a factor in the same sense that health is a factor. A person may perceive aging in ways that suggest physical decline, loss of vitality, loss of health, and loss of sexual performance. Many have heard the myth that once one reaches a certain age (most often around 40), sexual performance declines or ends. The beliefs and anxiety surrounding this myth may inhibit desire.

A medical problem that deserves special mention is infertility, which often leads the partner(s) to focus on sex for the purpose of procreation. At the same time, each month that fertilization does not occur, the couple is open to a host of unpleasant feelings, such as anger, loss, fear, and depression. Sex may become routine, mechanical, and pressured—in other words joyless. The partner who presumes responsibility for the infertility may begin to feel less masculine or feminine, defective, or sexually unattractive. The couple may begin to fear that parenthood is unattainable. In our experience, it is very common for these individuals to lose some desire and to experience other sexual difficulties, such as erectile dysfunction and inorgasmia. In a previous volume, Mahlstedt (1987) discusses the issues of infertility for the individual and the couple.

Individual psychopathology. ISD may be secondary to other psychological problems, including, but not limited to, depression, anxiety reactions, psychotic reactions and decompensation, obsessive-compulsive reactions, fetishes, and histrionic, borderline, and obsessive-compulsive personality disorders. The issue for the clinician is to fully diagnose the client and investigate the connection between the individual psychopathology and the lack of desire.

In some cases, this connection is easier to establish than in others. Depression is an obvious case. Virtually all clinicians are familiar with the effects or symptoms of depression and how sexuality may be affected. The client who is chronically anxious may have difficulty experiencing any pleasant feeling, let alone sexual desire. Obsessive-compulsive persons attempt to keep tight control over feelings. They may experience sexual feelings as a threatening loss of control, and may also fear the sexual act as one that cannot be performed perfectly and is "messy." It is interesting that we sometimes think of histrionic and borderline individuals as oversexed because of their sexual acting out. The question is whether the acting out is really from desire or for other reasons, such as the need for attention, approval, and even the compulsion to repeat earlier traumas, such as sexual abuse.

Body image. In our culture, appearance is exalted. We are constantly bombarded with images of what is attractive and told to aspire to those images. Most of these images are directed toward women, so it is no surprise that body image is very often a factor for women with ISD. Appearance is no indication of how a client sees his or her own body. The client who is preoccupied with body image and who has perfectionistic ideals may appear to fit the cultural stereotype of beauty, femininity, or masculinity. The key is to assess the client's view of his or her appearance. Those who believe themselves is unattractive, sexually unattractive, or unappealing because of some specific aspect of appearance may show this concern sexually. The specific complaints that emerge most frequently are weight (too thin or too heavy), breasts (too small or too large), and penis size (always too small). In addition to the obsessive concern expressed by the individual partner, the other partner may contribute to the concern by expressing overt or covert disapproval of these aspects. When this happens, the issues also becomes relational, not just individual. In a sexual interaction, a person expresses sexuality through the body. Both partners are aware of how they believe they appear to the self and the other and how they move their bodies in sexual ways. If a partner is unhappy and preoccupied with his or her personal appearance, then this state will inhibit the ability to generate feelings of desire.

Sexual mythology. Masters and Johnson (1970) suggested that lack of appropriate sex education and information was a factor in practically every case of sexual dysfunction. As mentioned earlier, they had not identified ISD. Their formula was quite simple—lack of information leads to dysfunction.

Over the past decade, researchers have investigated this relationship further. Many individuals grow up with a lack of appropriate sex education and reliable sources of information. However, this fact does not mean that people are sexually uninformed, but rather are misinformed. Most people seek out sex information, and in the absence of reliable information, acquire it from unreliable sources. The first source of information is one's childhood and adolescent peers. Later on, it becomes the media. Many men have gained information from men's magazines, such as *Playboy* and *Penthouse*, and from X-rated movies. References in these media to extraordinarily large penises may, in part, account for why so many men believe their penis is too small. Women have fared a little better. Women's magazines of the last two decades have attempted to provide scientifically based information on sexuality. Unfortunately, for some it is too late. The misinformation gained earlier in life has already done its damage. Mosher (1979) has been able to demonstrate empirically that this misinformation leads directly to sex guilt and sex anxiety. It is guilt and anxiety that leads directly to sexual dysfunction. These elements were missing in Masters and Johnson's (1970) simple formula. The level of sex guilt and anxiety may be so great as to dissuade the individual from acquiring any additional, and perhaps harmful, information. Thus, many clients presenting with ISD will report that they avoid all sexual material. They will not read books or articles, or even watch a sexy television show or movie.

Sexual fantasies. For some reason sexual fantasies have received little attention in the literature on ISD. Of all the contributors to Leiblum and Rosen's (1988b) volume on sexual desire, only one theorist mentioned the use of fantasy in treatment. This omission in the literature is striking in light of the fact that DSM-IV defines hypoactive sexual desire (ISD) in terms of a deficiency in sexual fantasies and desire for sexual activity. Nutter and Condron (1983) are the only researchers to examine the lack of sexual fantasies among ISD patients. They examined 25 women presenting at a sex therapy clinic with the diagnosis of ISD. They found that the women had significantly fewer fantasies during foreplay, coitus, masturbation, and general daydreaming. The content of the fantasies they did have was similar to those of women in the control group, and there was not a total lack of sexual fantasy. Clearly, more research needs to be done to confirm the relationship between fantasy and ISD.

In the meantime, our experience with ISD clients is that many have no sexual fantasies whatsoever. In fact, asking this question of them can produce an embarrassing reaction. We further suspect that the type of ISD is important. Our hypothesis is that those partners with primary, or lifelong, ISD are most likely not to have fantasies. Those with situational ISD, especially when they are having or have had an affair, are the most likely to have fantasies.

Sexual fantasies may be an important factor because their most common function is to help a person become aroused, stay aroused, and increase the level of sexual arousal (Sue, 1979). Loren and Weeks (1986) studied a group of college students. Their subjects reported that the most common reason for a sexual fantasy was to get or stay sexually aroused. If we subscribe to a cognitive model of behavior, then we feel how we think. An absence of fantasies may then lead to an absence of sexual desire. This last point will be elaborated in the section on treatment.

Fusion of sex and affection. This factor is probably both an effect of ISD and a cause. Sex and affection become fused and confused in many people. We see this difficulty in virtually every sex therapy case, especially ISD cases. One partner, usually the man, believes affection is to be expressed through the sexual act. He often denigrates affection as a useless display. The other partner, usually the woman, sees affection as having intrinsic value and perceives any attempt by the partner to show affection as a means for him to achieve a sexual interaction. Simply put, men tend to see affection as a means to an end, whereas women are more likely to see it as an end in itself. Couples caught in this kind of confusion begin to exchange what they can get for what they value. Women will then submit to sex in order to gain affection, and men will submit to showing affection in order to gain sex. Neither is happy with this arrangement, but the awareness and skills needed to break the cycle are not in place. As time goes on, anger and resentment build over this issue, and these feelings impact negatively on desire. The quality of the sexual interaction usually declines because the one who is giving sex to gain affection is not interested in the act and, therefore, does not have the feelings to sustain it. This factor is usually stronger for the woman than for the man. She feels she must trade sex just to get affection—something she deserves anyway. She may begin to feel less and less valued as a person because of his lack of affection. The problem generalizes to the point where she does not wish to be with someone who does not wish to show caring and affection.

The ISD client is disinterested in having sex. The partner is usually sexually frustrated, engaged in an ongoing struggle to get the client to have sex whether or not it is wanted. When the non-ISD partner shows affection for whatever reason, it is almost always interpreted as an effort to coerce a sexual interaction. The ISD partner fuses the two—to accept affection means I must accept sex. The consequence is that the ISD partner rejects affection, which leads to deterioration in the couple relationship, and, in turn, to further deterioration in the sexual relationship.

INTERACTIONAL FACTORS

Kaplan's (1979) analysis of the etiological factors for ISD was a major contribution. Unfortunately, her psychodynamic bias was so strong that it was difficult to place those factors in a systems framework. In fact, her basic approach to treating ISD consisted of combining behavioral-oriented sex therapy with an individually oriented psychodynamic approach. Masters and Johnson (1970) were even more limited in their theoretical approach. Despite their statement that there was no such entity as an uninvolved partner, they did not move to an interactional or systems perspective. This perspective was still emerging in the field at large.

There are still many sex therapists today who take an individually oriented behavioral approach along the lines of Masters and Johnson (1970). The first book on the integration of sex and marital therapy did not appear until 1987 when the authors published *Integrating Sex and Marital Therapy: A Clinical Guide* (Weeks & Hof, 1987).

From a systems perspective (Weeks, 1993), each partner is viewed as playing a role in the lack of desire. Of course, when there is an individual factor, such as a drug effect, this may not be the case. If individual factors are ruled out because they have been eliminated or treated, then the clinician must look to interactional variables. The Intersystem Approach (Weeks, 1994) requires that we examine each problem from multiple perspectives.

Anger. The inability to deal with anger is one of the most common of all couple problems (L'Abate & McHenry, 1983). Anger is highly incompatible with feeling sexual desire. We can all relate to this feeling at a personal level. However, in cases of ISD, the matter is not quite so simple. The type of anger that leads to ISD is chronic and suppressed. It is akin to feeling smoldering resentment. Chronically suppressed anger pervades the client's emotional life, leaving the person to feel little else—certainly not desire for the partner, who is perceived as being the source of the anger. This has been a factor slightly more often in the men this author has treated than in the women. These men believe in peace at any price. Rather than being overly explosive or inappropriately angry as some men are, these men have adopted an attitude of resignation about what troubles them in the relationship. They appear depressed, anxious, and withdrawn. They are more likely to disengage from their partners in order to remain quietly angry.

The problem with the inexpression of anger is not just within the person. Couples develop interlocking ways of handling anger and other feelings. The obvious question is why the other partner does not pick up on the smoldering anger, or become concerned by the absence of anger, and attempt to deal with it. It appears that the problem not only meets the underlying needs of the inexpressive partner, but of the other partner as well. The pattern may serve to protect the relationship. The partner may contribute to this pattern because s/he too is afraid of anger, needs to be able to criticize or put the other down, or needs to feel in control of the relationship without being questioned or challenged. The partners may create an unconscious collusion in which both avoid anger and conflict. This type of couple is said to be conflict-avoidant. They may have been taught that anger is bad and is bad for a relationship, that one should never express anger openly (just count to 10), or that if one pretends it is not there, the problem will eventually go away. In this case, both partners share the same irrational ideas about anger and conflict.

In other relationships, there are complementary beliefs. One might think, "Anger won't change anything so why say anything," whereas the other thinks, "Let it all out and it will be better." Or one partner might think, "Anger communicates a lack of love," and the other might think, "Anger isn't about the person, but the issue." The partner with the belief system that leads to a suppression of anger may become chronically angry as described. In the cases we have treated where the men do not, or rarely, get angry, the pattern is one of not fighting and not wanting sex.

On the other side of the coin are those individuals who are chronically and overtly angry. They do not know how to express anger without being hurtful. They are likely to attack the other person, not just the issue. One of the functions of this type of anger may be to regulate the distance in the relationship. They do not desire closeness. By being angry they communicate this to their partners indirectly, and the partners respond by withdrawing sexually. Why would one want to have sex with someone who is always angry? Then the question arises of why that partner stays with someone who is chronically angry. This partner also has a need to avoid closeness, and achieves this, indirectly, by marrying someone who will not allow closeness to happen.

Power and control. Every relationship must deal with how power and control are distributed. In some relationships, these issues have not been successfully negotiated. An imbalance exists in which one partner assumes too much power and control and the other too little, or they both assume too little, or they both assume too much. Cases involving ISD may involve one partner being overcontrolling and the other being undercontrolling. When the man is overcontrolling and the woman is undercontrolling, the woman will often develop a lack of desire.

These issues may be played out in two ways. One manifestation of the problem has to do with one partner assuming too much power and control and the other assuming too little. The partner who assumes too little has a feeling of being out of control, of being disempowered, and of resentment and anger toward the other partner for taking too much. This struggle for power and control may be overt. The partners may fight over numerous issues regarding who is to be in charge. When the struggle is covert, the clinician may not perceive the conflict initially because it is not offered as a complaint. However, observation of the couple will quickly show that one partner responds submissively to the other's aggression. In the relationship, sex may become the battleground for this unresolved struggle. We own our own bodies and our sexuality. Others may force us to behave in certain ways, but they cannot dictate our feelings. The resentment, anger, and frustration over not having compatible power and control suppress the ability to respond sexually. Feeling a lack of sexual desire and withholding sex is an indirect way of taking control. Of course, ISD clients almost never articulate this feeling, although their partners often remark that the one with the ISD is completely in charge of what happens sexually.

In the other two situations, where both partners assume too much or too little control, the struggle is over who will have the power or who will take care of whom. For example, if each one wants the other to take charge, then the issue is really one of dependency. Neither feels taken care of so they resent each other and that feeling suppresses desire.

The deeper manifestation of this problem of how power and control are distributed actually has to do with the partner's sense of identity. A partner with a poor self-image and weak ego does not know who s/he is or what s/he wants. How can one possibly feel empowered in a relationship if one doesn't feel empowered as an individual? In the family therapy literature, we refer to this phenomenon as a lack of self-differentiation (L'Abate, 1976). The differentiated individual defines self as being similar to *and* different from others. The undifferentiated individual defines self in terms of being opposite to *or* the same as others. In other words, undifferentiated individuals will view themselves either in terms of being the same as another person, such as a parent or partner, or as being the opposite of another person. The behavior of an undifferentiated individual is reactive or is determined by others. Self-determination is weak or nonexistent. ISD can result from either pattern of a lack of differentiation. It is easy to see how the partner who reacts oppositionally would not desire sex if the other partner does. Not wanting sex would be a way of affirming a sense of identity through opposition.

The partner who defines self in terms of sameness has a different dilemma. Sameness can be tolerated up to a point. When individuals do strive toward greater differentiation, what worked at one point in the relationship will no longer work. The classic case is the marriage of early inception and long duration. These partners married before they could develop a strong sense of self. They may have lived in harmony because they worked at being alike. Then, as they reach middle age and the children begin leaving home, they may begin to examine what they want for themselves. One partner may change and decide to be different. Being different is not easy when all one has ever known is sameness. The first step in this growth may be to become opposite. The result is the same as that noted.

Fears of intimacy. What gets presented as a lack of sexual desire in a relationship may actually be masking a much larger problem of a lack of intimacy or a fear of being more intimate. Intimacy is that balance of individuality and separateness in a relationship. It refers to the degree of closeness and bondedness with and caring for the other. Every person comes to a relationship with a particular tolerance of intimacy based on experiences in the family of origin and in previous relationships. Some partners enter a relationship with deeply buried fears of getting close to another. These fears can be disguised and hidden through a number of tactics. Our species is biologically programmed to respond to fear by either fleeing or fighting. The partner who fears intimacy may find things from which to flee or about which to fight. S/he may even generate anger as a pervasive feeling in order to avoid the feeling of fear.

These fears were described in Chapter 2 and include fears of dependency, feelings, anger, abandonment and rejection, exposure, and losing control or being controlled.

Examples of some other fears might be helpful at this point. One woman was afraid of losing control of her underlying anger and rage. She could later verbalize that she feared she might kill her husband in a rage. This fear prevented her from having sex with her husband. She was afraid that close physical contact might release this rage, and so she turned off all her feelings, including sexual desire, in order to avoid this catastrophic encounter. Another woman was afraid of exposure. She believed that if her partner knew what she was really like, he would not want to be with her. This fear was symbolically represented in her statement that if she were to have an orgasm, her appearance would be ugly, repulsive, and animalistic. In another case, a woman who had been suddenly abandoned just prior to marriage could not let herself trust her husband. In the prior relationship, she had had sex with her fiancé just before his disappearance. She associated sex with being abandoned. One intimacy fear that causes men much difficulty is the fear of being hurt. Men find it difficult to feel or express hurt. It is much easier for them to be angry. The view is that hurt symbolizes weakness and vulnerability—

unmanly traits. In order to deal with hurt, some men withdraw emotionally and sexually.

Just as the ISD masks a larger problem of intimacy for one partner, it also masks a problem for the other. If one partner has a fear of intimacy, it follows that the other must have some fear. Partners may have different fears or the same fear. The reason they are together is to maintain the distance between them so that the fears will not have to be exposed. In a sense, the ISD that is manifest in one partner benefits both. It is easy to become overfocused on the partner who presents with the symptom. Couple therapy involves knowing how to see the symptom as a relational problem. In one type of case, the wife will express dissatisfaction with the husband's distancing. Once he begins to approach her, she finds reasons to create distance, such as being angry that he waited so long. The question becomes one of why she was attracted to him in the first place. By focusing on his problem, she does not have to focus on herself. Assessment must remain relationship focused in order to avoid the traditional trait-type diagnosis, which only serves to pathologize one partner while letting the pathology of the other go unrecognized.

INTERGENERATIONAL FACTORS

Intergenerational factors in the etiology of ISD continue to be ignored in the literature. The term "intergenerational" is completely absent in the index to Leiblum and Rosen's (1988b) edited volume on the treatment of this disorder. Thus far, there has been no attempt systematically to research this factor in any kind of sexual dysfunction. This gap in the literature is striking given the popularity of family-of-origin approaches in family therapy. Intergenerational factors have been highlighted in previous works only by this author (Weeks, 1987) and his colleagues at the Marriage Council. Hof and Berman (1986) and Berman and Hof (1987) were the first to write specifically about the intergenerational transmission of sexual messages. In 1986, they published a paper that described the use of the sexual genogram as a way to assess the messages given to children about sexuality, gender roles, and other issues and how they might influence sexual functioning. The rationale was that just as we learn about love, loyalty, values, and the like, in the family, we also learn about sex.

Intergenerational messages may be transmitted in two ways. First, in just living in a family and experiencing whatever happens one absorbs even subtle influences. For example, in one of the cases described by Hof and Berman (1986), the wife had longstanding ISD. It turned out she had been abandoned by her father when she was an adolescent. She had unconsciously decided that she would never allow herself to be hurt so badly again by never getting close to anyone. It is interesting that in this case the husband had also been abandoned and had his own fears of getting close.

What the child observes and experiences become part of the learning about sexuality. Many children grow up in homes where there is little discussion of sex. As a result, they begin to think that there must be something bad, dirty, or sinful about sex. If something cannot be mentioned, there must be a good reason, and a good reason is that it is too dangerous to discuss. The child begins to think that sex is dangerous.

The second way intergenerational sexual messages are transmitted is verbally, and the messages may be either direct or implied. It is our experience that direct negative messages about sex appear often in our primary ISD cases. These are the old messages of sex being bad, sinful, dirty, and wicked. One woman with ISD could only vaguely remember that whenever sex was discussed by her mother it was always in negative terms. Her mother's position was that men always wanted sex and women just had to put up with it. She could not remember direct negative messages, but rather that the messages were negative by implication.

One of the most fascinating cases involved a man in his 40s who experienced situational ISD. His father, a wealthy executive whose wife had died when the client was a child, did not remarry. The father was a playboy in every sense of the word. He told his son that, if he were successful, he would always be surrounded by women who would want to have sex with him. As an adult, the son found that, in spite of his success, women, in general, were not trying to seduce him, and neither was his wife. No women behaved at all in the way his father had described them. He felt that something must be wrong with him because women were not interested in him sexually and his wife did not assume full responsibility for the sexual relationship. He became more and more anxious that he was the cause of his wife's lack of desire. This anxiety reached a point where he eventually had difficulty getting aroused. He once commented that if he were to initiate sex, it would mean he was a "nothing." This statement could be traced to his father's injunction that a successful man never has to ask for sex.

Two more family patterns should be mentioned. To our knowledge, the first has never been discussed in the literature. The term "parentification'' refers to a child's being treated like an adult (see Sauber, L'Abate, Weeks, & Buchanan, 1993). The parentified child is given a great deal of responsibility for taking care of things that adults should be doing— being asked to make difficult decisions or to help the parent deal with emotional crisis. Parentified children do grow up, but do not grow out of this pattern of behavior. Some become caretakers in their own marriages. What they continue to carry is a sense of omnipotence, the belief that they can resolve any difficulty presented by another, and an underlying feeling of rage at being asked to do the impossible. During the course of a relationship, these partners may fall more and more deeply into this same childhood pattern as the relationship presents opportunities to take care of the other. At some point, the underlying rage takes over and motivates this partner unconsciously to withhold sex. Desire diminishes as the underlying rage takes over. Rarely is this rage expressed directly; most of these adults are unaware of its existence. They begin to see their partner as the parent who took their childhood and left them feeling empty and burned out. The partner becomes less and less attractive, in general, because of this unique transference reaction. The clinician needs to assess for parentification by asking whether the family was intact, who took care of whom, and who the ''boss'' was in the family. Parentification is more likely to occur in single-parent families and where there is substance abuse. The clinician also needs to determine whether there was an appropriate generational hierarchy where parents took care of their children and took care of their own emotional needs without imposing those needs on their children.

The other intergenerational phenomenon to assess is whether child abuse, particularly sexual abuse, has occurred. The literature on sexual abuse recently detailed some of the long-range effects of sexual abuse (Courtois, 1988). Abused partners may develop an ongoing lack of sexual desire, any number of sexual dysfunctions, and specific dislikes, if not phobic reactions, to sexual behaviors that occurred during the trauma. For example, a woman may feel disgusted by oral sex or by being touched in a certain way or in a certain place. Abused partners may feel guilt over sex, ''numb out'' or dissociate during sex, or feel out of control. Some may even experience flashbacks that are painful and frightening. Sexual abuse as a factor in ISD may become manifest in a number of ways, and may lead to primary ISD.

One of our cases involved a woman who had been sexually abused as a child by an older neighbor boy. Her mother would leave the children with this boy's family when she needed to go out. The abuse lasted for several years. When asked why she did not tell anyone, this client said she could never talk to her mother, especially about things that troubled her. She felt that her only option was to accept the abuse. This experience of being used left her with a fear of getting physically or sexually close to anyone. She married a kind and gentle man who was not sexually demanding. They acted more like brother and sister.

Sexual abuse can also appear in cases of secondary ISD. In these cases, something happens in the relationship that triggers the trauma. One client thought she could trust her partner of several years. During this time, she had no difficulty being sexual with him. He had a brief affair, which meant to her that he was no longer trustworthy. From that point on, she equated his behavior with that of her father, who had sexually abused her as a child. In her mind, he (father or partner?) had betrayed her mother (an affair) and her. Assessing sexual abuse and its impact on sexual function/dysfunction is a very sensitive matter. The reader who is unfamiliar with this problem should consult Courtois (1988) or Maltz (1988, 1991).

Some ISD clients have not been sexually abused, but have been abused physically. One of the most striking examples this author can remember was a client who had been abused severely and consistently during childhood. As an adult, any kind of touch was perceived as painful. She would not allow anyone near her physically. As a result, she had suppressed sexual desire, deeming it a potentially dangerous physical experience.

TREATMENT

The one point on which all therapists agree is that ISD is a difficult disorder to treat. Most sexual dysfunctions can be treated briefly, in 10 sessions or less, and with a high degree of success. We believe ISD can also be treated effectively, but not using a brief therapy model. For example, Kaplan (1979) reported a success rate of only 10–15 percent after 15 sessions of therapy. Her approach consisted of behavioral oriented sex therapy combined with a psychodynamic approach. Leiblum and Rosen's (1988) edited volume provides us with a number of specific treatment models, none of which is truly eclectic or integrative when considered within the framework of this book. In addition to the approaches mentioned in this book, there are other approaches developed by McCarthy (1984), Regas and Sprenkle (1984), and Fish, Fish, and

Sprenkle (1984). It is also clear that the same concepts cut across different models of treatment. For example, using some of the traditional behavioral-oriented sex therapy exercises and redefining the ISD as a couple problem are common strategies. The approach we utilize follows the Intersystem Model, inasmuch as we consider the individual, interactional, and intergenerational factors in assessing and treating the problem.

Getting Started

It is best to start treatment by seeing the couple together. Sometimes partners are reluctant to come to therapy or they do not see the point because they believe the problem is an individual one. From the moment of the initial telephone contact, the therapist should make a case for them coming together for conjoint sessions. It may be necessary to present the therapy in terms of the solution which requires the presence of both partners, or by noting that sex requires two people. The therapist could also talk about the other partner's presence in terms of providing information that might be useful. If the therapist insists on both partners coming to therapy, they probably will. Unfortunately, therapists sometimes give up too easily and let the other partner get out of coming.

Once the initial diagnosis of ISD has been made, there are several matters to handle before getting started with treatment. First, it is important that the couple have an understanding of the disorder. Many clients have read some articles about lack of sexual desire, and some have even read Kaplan's (1979) book. Therefore, it is important to find out what clients already know and believe about the problem. Some of our clients have come to therapy expecting it to fail based on some articles they had read. The clinician needs to educate the couple about the problem—define it and discuss the course of therapy. An excellent resource for couples is the book *ISD: Inhibited Sexual Desire* by Knopf and Seiler (1990), which is both accessible to the layperson and authoritative. It is also a useful book for clinicians who are just learning about this disorder. Zilbergeld's *The New Male Sexuality* (1993), which contains two chapters on lack of desire and covers many of the other male sexual dysfunctions, is also a good choice.

In addition, the therapist also needs to instill some hope (Hof, 1993). The couple need to know that what they are bringing to therapy is treatable and that ISD is a problem that does not demand immediate attention. The couples we have treated had experienced ISD for months, sometimes years, prior to getting help. Donahey and Carroll (1993) found that women presenting with ISD had the problem for an average of 4.7 years and men for an average of 3.4 years. The couple has to understand the course of treatment and have realistic expectations. The problem is not one that can be treated with brief therapy. Most of the cases require six months to two years. We tell this to the couple within the first four meetings after the diagnosis has been confirmed. The duration of treatment depends on the number and severity of factors contributing to the lack of desire. By the time the initial assessment is done, most couples have some idea about what needs to be changed in order to resolve the ISD. Some couples may choose not to continue treatment because of the commitment, time, and financial cost involved. We believe strongly that informed consent to treatment, to the extent that we understand what is required, is crucial to the establishment of a workable therapeutic contract.

Another prerequisite to getting started is the assurance that both partners are invested in the process. In explaining that the problem usually has to do with their relationship, at least in part, the therapist clarifies the need to work together to take care of the relational problems suppressing desire. The non-ISD partner is also needed to help with those aspects of the problem that are not relational.

The therapist will need three to four sessions to conduct an initial evaluation. Clients should be informed about this evaluation procedure. Part of the initial evaluation needs to be done individually. The therapist may see the partners for separate sessions or may split one session between the two of them. There are several reasons for seeing partners separately, in spite of the fact that such a procedure is generally considered unwise in couples work. The ISD partner may minimize the lack of desire in the presence of the partner. In order to get a better idea of just how turned off the partner might be, it is essential to see that partner separately. There is other information that is difficult to divulge in front of a partner. The therapist may learn that there has been, or is, an affair. The client may experience desire for another, but not for the established partner. Sometimes a partner has been sexually abused, but is not ready to tell the partner for fear of the partner's reaction to him or her and to the abuser. Prior to splitting the couple, it is absolutely essential to make the rules of confidentiality clear. These rules were outlined in Chapter 8, where extramarital sexuality and affairs were discussed.

A final reason for individual sessions is to take care of those concerns that women usually have when their husbands lack desire. When women present with ISD, men do not seem especially puzzled by its presence in the relationship. Men can accept that women sometimes lack desire and that the condition might continue for a long time. However, in this culture, men are supposed to be sexual all the time. Some women expect men to be chronically turned on. If this is not the case, the woman often begins to wonder whether he is having an affair or has "turned gay." Female partners will sometimes ask about other women, but none of our clients have directly confronted their partners about being gay. If the woman does not bring the concern up, ask whether it has crossed her mind. If it has, then explore the matter with her, and, if appropriate, provide her with some reassurance that his becoming homosexual is highly unlikely. It is important for women to know that ISD can occur in men and nothing they can do or say will be effective in sexually stimulating them. We have seen women take classes in belly dancing, stripping, and flirting in order to become more seductive. When these techniques fail, they blame themselves or worry about extramarital affairs. The therapist also needs to spend time discussing how the women have unnecessarily blamed themselves, thinking they are unattractive, boring, sexually incompetent, or any among a host of other self-denigrating options.

Rapid Assessment of ISD

Because ISD may involve so many factors in its etiology, the assessment of this problem may be protracted and complex. The clinician and the couple would both prefer as quick an assessment of the problem as possible. The following two techniques provide a great deal of information in a short period. It is certainly possible to employ these two techniques within the three- or four-session evaluation period and to continue to assess throughout treatment as issues emerge.

A general assessment of the sexual relationship should take place. The clinician may use any one of several formats described in the literature (Kaplan, 1983). Five additional questions help the clinician assess for ISD. First, the couple should be asked about the frequency of sex. This is obviously a behavioral question. The couple should be asked about the frequency of sex from the inception of the relationship to the present day, noting any changes. It is also useful to ask who initiates sexual encounters. The clinician may note where there was a sudden or gradual loss of desire, and if one partner was always the initiator. This question can then be expanded to include prior relationships. Clients with primary

ISD will report a low frequency of sex in prior relationships or that they went along with sexual acts because their partners initiated them. Just because a person has sex does not mean s/he desires it. ISD clients usually have had sex on some regular basis because they felt their partners demanded it or had a right to sexual contact.

The second question, then, is whether the person experiences a desire for sexual contact. The therapist should clarify that the first question deals with behavior, whereas the second deals with a feeling—a feeling of sexual desire. The history of sexual desire should be explored just as the history of frequency of contact was examined, including desire predating the current relationship.

The third question has to do with the degree to which desire is felt. The clinician may ask the client to imagine a scale from $+10$ to -10, with one end representing intense sexual desire and the other representing sexual revulsion and disgust. Zero represents sexual neutrality, a take-it-or-leave-it attitude. The clients are asked how they would rate their level of desire most of the time, when they are with their partner physically, as well as the intensity of their feelings when their partner makes an advance. Most of our ISD patients place themselves from -2 to -5 when asked to state their sexual desire globally. The more difficult cases to treat have been those with the most intense negative ratings.

The fourth question applies to some, but not all, cases. This question has to do with situations when desire is felt and then lost. The client who reports never feeling stimulated will not be able to answer this question. Other clients feel desire at various times, but then report that it disappears. Some describe the experience as like a switch being turned off. This information gives the clinician an opportunity to learn what the turn-off triggers might be. It is also useful because the client can then focus on those moments in order to learn more about the mental mechanism that is causing the loss of desire. Some of the reported triggers occur when the partner starts to get ready for bed, when the partner makes a sexual overture, when the partner walks into the house, and when the partner's headlights flash through the window. This and the previous question also need to be checked out with regard to other people. It is often wiser to ask about desire for others in the individual session.

The final question is whether there are physical problems. Are there other sexual dysfunctions in the relationship, such as erectile problems, premature ejaculation, inorgasmia, or vaginismus? Concurrent sexual dysfunctions may serve to increase the level of anxiety even further and lead the partner(s) to feel turned off because they expect another sexual failure. ISD may also result from a sexual dysfunction. The dysfunction may create anxiety and fears of performance that make sexual interactions unpleasant. Just the thought of a sexual interaction may become an aversive event. This feeling can then lead to a suppression of desire. Donahey and Carroll (1993) have empirically shown that of patients seeking help for ISD, only 15 percent of men and 25 percent of women reported no other sexual dysfunction. The clinician must often decide how to weave together the treatment of multiple sexual problems.

The next procedure is both diagnostic and therapeutic. As such, it must be introduced as being both. The therapist describes the procedure and talks about using it over a number of sessions. This procedure involves assessing the clients' cognitions about sex. Before actually beginning this process, the therapist asks the couple to think about how it is they create a state of sexual desire. The therapist explains that sexual desire and sexual inhibition are mirror images, such that if we can discover how to start the turn-on mechanism, we will be able to shut down the turn-off mechanism. The therapist may need to explain that s/he is not talking about the relationship in general or about other global factors that might interfere with sexual desire. The focus is specifically on how to create sexual desire. Most couples will respond to this question of how desire is generated by talking about physical stimulation and sexual fantasy. The therapist wants the couple to see that sexual feelings derive from sexual thoughts and images (fantasies). Clients with ISD usually report that they lack fantasies and do not have sexual thoughts regarding their partner or have negative sexual thoughts regarding their partner. Most will have negative sexual thoughts. We refer to this concept as having positive sexual self-talk (+ SST) or negative sexual self-talk (− SST).

Clients are most often aware of some of their negative sexual self-talk. They may not immediately grasp the idea of positive sexual self-talk. Much of the positive self-talk is unconscious or transparent to the individual. In other words, we do not usually stop to think about what we are thinking. So, when we say to ourselves such things as, "My partner looks sexy tonight," or "I want to have sex," or "Sex would feel good," or "I'm horny," we do not realize we are talking ourselves into a state of sexual desire. As a diagnostic tool, the first task is to help the couple catalogue their negative sexual self-talk. To facilitate this process, the therapist asks the partners to think about their cognitions in four categories: the negative thoughts about the self, about the partner, and about the relationship, and the negative messages from the family of origin. Although this procedure is of more importance for the ISD partner, we collect the thoughts from both partners. Sometimes the non-ISD partner is also carrying some negative thoughts that feed into the negative thoughts of the ISD partner, and also affect the ability to become aroused. Clients are asked to start listing these thoughts in the session and to continue this process at home. As time goes on, more thoughts are likely to emerge. It is best to link this assignment to a behavioral assignment involving touch. By putting the partners in physical contact, underlying negative thoughts are more likely to surface. The touching exercise should be something they can do without generating anxiety. For example, the most common exercise is a "pleasuring" experience involving nongenital stimulation.

Partners are also asked if they need to see the therapist individually in order to fully disclose some of their negative thoughts. Partners may feel that if they say certain things, it will be unnecessarily hurtful to the partner. If they believe they need this opportunity, the therapist should provide it as soon as possible under the guidelines suggested about confidentiality.

Most partners will list 5 to 10 negative thoughts for the first three categories. Occasionally, someone will list more. One man with ISD listed four pages of negative thoughts without being redundant. His therapy took five years and involved individual therapy with another therapist concurrent with the marital/sex therapy. The following case example shows the thinking of a women with ISD who was in a very destructive marriage.

Negative Sexual Self-Talk

Self
I won't be able to get lubricated, so sex will be painful.
I'm always tired at night when he wants sex.
I won't be able to have an orgasm.
It's been so long since we've had sex, it's hard to imagine.
I can't approach my husband for anything.
I don't feel his hugs or affection are real.
Partner
He will yell at me if I don't want sex.
He will yell at me if I don't get it right.

He's selfish.
He's cold.
He's insensitive to what I need sexually.
He will reject me after sex.
   Relationship
When we had sex, it was routine.
We are too restrictive in what we do.
We have too many differences.
We don't have any mutual goals.
Everything is my fault.

This example demonstrates a number of points. First, clients will categorize items in general ways. Some items could go under multiple headings; sometimes they are misplaced. Gathering the information is the important issue, not having it neatly organized. Second, clients may list thoughts that are not directly related to sexual functioning, but still have a very significant impact on the level of desire. Third, the thoughts are a point of departure for discussion. Each item should be reviewed in order to find out what it means to the client and to the partner. More than anything else, this procedure provides information quickly and informs the clinician about what factors are individual, interactional, and intergenerational. In the above example, the ISD was secondary and was based on relationship dynamics. The focus of treatment was marital therapy.

Early Phase of Therapy

The first phase of therapy consists of continuing the diagnostic procedure and a number of other tasks. Once the negative sexual self-talk has been identified, the next step is to sort out which thoughts need to be worked on from an individual perspective and which point to relational difficulties that involve working with the couple. Let us start with those thoughts that can be worked on individually. These thoughts are treated from a cognitive therapy perspective (Ellis & Harper, 1975). The client is asked to think of counter ideas, or more rational or productive ideas. The therapist may need to provide more or less help in developing these ideas, depending on the client's ability to follow through. In addition, the client is asked to think of as many positive ideas as possible for each category.

These ideas may be general, as well as specifically sexual. The client is encouraged to continue this process weekly until a long list of positives has been created. These thoughts need to be practiced daily. The client should review the counter ideas so that when one of the negative thoughts occurs, it can be rapidly countered, and the couple should think about the positive thoughts at least twice daily.

Proceeding in this manner helps to create more positive thoughts about the relationship and sexual interactions. It is also useful to help the client develop a fantasy life. The therapist may first need to remove any barriers to having sexual fantasies by discussing the issues. Giving the couple information about the fact that most people have fantasies, and use them to become aroused, stay aroused, or become more aroused, is helpful. It is especially important to let them know that anything they fantasize about is normal, and that in long-term relationships partners almost never fantasize about their established partner (Masters & Johnson, 1979). The couple may also need to talk about whether fantasies are to be shared or kept private. Several books are useful in normalizing sexual fantasies and in getting the client primed to have fantasies. *Shared Intimacies* (Barback & Levine, 1980) provides some basic information in a personal way. Nancy Friday has compiled fantasies of both men and women in several books, including *My Secret Garden* (1973), *Forbidden Flowers* (1975), *Men in Love* (1980), and *Women on Top* (1991). The ISD partner is encouraged to read one or two fantasies each day, skipping those that are not enjoyable. The purpose of this exercise is to help the client create a fantasy life by borrowing from the fantasies of others. Since some clients do not respond to these books particularly, they are given the mission of going to the local bookstore to find whatever erotic books work for them. Men sometimes prefer erotic magazines and movies.

In this first phase, the therapist is setting the therapeutic agenda with the couple. It is extremely important to collaborate on the development of this agenda. ISD partners may not be ready to undertake anything sexual for a period of time, whereas others are ready to begin very gradually. Pacing the work is important. Going too quickly can arouse anxiety, which works against the therapy.

Couples presenting with ISD are usually out of touch with each other physically. The sharing of affection may have dropped out of the interactions as a result of being fused with sex. The therapist needs to suggest that the couple begin slowly by agreeing not to attempt a sexual interaction, but rather some agreed-upon physical interactions worked out in the therapist's office. The couple is encouraged to begin or renew a show of spontaneous affection. They are also given one of the traditional sex therapy exercises that involves nongenital stimulation (Masters & Johnson, 1970). The therapist may have to start with exercises that are below the starting point recommended by Masters and Johnson. Holding hands, caressing each other's hands, or doing a back rub, in the living room, fully clothed, may be the starting point. As we have stated, it is important to understand that some clients are unable to tolerate any physical interaction until other work is done. Over time, the touching exercises follow the traditional path outlined by such therapists as Kaplan (1979). This progression goes from nongenital touching, to genital touching for the purpose of exploration and sensation, to genital touching for the purpose of sexual arousal and orgasm, to sexual interactions that are not goal oriented.

Early on in treatment, the couple should understand the role of anxiety. Performance anxiety is a term that was developed by Masters and Johnson (1970) to refer to the type of anxiety that interferes with sexual performance. Simply put, as anxiety increases, sexual performance decreases. Apfelbaum (1988) has formulated a concept that explains the anxiety experienced by the ISD patient, which he labeled response anxiety. ISD clients feel they must respond emotionally when, they are expected to be sexual. Such expectations may be self-imposed or on the part of the partner. The anxiety occurs when they are feeling turned off when they "should" be feeling turned on. Suppose a man with ISD were approached by his wife for sex. He might be able to perform sexually, but he knows this is insufficient. He believes he must also generate sexual feelings and feel sexual pleasure when they are together. But he knows this is not going to happen. The disparity creates anxiety. The more he tries to force himself to feel desire, the less he is able to do so. The couple must understand how response anxiety works and be given permission to feel whatever they feel. Feelings cannot be dictated, prescribed, or forced. Once the ISD partner knows it is acceptable to feel whatever is experienced, the response anxiety is lowered, and the probability of feeling stimulated increases.

In summary, the first phase of therapy involves setting the agenda, completing the rapid assessment and beginning to work with the cognitions to see which ones are individually oriented and which are relationally oriented, and discussing the role of response anxiety in order to eliminate it.

Second Phase of Therapy

The combination of the foregoing techniques during the initial phase of treatment may, for some couples, enhance desire. However, these techniques alone are rarely enough to sustain the desire. The rapid assessment procedure has helped to identify the individual, interactional, and intergenerational factors that suppress desire. As the therapy continues, these factors will be examined one by one, and new factors will probably emerge as a result of continued discussion, along with the touching exercises being done at home. The therapist must weave together a variety of techniques to take care of each problem or factor.

For the individual variables, the therapist may need to make a referral to the appropriate physician to rule out medical problems, correct hormonal deficiencies, or change medications that might affect sexual desire or performance. Appropriate therapeutic measures must be implemented in order to deal with each individually oriented concern, such as negative body image or feelings of sexual guilt or anxiety as a result of sexual mythology. We suggest that this work be done in the presence of the partner unless there is a strong rationale for not doing so. Working together helps to strengthen the relationship, to increase support and empathy, and to reveal ways in which the partner may have contributed to problems in the ISD partner. For example, there was a case in which one of the problems of the ISD partner was his preoccupation with the size of his penis. He believed that it was too small. He required education and a change in his belief system. It turned out that his wife liked to talk about her past sexual experiences and she would always point out that all of her previous lovers had larger penises. On first look, his problem appeared to be strictly individual. However, the additional information clarified the importance of the interactional factors, making the involvement of the wife necessary. There was an opportunity to explore why the woman needed to put her husband down and to keep him sexually distant.

Much of the work that needs to be done is actually marital therapy and not sex therapy, as traditionally defined. The section on etiology revealed just how many relational factors may be involved. When relational factors are involved, the therapy proceeds along two tracks. One track deals with the sexual desire per se (cognitive work, fantasy work, etc.) and the other deals with the relationship problems. Because of the variety and complexity of the relational problems, an entire volume could be devoted to describing how to deal with each one. We have addressed the treatment of these problems in our previous books on couples therapy and in other chapters of this volume (Weeks [1989], Weeks & Hof [1987, 1994], Weeks & Treat [1992]. The most significant interactional factors of anger, control, and intimacy are discussed in detail in *Couples in Treatment: Techniques and Approaches for Effective Treatment* (Weeks & Treat, 1992).

Although the etiology of the problem may, in large measure, be due to relationship issues, that is not always clear to the couple, nor is it something that partners are often willing to accept. The first step in doing the marital work is to reframe the problem systemically. The technique of reframing is also discussed in *Couples in Treatment* (Weeks & Treat, 1992). The couple must see how the ISD partner is exhibiting a problem in the relationship. The most effective way to accomplish this goal is to lead the couple to this insight by asking questions that inevitably lead to this conclusion. First, relationship problems must be established. Someone has to say that this kind of problem exists. Second, the therapist establishes a link between the ISD and the relational problem by asking the ISD partner about the effect of the relational problem on feelings of sexual desire. This is a matter of feeling and is undeniable. Third, the relationship problem must be defined as such. The therapist asks questions that make the roles of the actors in the interaction clearer, and the role of the non-ISD partner apparent in maintaining or creating this interaction.

Suppose, for example, that a man presents with ISD and he is suppressing his anger. The first step is to reveal that he is angry, that he is suppressing his anger, and that this act is leading him to be sexually disinterested. What may appear to be just his individual problem is then contextualized. When questions are asked about the way the couple deals with anger, it might be learned that the wife came from a family where anger was violently expressed. She came to the marriage with the unconscious need to find someone who would not threaten her by being angry. She would then send him subtle or not so subtle messages about not being angry. In one case, a woman told her husband that if he were ever like her father, she would leave him immediately. He fully understood this message, although it was not talked about beyond her cryptic statement. Once both partners understand that they are contributing to the problem in the relationship, which becomes manifest in terms of ISD, it is possible to proceed with the marital/couple therapy.

The third area that may cause difficulty is the intergenerational. Intergenerational work can be done in a variety of ways. It can be done with the individual alone or with the couple together, and may include other family members. Again, we prefer to do this work with the couple together unless there is a compelling reason not to do so.

The simplest of the intergenerational factors would concern sexually negative messages from the parents. Making these messages explicit and helping the client to counter them with sex-positive messages through giving permission, education, and factual information is useful. Understanding the impact of subtle messages and patterns on the family may also be necessary. Once the clients begin to make these connections, they are free to move on and make their own choices without the unconscious loyalty to the family.

A parentified adult may not know that s/he is a parentified adult. S/he may define herself or himself as a caretaker while not completely appreciating the origin of this behavior. This partner is not in touch with the underlying contradictory feelings of omnipotence and rage toward the other. The therapist helps the client understand these feelings and the reason these feelings could not be acknowledged in childhood or adolescence and how the denial is still working. Freeing the client from this complex web of emotion will change many aspects of the emotional relationship and be a difficult transition for the couple.

One of the most effective ways to access the intergenerational messages that may be influencing sexual function/dysfunction is to use the sexual genogram (Berman & Hof, 1987; Hof & Berman, 1986). The process involves five component parts: introduction, creation and exploration of a genogram, creation and exploration of a sexual genogram, exploration and discussion of genogram material/issues with family members, and a review of the total process and integration with the treatment plan.

The process is facilitated by a cognitively oriented explanation of the concepts and goals, with an emphasis on the role of early learning and intergenerational processes in the development of individual, couple, and family systems. As the partners grasp the concept, they are helped to speculate as to how these concepts might relate to the presenting sexual problem, usually with an increase in motivation to continue the process.

Each partner is then requested to create a genogram. This can be done by each partner within the session, with the therapist and each partner in private sessions, or by the partners at home in private, with sharing and discussion between the partners after the work has been completed. Which approach is utilized is a matter of therapist preference, available time, and the clients' needs for either sharing or privacy.

After the genogram has been created and explored, each partner is asked to reconsider it during the following week, with a specific focus on sexual-genogram questions related to overt/covert messages in the family regarding sexuality, intimacy, masculinity, femininity; how sexuality and intimacy were encouraged or discouraged; what secrets might have existed in the family regarding sexuality and intimacy; and so forth. Answers are to be written, and in subsequent therapy sessions, meanings, insights, and ideas are explored, with a focus on which issues might need further exploration with other family members.

If further exploration is indicated, a family journey is carefully planned to explore and discuss genogram material with family members and to facilitate resolution of emergent issues. Conjoint therapy continues during the extended process to provide support and empathy for and to increase understanding by both partners. This is followed by a reflective review of the total process. Insights regarding the etiology and maintenance of the sexual problem often lead to diminished blaming and a positive sense of reciprocity. These learnings and ideas of the clients and the therapist are then merged with the other components of the treatment plan. Once released from the underlying feelings of rage and the need to take care of the partner, the person is free to experience feelings of sexual desire toward the other. In many of these relationships, the presentation is that of one partner (the ISD partner) feeling overwhelmed by the needs of the other. This represents a dynamic in the relationship and opposing needs in the parentified partner to take care of and be cared for.

Sexual trauma and incest require special attention and treatment. If the ISD partner has been sexually victimized, then this factor must be dealt with first. It is generally considered advisable to have a therapist of the same gender as the abused person when dealing with sexual trauma. Treatment is usually extended. Once this factor has been identified, the link to the lack of desire must be established. Once this is done, the incest survivor should be seen individually by the couple therapist or another therapist. It is usually better to make a referral to another therapist. Maltz (1988, 1991) and Trepper and Barrett (1989) have described the couple therapy for incest and other abuse. The therapist should consult these works on how to coordinate the individual and couple therapies when sexual abuse has occurred. The ISD work will be very slow in the beginning. Any work on the sexual relationship may need to be delayed until some work is done on this issue. The couple need to be informed about how slowly the sexual work may go. In some cases, the fact of sexual abuse may have been hidden or denied, so that the first step is to make the client aware of the trauma and its effects. This revelation can be painful and shocking, and may anger the non-ISD partner for what s/he may perceive as a deliberate deception.

Earlier, we mentioned that the therapy follows two tracks—one sexual and the other marital. The other facet of the sexual work is to attend to other sexual dysfunctions. Treating the sexual dysfunctions will not be possible until the relationship is relatively free of problems and some desire has been created or restored. The timing of this work must be appropriate for each couple. If partners are fighting constantly and angry with each other or one is devoid of sexual desire, it is obvious that they are not amenable to working on sexual dysfunctions. When they do become ready, it is then a matter of determining which disorder to treat first, the relational problems or the sexual problems (his or hers), or determining how the problems may be treated concurrently. The treatment of the dysfunctions can be mixed with the marital work on an ongoing basis.

Final Phase of Treatment

This phase is defined as that point in treatment when the work is no longer remedial. The aspects of the relationship that needed to be restructured have been restructured, the relational problems contributing to the ISD have been resolved, and the other factors that were supporting the ISD have also been resolved. The couple is now functional, but is not necessarily functioning optimally. The couple that has undergone this therapy has invested a great deal of themselves, demonstrated a considerable amount of commitment to each other, and evidenced deep caring for each other. These couples expect more than do many couples who engage in short-term therapy, and perhaps more than most couples in general. These couples want their sexual relationship not only to be satisfying, pleasurable, and comfortable, but also to be creative, vital, and dynamic.

During this phase, the therapist has the rare opportunity to promote health and growth in the couple's sexual relationship. A variety of strategies can be used to achieve this goal. The therapist needs to encourage open and direct sexual communication throughout. This goal is achieved by talking in the office and throughout the exercises (pleasuring I, II, etc.). The couple can be further educated by prescribing a variety of readings. They can be sent to the local bookstore to browse in the section on sexuality to find books they want to use to enhance their relationship. We also send couples to sexual enrichment workshops or Sexual Attitude Readjustment (SAR) workshops. These workshops give them an opportunity to talk to other people, become exposed to explicit sexual information, and examine attitudes, beliefs, values, and so on. The first three videotapes of *The Better Sex Video Series* (1989) are also helpful in showing couples new techniques and the value of fantasy. Sexual expectations may now be clearly stated in the newly found sense of comfort in talking to each other about sex. The partners are encouraged to continue expressing affection without its having to lead to sex. They are taught how to share sexual responsibility so that each can initiate, and each is free to say "no" and suggest some other activity. The cultural norm is to place performance expectations on sex. The therapist must help the couple learn how to avoid getting caught up in performance and think instead in terms of pleasure. Once they have internalized this concept, sex can be anything they want it to be as long as the ultimate goal is mutual enjoyment and pleasure.

The couple may also want to develop their sexual abilities even beyond this point. Women who were occasionally orgasmic may want to learn to be orgasmic more frequently. Men who have fairly good ejaculatory control may wish to improve their ability to control ejaculation. Some couples may even want to experiment with extended sexual orgasms (Brauer & Brauer, 1990). Working on these behaviors would seem to suggest that the couple is hooked on performance. These behaviors should only be encouraged if they represent a search for greater pleasure and enjoyment for both the individual and the couple.

CONCLUSION

ISD has become one of the most common problems seen by sex and marital therapists. It is also one of the most difficult and complex problems to treat. The traditional approach to sex therapy, time-limited behavioral oriented treatment, is not effective. Numerous other approaches have now been developed, each of which assumes a particular theoretical stance toward ISD. The purpose of this chapter was to present an integrated and systematic approach to the problem based on the Intersystem Model of therapy. ISD is a multicausal problem; a confluence of factors contribute to its creation. In the Intersystem Model, these factors are examined from the individual, interactional, and intergenerational perspectives. Likewise, treatment must be multileveled and flow from an understanding of the different kinds of factors.

ISD is a challenging problem because it requires therapists to leave theoretical dogma behind. A single theoretical approach or the use of limited techniques is likely to fail. The therapist must be flexible and creative. The model of treatment must be integrative. This, in turn, means that the therapist must be well versed in individual, sex, marital, and family therapy. How many therapists can make such a claim? In the past, sex therapists have too often overlooked or underemphasized the relationship and marital therapists have overlooked or ignored the sexual difficulties. These modalities must be integrated if we are to work effectively with this problem. Even with this arsenal of techniques and approaches, treatment is difficult and extended. The therapist must attend to the couple's discomfort in talking about such personal matters. The therapist must also be personally comfortable in dealing with sexual matters in a detailed and frank manner. A therapist cannot do something *to* a couple—the therapist practices his or her art *with* the couple. The therapy will work only if it is collaborative. The couple have to assume responsibility for their therapy. They are not expected to be experts, but to discuss what they are ready and able to do, to communicate about sex, to accept personal responsibility. These issues are not simple; after all, it was the scope of these deficiencies that led to, or contributed greatly to, the problems in the first place.

ISD is a problem among many problems. The problem must be constructed contextually. There may be many connections, some clear, some obscure. The sex therapist who approaches the problem as a technician will quickly find the tools of little value. The effective therapist will have an integrative theory, develop a comprehensive case formulation, be flexible, and be well trained in many modalities and techniques. Such a therapist will find no more exquisite a problem to treat than ISD.

REFERENCES

American Psychiatric Association. (1987). *Diagnostic and statistical manual of mental disorders* (rev. 3rd ed.). Washington, DC: Author.

American Psychiatric Association. (1994). *Diagnostic and statistical manual of mental disorders* (4th ed.). Washington, DC: Author.

Apfelbaum, B. (1988). An ego-analytic perspective of desire disorders. In S. Leiblum & R. Rosen (Eds.), *Sexual desire disorders* (pp. 57–106). New York: Guilford.

Bahr, J., & Weeks, G. R. (1989). Sexual functioning in a nonclinical sample of male couples. *American Journal of Family Therapy*, *2*, 110–127.

Barbach, L., & Levine, L. (1980). *Shared intimacies*. Garden City, NY: Archer/Doubleday.

Berman, L., & Hof, L. (1987). The sexual genogram—assessing family-of-origin factors in the treatment of sexual dysfunction. In G. R. Weeks & L. Hof (Eds.), *Integrating sex and marital therapy: A clinical guide* (pp. 37–56). New York: Brunner/Mazel.

Brauer, A., & Brauer, D. (1990). *The ESO ecstasy program*. New York: Warner.

Courtrois, C. A. (1988). *Healing the incest wound*. New York: Norton.

Donahey, K., & Carroll, R. (1993). Gender differences in factors associated with hypoactive sexual desire. *Journal of Sex and Marital Therapy*, *19*, 25–40.

Ellis, A., & Harper, R. (1975). *A new guide to rational living*. Englewood Cliffs, NJ: Prentice-Hall.

Fish, L., Fish, R., & Sprenkle, D. (19840. Treating inhibited sexual desire: A marital therapy approach. *American Journal of Family Therapy*, *12*, 3–12.

Frank, E., Anderson, G., & Rubinstein, D. (1978). Frequency of sexual dysfunctions in normal couples. *New England Journal of Medicine*, *3*, 111–115.

Friday, N. (1973). *My secret garden*. New York: Trident Press.

Friday, N. (1975). *Forbidden flowers*. New York: Pocket Books.

Friday, N. (1980). *Men in love*. New York: Dell.

Friday, N. (1991). *Women on top*. New York: Pocket Books.

Hof, L. (1993). The elusive elixir of hope. *The Family Journal: Counseling and Therapy For Couples and Families*, *1*(3), 220–227.

Hof, L., & Berman, E. (1986). The sexual genogram. *Journal of Marital and Family Therapy*, *12*, 39–47.

Hyde, J. (1979). *Understanding human sexuality*. New York: McGraw-Hill.

Kaplan, H. (1979). *Disorders of sexual desire*. New York: Brunner/Mazel.

Kaplan, H. (1983). *The evaluation of sexual disorders*. New York: Brunner/Mazel.

Kaplan, H., & Owen, J. (1993). The female androgen deficiency syndrome. *Journal of Sex and Marital Therapy*, *19*, 3–24.

Knopf, J., & Seiler, M. (1990). *ISD: Inhibited sexual desire*. New York: Morrow.

L'Abate, L. (1976). *Understanding and helping the individual in the family*. New York: Grune & Stratton.

L'Abate, L., & McHenry, S. (1983). *Handbook of marital interventions*. New York: Grune & Stratton.

Lazarus, A. (1988). A multimodel perspective on problems of sexual desire. In

S. Leiblum & R. Rosen (Eds.), *Sexual desire disorders* (pp. 145–167). New York: Guilford.

Leiblum, S., & Rosen, R. (1988a). Introduction: Changing perspectives on sexual desire. In S. Leiblum & R. Rosen (Eds.), *Sexual desire disorders* (pp. 1–20). New York: Guilford.

Leiblum, S., & Rosen, R. (Eds.). (1988b). *Sexual desire disorders.* New York: Guilford.

Levine, S. (1988). Intrapsychic and individual aspects of sexual desire. In S. Leiblum & R. Rosen (Eds.), *Sexual desire disorders* (pp. 21–44). New York: Guilford.

Lief, H. I. (1977). Inhibited sexual desire. *Medical Aspects of Human Sexuality*, 7, 94–95.

Lief, H. I. (1985). Evaluation of inhibited sexual desire: Relationship aspects. In H. S. Kaplan (Ed.), *Comprehensive evaluation of disorders of sexual desire* (pp. 59–76). Washington, DC: American Psychiatric Press.

LoPiccolo, L. (1980). Low sexual desire. In S. R. Leiblum & L. A. Pervin (Eds.), *Principles and practice of sex therapy* (pp. 44–64). New York: Guilford.

LoPiccolo, L., & Friedman, J. (1988). Broad spectrum treatment of low sexual desire: Integration of cognitive, behavioral and systemic therapy. In S. Leiblum & R. Rosen (Eds.), *Sexual desire disorders* (pp. 107–145). New York: Guilford.

Loren, R., & Weeks, G. R. (1986). Comparison of the sexual fantasies of undergraduates and their perceptions of sexual fantasies of the opposite sex. *Journal of Sex Education and Therapy*, 12, 31–36.

Mahlstedt, P. (1987). The crisis of infertility: An opportunity for growth. In G. Weeks and L. Hof (Eds.), *Integrating sex and marital therapy: A clinical guide* (pp. 121–148). New York: Brunner/Mazel.

Maltz, W. (1988). Identifying and treating the sexual repercussions of incest: A couples therapy approach. *Journal of Sex and Marital Therapy*, 4(2), 116–144.

Maltz, W. (1991). *The sexual healing journey.* New York: HarperCollins.

Masters, W., & Johnson, V. (1970). *Human sexual inadequacy.* Boston: Little, Brown.

Masters, W., & Johnson, V. (1979). *Homosexuality in perspective.* Boston: Little, Brown.

McCarthy, B. (19840. Strategies and techniques for the treatment of inhibited sexual desire, *Journal of Sex and Marital Therapy*, 10, 97–104.

Mosher, D. (1979). Sex guilt and sex myths in college men and women. *Journal of Sex Research*, 15, 224–234.

Nutter, P., & Condron, M. (1983). Sexual fantasy and activity patterns of females with inhibited sexual desire versus normal controls. *Journal of Sex and Marital Therapy*, 9, 276–282.

Regas, S., & Sprenkle, D. (1984). Functional family therapy and treatment of inhibited sexual desire. *Journal of Marital and Family Therapy*, *10*, 63–72.

Rosen, R. C. (1991). Alcohol and drug effects on sexual response: Human experimental and clinical studies. In J. Bancroft (Ed.), *Annual review of sex research* (pp. 119–179). Lake Mills, IA: Society for the Scientific Study of Sex.

Rosen, R. C., Leiblum, S. R., & Hall, K. (1987). *Etiological and predictive factors in sex therapy.* Paper presented to the annual meeting of the Society for Sex Therapy and Research, New Orleans.

Sauber, R., L'Abate, L., Weeks, G., & Buchanan, W. (1993). *The dictionary of family psychology and family therapy* (2nd ed.). Newbury Park, CA: Sage.

Schover, L., & LoPiccolo, J. (1982). Effectiveness of treatment for dysfunctions of sexual desire. *Journal of Sex and Marital Therapy*, *8*, 179–197.

Segraves, R. (1988a). Hormones and libido. In S. Leiblum & R. Rosen (Eds.), *Sexual desire disorders* (pp. 271–312). New York: Guilford.

Segraves, R. (1988b). Drugs and desire. In S. Leiblum & R. Rosen (Eds.), *Sexual desire disorders* (pp. 313–348). New York: Guilford.

Sue, D. (1979). Erotic fantasies of college students during coitus: *Journal of Sex Research*, *15*, 299–305.

The better sex video series. (1989). Ft. Lauderdale, FL: Learning Corp.

Trepper, T. S., & Barrett, M. J. (1989). *Systemic treatment of incest: A therapeutic handbook.* New York: Brunner/Mazel.

Weeks, G. R. (1987). Systemic treatment of inhibited sexual desire. In G. Weeks & L. Hof (Eds.), *Integrating sex and marital therapy: A clinical guide* (pp. 183–201). New York: Brunner/Mazel.

Weeks, G. R. (1994). The Intersystem Model: An integrative approach to treatment. In G. Weeks and L. Hof (Eds.), *The marital/relationship therapy casebook: Theory and application of the Intersystem Model* (pp. 3–34). New York: Brunner/Mazel.

Weeks, G. R. (Ed.). (1989). *Treating couples: A clinical guide.* New York: Brunner/Mazel.

Weeks, G. R., & Hof, L. (Eds.). (1987). *Integrating sex and marital therapy: The Intersystem Model of the Marriage Council of Philadelphia.* New York: Brunner/Mazel.

Weeks, G. R., & Hof, L. (Eds.). (1994). *The marital-relationship therapy casebook: Theory and application of the Intersystem Model.* New York: Brunner/Mazel.

Weeks, G. R., & Treat, S. (1992). *Couples in treatment: Techniques and approaches for effective practice.* New York: Brunner/Mazel.

Zilbergeld, B. (1993). *The new male sexuality.* New York: Bantam.

Zilbergeld, B., & Ellison, L. (1980). Desire discrepancies and arousal problems in sex therapy. In S. Leiblum & L. Pervin (Eds.), *Principles and practice of sex therapy* (pp. 65–101). New York: Guilford.

NAME INDEX

Alberti, R., 82
Alder, A., 22
Anderson, G., 218
Apfelbaum, B., 242

Bach, G., 59, 63, 71, 82
Bahr, J., 219
Bandler, R., 11, 12
Bandura, A., 67
Barback, L., 241
Barnard, C. P., 5, 8
Barrett, M. J., 246
Beach, S. R. H., 95
Beavers, W. R., 1, 2, 8, 12, 13, 208, 210, 211
Beck, A., 7, 13
Becvar, D., 2
Becvar, R., 2
Bengston, V. L., 207, 209
Berland, D. I., 196
Berman, B., 245
Berman, E. M., 120, 162, 183, 230, 231
Bifulco, A., 99
Biglan, A., 101
Boszormenyi-Nagy, I., 47, 183
Bowen, M., 35, 182, 183, 184
Brandt, J. O., 180
Brauer, A., 248
Brauer, D., 248
Bridge, L., 99
Brody, E. M., 201
Brown, E. M., 161
Brown, F. H., 181
Brown, G. W., 97, 99
Buchanan, W., 232
Burchill, S. A. L., 97, 100
Burns, D., 66
Burton, L. A., 16

Cafferata, G. L., 201
Cameron-Bandler, L., 11
Carnes, P., 126, 129, 130, 131, 138, 141
Carroll, R., 234, 238
Charny, I. W., 161
Chelune, G., 33
Christensen, A., 108
Clarkin, J. F., 2
Cleary, P. D., 97
Clinebell, C. H., 34, 62
Clinebell, H. J., 34, 62

Colarusso, C., 164
Condron, M., 224
Corley, A., 129
Corrales, R. G., 5, 8
Courtois, C. A., 186, 232, 233
Covelman, K. W., 155
Covelman, S., 155
Cowley, M., 195
Coyne, J. C., 97, 100, 101, 103, 106, 107, 108
Crichton, J., 196
Crispell, D., 196

Dayringer, R., 71
de Beauvoir, S., 195
DeLongis, A., 97
Dienelt, M. N., 96
Dobson, K., 96
Doherty, W. J., 14, 63, 64, 66, 67
Dolan, Y. M., 142, 143
Donahey, K., 234, 238
Dow, M. G., 112
Dumont, C. P., 112

Elliot, M., 33
Ellis, A., 69, 240
Ellison, L., 217
Emmons, M., 82
Erikson, E. H., 22, 197
Everett, C. A., 196

Feldman, L. B., 59, 92, 93, 101
Fish, L., 233, 234
Fish, R., 233, 234
Fisher, H., 191
Fisher, R., 72
Framo, J. L., 183, 204
Frank, E., 218, 219
Frank, J. B., 2, 12
Frank, J. D., 2, 12
Freud, S., 22, 196
Frey, W. H., 196
Friday, N., 241
Friedan, B., 195
Friedman, J., 219
Fruzzetti, A. E., 96

Garfield, S. L., 196
Geographic Profile, 196
Gerson, R., 183
Glass, S. P., 161

Glick, I., 2
Goldberg, H., 59, 71, 82
Goldberg, M., 166
Goldenberg, H., 2, 11
Goldenberg, I., 2, 11
Greden, J., 97
Griffith, J. L., 16
Griffith, M. E., 16
Grinder, J., 11, 12
Group for the Advancement of Psychiatry, 16
Guerin, P. J., 79, 183
Gurman, A. S., 2

Hall, K., 219
Hallowell, E. M., 166
Harper, J., 33
Harper, R., 240
Harris, T., 97, 99
Heavey, C. L., 108
Hendix, H., 79
Herceg-Baron, R. L., 98
Herr, J. J., 205
Hof, L., 11, 14, 15, 25, 36, 62, 63, 72, 88, 106, 111, 120, 121, 132, 176, 183, 226, 230, 231, 234, 244, 245
Holman, B., 146
Holmes, T. H., 179
Holtzworth-Monroe, A., 98
Hooley, J. M., 98
Hops, H., 96, 101
Horney, K., 22
Hunt, B., 15, 43
Hunter, R., 126
Hyde, J., 217

Imber-Black, E., 189

Jacobson, N. S., 96, 98, 103, 104, 106
James, M., 79, 80
Jessee, E. H., 95, 97, 105, 106, 112
Johnson, G., 47
Johnson, V., 136, 215, 216, 223, 225, 226, 241, 242
Jongeward, D., 79, 80

Kaplan, H. S., 215, 216, 217, 221, 225, 233, 234, 236, 242

253

SUBJECT INDEX